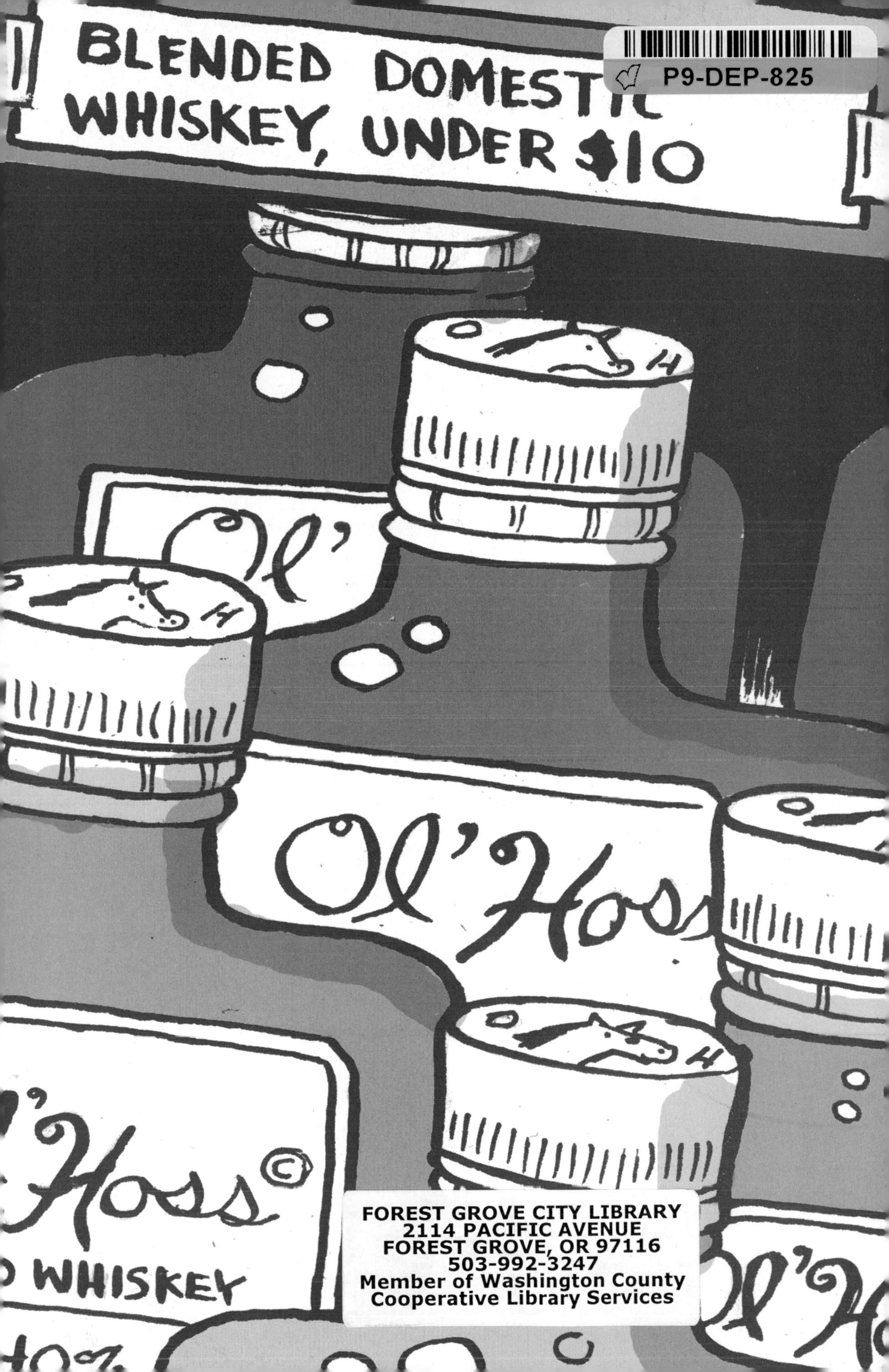
BLENDED DOMESTIC
WHISKEY, UNDER $10
Ol'
Ol' Hos
Hoss©
WHISKEY

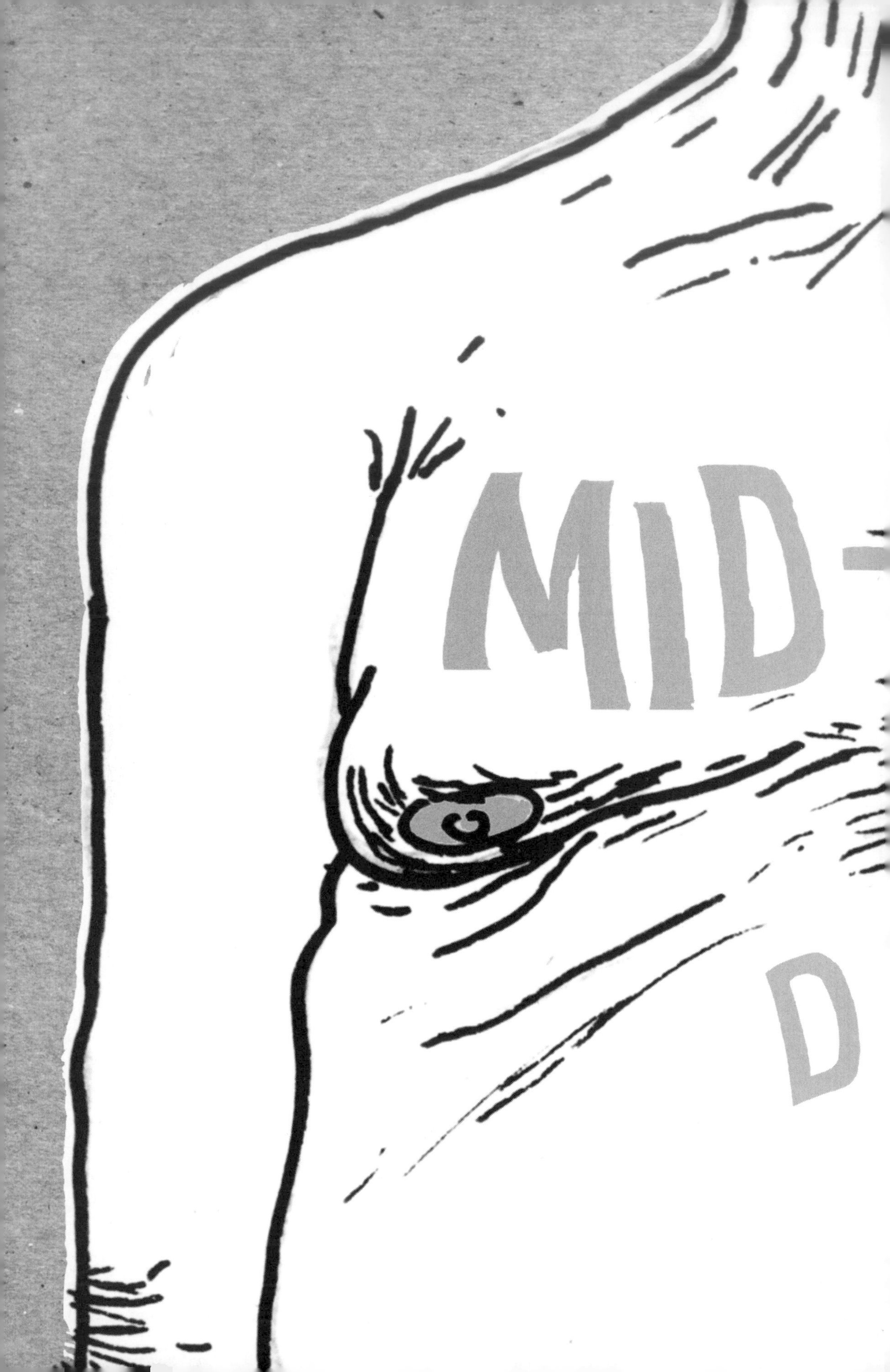
MID-
D

A COMIC BOOK
BY JOE OLLMANN

LIFE

Drawn & Quarterly, PO Box 48056, Montréal,
Quebec, Canada H2V 4S8

www.drawnandquarterly.com

First softcover edition: February 2011.
Printed in Canada
10 9 8 7 6 5 4 3 2 1
Library and Archives Canada Cataloguing in
Publication

Ollmann, Joe, 1966—
    Mid-life /Joe Ollmann

ISBN 978-1-77046-028-7

    I. Title.

PN6733.056M53 2011 741.5'971
C2010-906412-7

Distributed in the United States by Farrar,
Straus & Giroux, 18 West 18th Street,
New York, NY 10011
888-330-8477

Distributed in Canada by Raincoast Books
9050 Shaughnessy Street, Vancouver, BC V6P 6E5
800-663-5714

Distributed in the UK by Publishers Group UK
8 The Arena, Mollison Avenue, Enfield,
EN3 7NL   020 8216 6070

The author wishes to thank The Canada
Council for the Arts for their generous
support. ■✳■

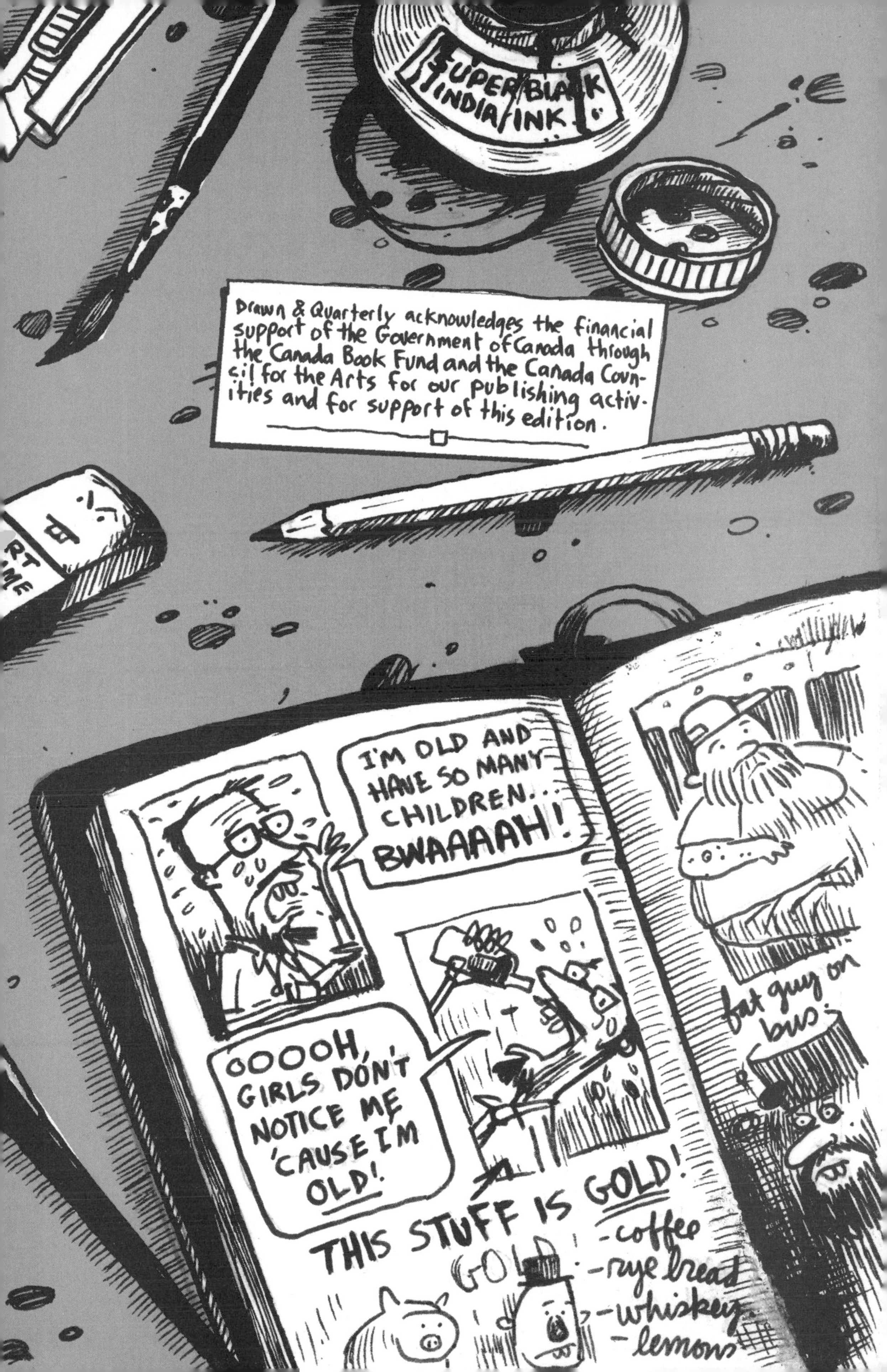
SUPER BLACK INDIA INK
Drawn & Quarterly acknowledges the financial support of the Government of Canada through the Canada Book Fund and the Canada Council for the Arts for our publishing activities and for support of this edition.
I'M OLD AND HAVE SO MANY CHILDREN... BWAAAAH!
OOOOH, GIRLS DON'T NOTICE ME 'CAUSE I'M OLD!
fat guy on bus:
THIS STUFF IS GOLD!
-coffee
-rye bread
-whiskey
-lemons

THIS BOOK IS
DEDICATED TO:
(IN ORDER OF AGE.)

TAIEN

MEAGHAN

LIZ

SAM

"HOMO SUM, HUMANI NIHIL A ME
ALIENUM PUTO."   (I AM A MAN,
I HOLD THAT NOTHING HUMAN IS
ALIEN TO ME.) - TERENCE,
ROMAN COMIC DRAMATIST,
185 BC-159 BC

THIS IS LARGELY A WORK OF FICTION.
EXCEPT WHERE IT ISN'T. PLEASE
SEE THE NOTES FOR EVEN LESS
CLARIFICATION.

IF, AFTER READING THIS BOOK, YOU FIND
YOURSELF ASKING: WHY WOULD A MAN
DRAW HIMSELF IN HIS UNDERPANTS SO
OFTEN AND REVEAL FICTIONALIZED
TIDBITS OF HIS LIFE IN CARTOON
FORM? I CAN ONLY RESPOND THAT
WHILE, BY AND LARGE, I'M NOT MUCH
OF A SOCIOPATHIC-EXHIBITIONIST OF
THE CURRENT REALITY-TELEVISION
SERIES SET, I STILL BELIEVE SOME
THINGS ARE UNIVERSAL TRUTHS AND
HOLD THAT, YES, THOSE TRUTHS MAY
INCLUDE DRAWING ONESELF IN ONE'S
UNDERPANTS. OH, AND ALSO, THAT
SOME OF THOSE TRUTHS ARE
FICTIONS. —JOE OLLMANN, 2010

MID-LIFE

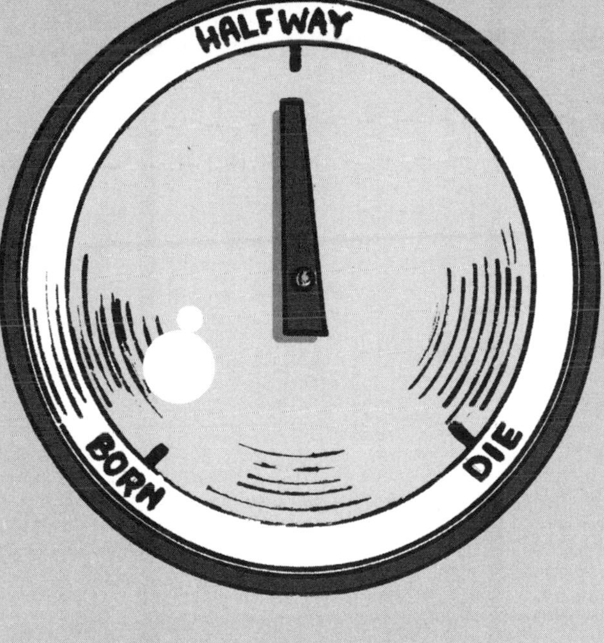
HALFWAY
BORN
DIE

D&Q
MONTREAL

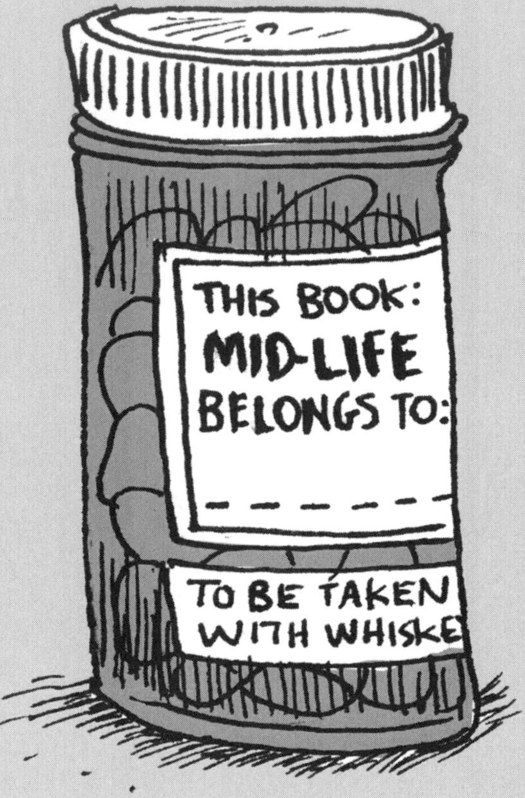
THIS BOOK:
MID-LIFE
BELONGS TO:
TO BE TAKEN
WITH WHISKE

MAY I DRAW YOU
A PICTURE?

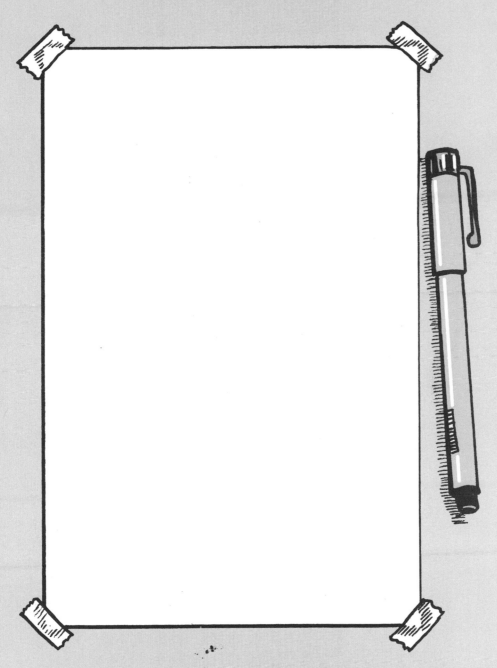

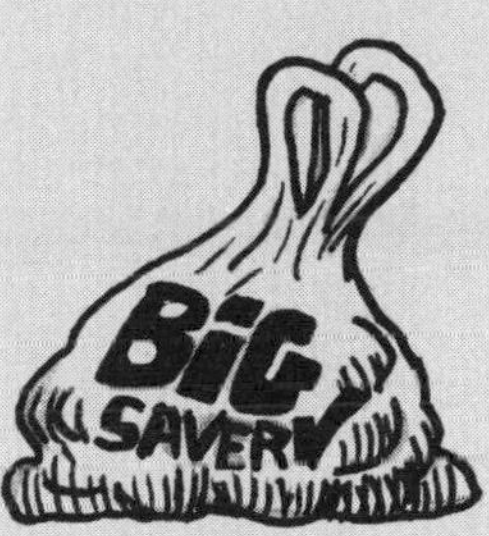
BIG
SAVER

MID-LIFE: PART ONE

CHAPTER ONE:

WERE YOU IN THE SHIT? YEAH, I WAS IN THE SHIT.

THE PLASTIC GROCERY BAG FULL OF CAT SHIT THAT I'M CARRYING BREAKS SUDDENLY.

RELEASING A REMARKABLY EL-EGANT CASCADE OF PISS-SOAKED LITTER, PUNCTUATED WITH HARDENED TURDS THAT CLICK IN DIFFERENT TONES, LIKE A XYLOPHONE-OR A VIBRAPHONE MAYBE-AS THEY HIT THE TILES. DINK-DINK-DINK!

"SHIT" IS ALL I MANAGE TO ADD TO THE SONG. LESS A LYRIC THAN A SONG-TITLE REALLY. THEN I BE-GIN SWEEPING UP THE MESS, BE-MOANING MY SAD, BULLSHIT CINDERELLA FATE.

AFTERWARD, MY SOCKS HAVE CAT-LITTER STUCK TO THEM. I PEEL THEM OFF AND, BACKING AWAY FROM ANY REMAINING LITTER...

...I STEP FULL INTO THE MID-DLE OF SAM'S ENVIRONMENTALLY-FRIENDLY AND SHIT-COVERED DIAPER COVER I'D LEFT ON THE BATHROOM FLOOR TO CLEAN.

PEOPLE MARVEL AT A SURGEON HOLDING A LIVING HUMAN HEART IN THEIR HANDS. I'M MORE AM-AZED AT THE EASE WITH WHICH A PARENT GETS USED TO HAND-LING BABY POOP.

I JUST KEEP WONDERING HOW MY LIFE HAS COME TO BE SO LITERALLY FULL OF SHIT. I MEAN, SERIOUSLY, THREE CATS AND A BABY MAKE FOR A LOT OF CRAP.

THERE'S MORE POOP IN MY LIFE THAN A GERMAN PORN FILM. HOW DID MY TEXT BOOK HIP-STER LIFE GET SO VERY BORING AND DOMESTIC?

CHAN IS ALWAYS REMINDING ME THAT IT WILL ONLY GET BETTER. SHE IS PRONE TO OPTIMISM, BUT SHE'S PROBABLY RIGHT, TOO.

I MEAN, I KNOW THIS FROM PERSONAL EXPERIENCE. I'VE DONE THIS BEFORE AND LIVED TO TELL THE TALE. SOMETIME AR--OUND TWENTY YEARS AGO, THE GIRLS STOPPED POOPING THEIR PANTS AND BEGAN SLEEPING MORE THAN TWO HOURS A NIGHT.

EVENTUALLY, THEY GET UP BEFORE YOU UNSUPERVISED AND YOU CAN EVEN TRAIN THEM TO MAKE COFFEE.

COFFEE'S UP, DAD...

DON'T GET ME WRONG, THE GIRLS STILL GIVE ME GRIEF, BUT IT RARELY INVOLVES POO, AND TONIGHT I'M MOST GRATEFUL FOR THAT.

I GOTTA CALL MARTHA TO--NIGHT AND BOOK HER A TRAIN TICKET. SHE MENTIONED WANTING TO VISIT HER LIT--TLE BROTHER.

WATCHA DOING?

OH, JUST SHIT WRANGLING. CLEANED THE LITTER AND THEN I STEPPED IN THAT GUY'S SHITTY FUCKING DIAPER...

SHOOKA SHOOKA

YOU'RE GONNA HAVE TO WATCH THAT SOON.

WHAT?

OH, A LITTLE BABY SAYING: "FUCKING SHIT, DADDY." YOU KNOW...

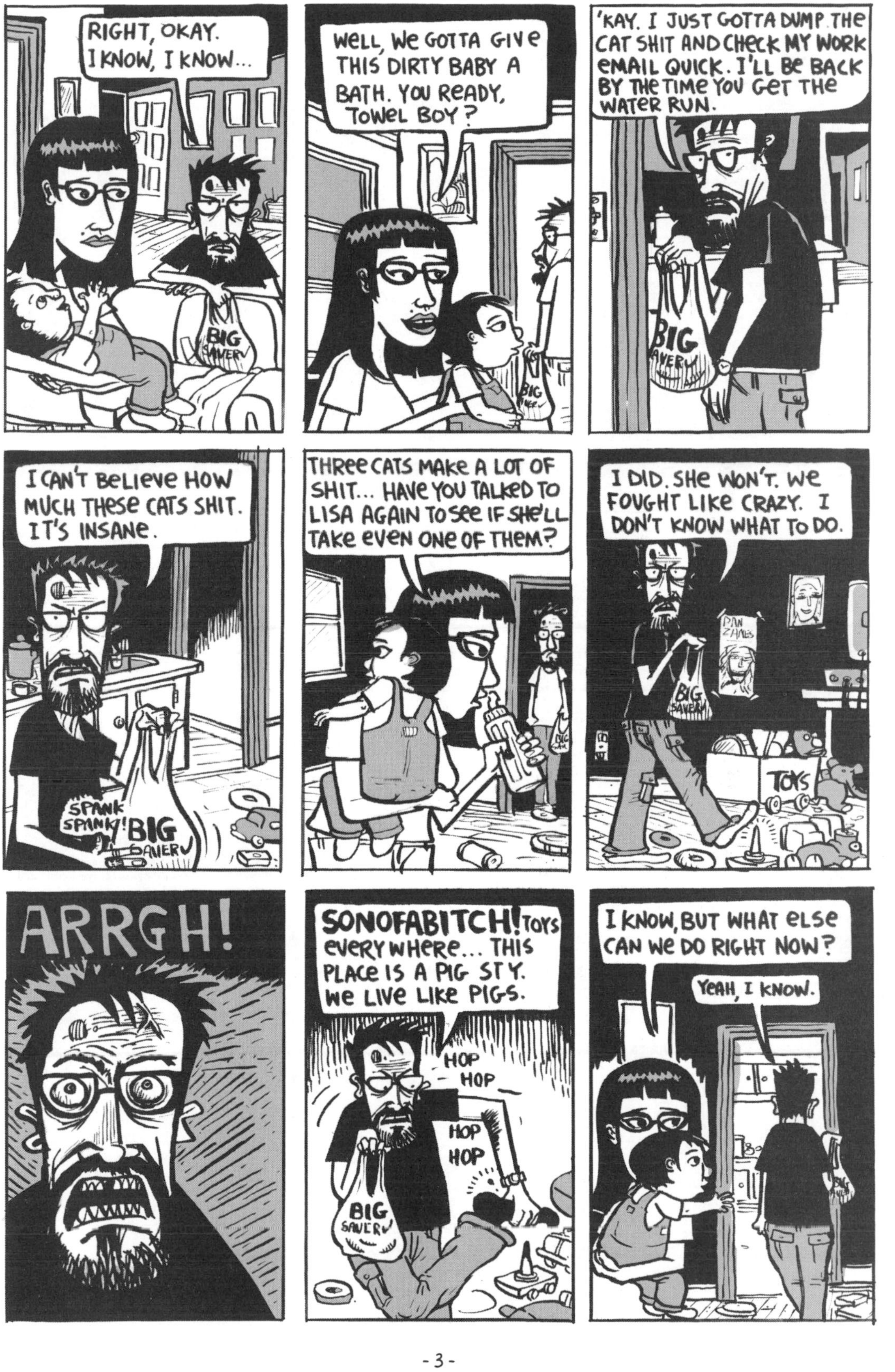
RIGHT, OKAY. I KNOW, I KNOW...
BIG SAVER
WELL, WE GOTTA GIVE THIS DIRTY BABY A BATH. YOU READY, TOWEL BOY?
'KAY. I JUST GOTTA DUMP THE CAT SHIT AND CHECK MY WORK EMAIL QUICK. I'LL BE BACK BY THE TIME YOU GET THE WATER RUN.
I CAN'T BELIEVE HOW MUCH THESE CATS SHIT. IT'S INSANE.
SPANK SPANK!
THREE CATS MAKE A LOT OF SHIT... HAVE YOU TALKED TO LISA AGAIN TO SEE IF SHE'LL TAKE EVEN ONE OF THEM?
I DID. SHE WON'T. WE FOUGHT LIKE CRAZY. I DON'T KNOW WHAT TO DO.
TOYS
ARRGH!
SONOFABITCH! TOYS EVERY WHERE... THIS PLACE IS A PIG STY. WE LIVE LIKE PIGS.
HOP HOP
HOP HOP
I KNOW, BUT WHAT ELSE CAN WE DO RIGHT NOW?
YEAH, I KNOW.

SHE'S RIGHT AGAIN; THERE'S NO-THING WE CAN DO. IF EITHER OF US WANT TO GET ANY OF OUR OWN CREATIVE WORK DONE IN THE MAY-BE ONE HOUR A NIGHT THAT SAM IS ASLEEP BEFORE WE FALL DOWN OURSELVES, WE HAVE TO LEAVE THE DISHES AND THE SWEEPING TO ROT.

I MEAN, REALLY, I DON'T WANT TO BE REMEMBERED SOLELY BY HOW CLEAN MY CARPETS ARE WHEN I'M DEAD.

HE... HE KEPT A VERY CLEAN HOUSE.

AND TO BE HONEST, CHAN AND I WEREN'T EXACTLY MARTHA STEWART IN OUR OLD LIFE BEFORE SAM ANYWAY.

YOU'RE... DOING... THE DISHES?

I NEEDED A PLATE.

BIG SAVER

MAYBE I SHOULD JUST KEEP A CLEANER HOUSE. IT'S NOT LIKE MY "CREATIVE WORK" IS SEAR-ING A GIANT SCAR ON THE COL-LECTIVE MEMORY OF MANKIND ANYWAY.

THERE'S ACTUAL DUST ON MY DRAWING BOARD.

AH WELL, MAYBE AFTER SAM'S BATH...

KLAK

WHA? I DON'T THINK SO...

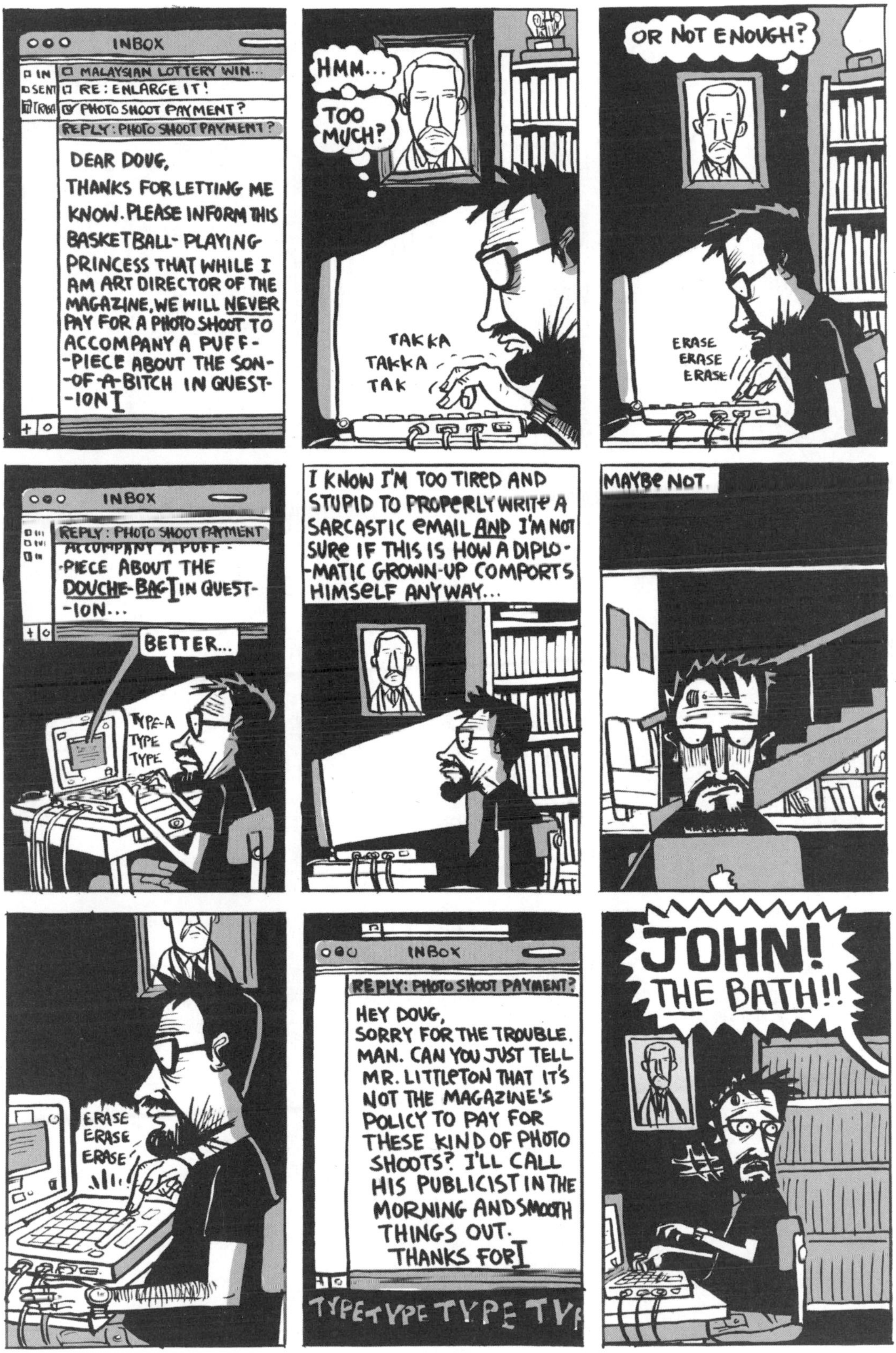
INBOX
IN
SENT
TRASH
MALAYSIAN LOTTERY WIN...
RE: ENLARGE IT!
PHOTO SHOOT PAYMENT?
REPLY: PHOTO SHOOT PAYMENT?
DEAR DOUG,
THANKS FOR LETTING ME KNOW. PLEASE INFORM THIS BASKETBALL-PLAYING PRINCESS THAT WHILE I AM ART DIRECTOR OF THE MAGAZINE, WE WILL NEVER PAY FOR A PHOTO SHOOT TO ACCOMPANY A PUFF--PIECE ABOUT THE SON--OF-A-BITCH IN QUEST--ION
HMM...
TOO MUCH?
TAKKA TAKKA TAK
OR NOT ENOUGH?
ERASE ERASE ERASE
INBOX
REPLY: PHOTO SHOOT PAYMENT
ACCOMPANY A PUFF--PIECE ABOUT THE DOUCHE-BAG IN QUEST--ION...
BETTER...
TYPE-A TYPE TYPE
I KNOW I'M TOO TIRED AND STUPID TO PROPERLY WRITE A SARCASTIC EMAIL AND I'M NOT SURE IF THIS IS HOW A DIPLO--MATIC GROWN-UP COMPORTS HIMSELF ANYWAY...
MAYBE NOT.
ERASE ERASE ERASE
INBOX
REPLY: PHOTO SHOOT PAYMENT?
HEY DOUG,
SORRY FOR THE TROUBLE. MAN. CAN YOU JUST TELL MR. LITTLETON THAT IT'S NOT THE MAGAZINE'S POLICY TO PAY FOR THESE KIND OF PHOTO SHOOTS? I'LL CALL HIS PUBLICIST IN THE MORNING AND SMOOTH THINGS OUT.
THANKS FOR
TYPE TYPE TYPE TYP
JOHN!
THE BATH!!

CHAPTER TWO: REPEAT OFFENDER

FIRST OFF, LET ME TELL YOU, I LOVE MY KIDS. ALL OF THEM.

BIP BIP BIP

BUT I AM SERIOUSLY GOING TO SMASH MY BALLS WITH A COUPLE OF BRICKS TO STOP MY PROPENSITY FOR REPRODUCTION.

RING RING.

MATTY! HEY KID, WHAT'S HAPPENING?

NOT MUCH, 'ADULT,' WHY ARE YOU WHISPERING?

SAM'S KIND OF ASLEEP ON ME. I CAN'T PUT HIM DOWN OR EVEN MOVE 'CAUSE HE'LL WAKE UP.

LUCKILY, I COULD REACH THE PHONE THIS TIME. I'VE BEEN TRAPPED UNDER A SLEEPING SAM FOR HOURS BEFORE, TRYING TO REACH SOMETHING TO READ: A HARDWARE STORE FLYER, A TAKE OUT MENU...

WOW, TRUE PARENTING STORIES. YOU DIDN'T SPOIL US LIKE THAT.

I'M PRETTY SURE I DID. ANYWAY, YOU'RE COMING TO TOWN; FALL ASLEEP ON MY ARM, AND I WON'T MOVE... GO CRAZY.

WHAT TIME YOU WANT ME TO BOOK YOUR TRAIN?

I GUESS THE FRIDAY EX--PRESS AND I'LL GO BACK SUNDAY AFTERNOON.

OH, SO SHORT...

OKAY JEWISH MOM, EASY ON THE GUILT. I DO HAVE A JOB YOU KNOW, DAD.

OKAY, OKAY! I'LL BOOK IT AND EMAIL YOU THE RESERVATION NUMBER.

OKAY. WHAT'S NEW THERE?

AFTER SOME TIME, I REALIZE I'VE LAUNCHED INTO A LONG, COMPLICATED STORY ABOUT MY JOB, HOW OFTEN I DO THIS, AND HOW BORING I'VE BECOME. I STOP MYSELF ABRUPTLY.

BLAH BLAH BLAH BLAH BLAH BLAH BLAH BLAH BLA...

...SO ANYWAY, THE FAMOUS BASKETBALL GUY WANTS TO GET PAID TO STAND STILL FOR A CAMERA FOR TEN MINUTES, BLAH, BLAH... IT'S ALL BORING, NOTH--ING NEW HERE. WHAT ABOUT YOU?

I'M GOING OVER TO MOM'S FOR DINNER TONIGHT.

ALWAYS A CONVERSATION STOP--PER. YOU CAN HEAR A NEEDLE BEING DRAGGED ACROSS A RECORD: ERRRR! BUT I'M DETERMINED TO BE A GROWN-UP.

OH...

...THAT'S... NICE...

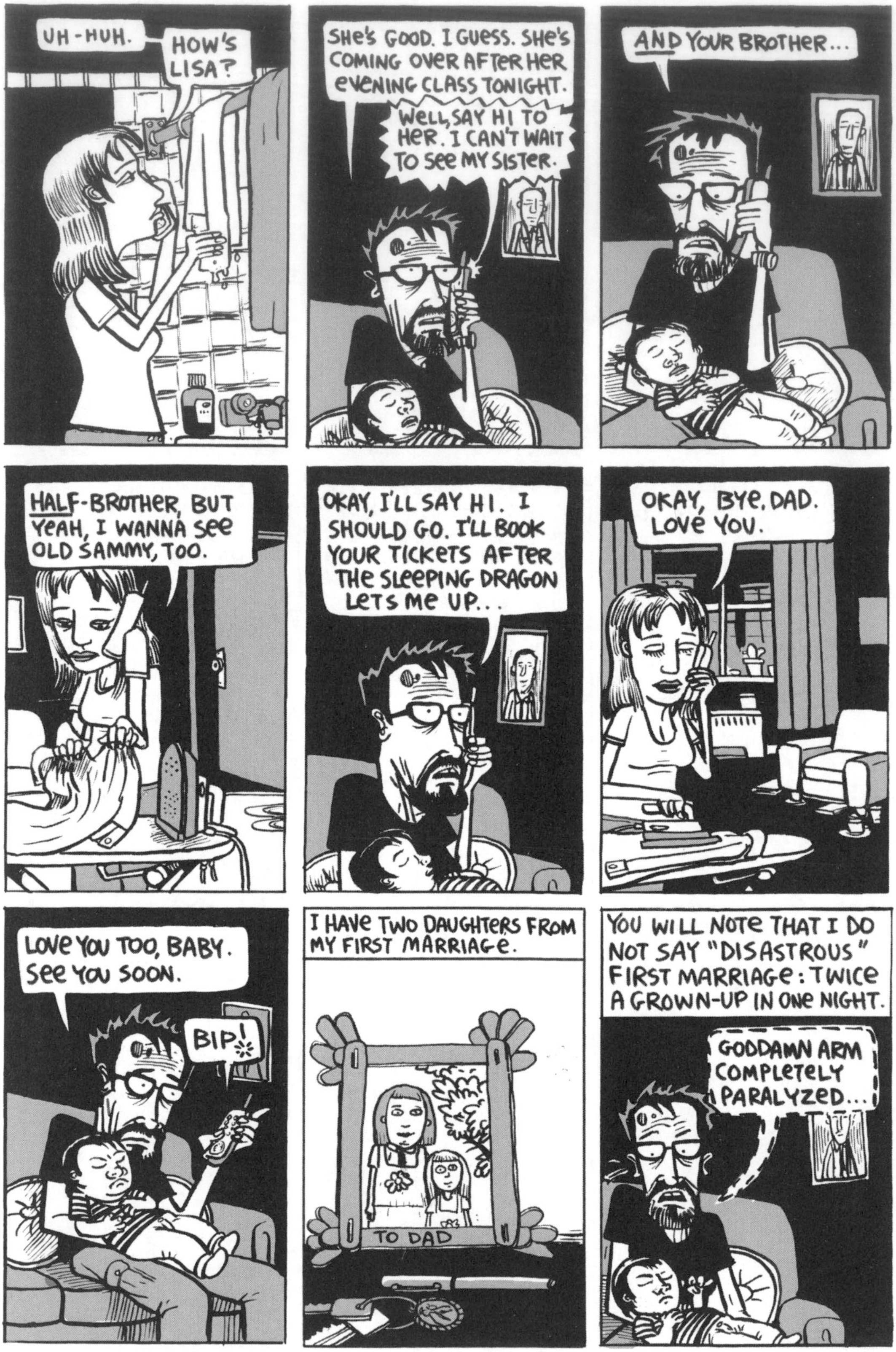
UH-HUH.
HOW'S LISA?
SHE'S GOOD. I GUESS. SHE'S COMING OVER AFTER HER EVENING CLASS TONIGHT.
WELL, SAY HI TO HER. I CAN'T WAIT TO SEE MY SISTER.
AND YOUR BROTHER...
HALF-BROTHER, BUT YEAH, I WANNA SEE OLD SAMMY, TOO.
OKAY, I'LL SAY HI. I SHOULD GO. I'LL BOOK YOUR TICKETS AFTER THE SLEEPING DRAGON LETS ME UP...
OKAY, BYE, DAD. LOVE YOU.
LOVE YOU TOO, BABY. SEE YOU SOON.
BIP!
I HAVE TWO DAUGHTERS FROM MY FIRST MARRIAGE.
TO DAD
YOU WILL NOTE THAT I DO NOT SAY "DISASTROUS" FIRST MARRIAGE: TWICE A GROWN-UP IN ONE NIGHT.
GODDAMN ARM COMPLETELY PARALYZED...

MATTY IS TWENTY-THREE AND LISA IS NINETEEN.

I'M FORTY YEARS OLD. I KNOW THE MATH. I WAS MARRIED, RIDICULOUSLY, AT SEVENTEEN AND SPAWNED CHILDREN AT THAT SAME TIME LIKE SOME HILLBILLY CHILD BRIDE.

PAM KURT

VE LACEY

JOHN OLSEN

CONTRARY TO WHAT YOU MIGHT THINK, HAVING ADULT CHILDREN WHEN I'M FORTY DOES NOT MAKE ME FEEL AS OLD AS THEIR LITTLE BROTHER DOES. HAVING A BABY AT FORTY WITH A SUBSTANTIALLY YOUNGER WIFE HAS AGED ME TWENTY YEARS IN MINUTES.

WHEN I'M OUT WITH MY GIRLS THERE IS STILL ALWAYS A CHANCE A STORE CLERK OR SOMETHING WILL COMMENT ON HOW YOUNG THEIR DAD IS. THOUGH IT HAPPENS LESS AND LESS AS I GET EVER CRAGGIER AND GRISTLED.

OMIGOD HE'S YOUR DAD? I THOUGHT HE WAS YOUR BOY- FRIEND!

EWWW!

WITH LITTLE SAM I'M JUST A NEAR-ELDERLY YUPPIE DAD, EMASCULATED BY THE DIAPER BAG...

...BY THE STROLLER...

LURCHING

MADE FOR TINY PEOPLE.

...BY FRONT CARRIERS AND VARIOUS "MAMA KANGAROO" SLINGS.

POOR SAM WILL NEVER KNOW HIS DAD AS A CAPABLE, VIRILE, STREET-FIGHTIN' MAN...

YOU WANNA DO THE MAN- -DANCE, PUNK? GIRLS, WAIT FOR DADDY IN THE CAR.

CREAM

...HE WILL ONLY KNOW A WEAK, SAGGY-BOSOMED OLD DAD.

BONK!

WHOOPS!

I HATE TO BE A CLICHE' HERE, BUT MY BODY IS FALLING APART. LET ME JUST LIST A FEW HIGH LITES:

FACE— LIVER SPOTS AND WRINKLES. THIS IS THE KIND OF SHIT MY GRAMMA HAD AT AGE 96. THIS IS THE KIND OF SHIT OLD GUYS IN CHINESE MEDICINE SHOPS HAVE.
AND NOW, SO DO I.

NECK — TURKEY WATTLES. MY FORMERLY MANLY NECK NOW LOOKS LIKE GOLDIE HAWN IN HER OSCAR DRESS.

SHOULDERS — SAGGING, PLUS BOSOMS! FOLDS OF FLESH WHERE THE CHEST AND SHOULDERS MEET, MAKING ME LOOK PREMATURELY LIKE CLINT EASTWOOD IN THE BRONCO BILLY SERIES OF FILMS: SHIRTLESS, SQUINTY- EYED AND SAGGY- BOSOMED.

STOMACH— CONTINUAL BLOATING, EMBARRASSING "INTERNAL FLATULENCE," NOT FARTS, BUT INTERNAL SHIFTING OF GAS WITH NO ISSUE, US- UALLY OCCURRING DURING BUSINESS MEETINGS. ALSO, CONTINUAL ALTERNATING DIARRHEA OR CONSTIPATION!

STOMACH (CONTINUED) — I HAVE A PICTURE, TAKEN FOUR YEARS AGO, WHICH SHOWS ME WITH ROWS OF PROMINENT AB- -DOMINAL MUSCLES, PURPORTEDLY A KEY ELEMENT TO BEING A WORTH- -WHILE MEMBER OF OUR SOCIETY. TAKE AWAY DAILY EXERCISE AND SUBSTITUTE A BAG OF CHIPS. RESULT: GUT.

PLUMBING, ETC — NO REAL COM- -PLAINTS ON THE RECREATIONAL ASPECTS YET, BUT YOU KNOW HOW OLD MEN SHAKE IT FOR HOURS AFTER PISSING IN PUBLIC TOILETS? I DO THAT TOO.

KNEES — BENDING TO PICK UP MY YOUNG SON IS ACCOMPANIED BY A SOUND LIKE FOUR CHOPSTICKS BREAKING.

LEGS — THE HAIR IS FALLING OFF AND THERE ARE VARICOSE VEINS. BOTH OF WHICH ARE ABOUT AS MANLY AS HAVING A BLADDER INFECTION.

MIGHT AS WELL JUST... TRY... AN... FALL ASLE—

UNGH!

HEY, LITTLE GUY...

NO!

HE ALWAYS WAKES UP ANGRY. IT'S A LEGACY I PASS ON TO ALL MY KIDS.

JEWS!

WHAT?!!

OH; JUICE, YOU WANT A DRINK...

THERE YA GO: JEWS. YOU WANNA WATCH A VIDEO?

THIS IS A GREAT EXAMPLE OF WHAT'S WRONG WITH THE "MIDDLE-AGE PARENT SYNDROME". I HARDLY EVER LET MY FIRST KIDS WATCH ANY TV AND WHEN THEY WERE OLDER, I LECTURED THEM ENDLESSLY ON THE CON--SUMPTION-FUELED CRAP ON TV.

WELL, IF YOU WANT TO WATCH A SEXIST PILE OF CONSUMER CRAP, THEN BY ALL MEANS, DO WATCH MY LITTLE PONY...

SAM GETS SAT IN FRONT OF THE TV. WITH A WORN-OUT DAD WHO JUST WANTS A MINUTES PEACE TO THINK ABOUT HOW SORE HIS SWOLLEN FEET ARE.

SKUHGGG...

"YAY," SAM, VIDEOS.

I KNOW THAT THINKING LIKE THIS ONLY AGES ME PREMATURELY. I SHOULD BE RAGING AGAINST ALL OF THIS BUT I FIND I'M MOSTLY TOO TIRED TO DO ANYTHING BUT GO QUIETLY INTO THAT GOOD NIGHT.

THOMAS?

RAFFI?

THOMAS!

I'VE HAD EXTENDED EXPERIENCE WATCHING KID SHOWS, BOTH FIRST-HAND BEFORE I WAS MARRIED AT AGE SEVENTEEN...

SUFFERIN' PSYCHE!

LED ZEP ZOSO

...THEN, WHEN SATURDAY MORNING CARTOONS WERE REPLACED BY CONNUBIAL LIFE, I WATCHED A LOT OF ANIMATION WITH MY OFFSPRING.

MOST KID SHOWS ARE VARYING DEGREES OF CRAP: CLOYING AND CUTESY OR FARTY AND INAPPROPRIATELY RIBALD. THEY INSULT THE INTELLIGENCE AND DUMBFOUND WITH THE LACK OF EFFORT THEIR CREATORS APPARENTLY PUT FORWARD.

THE BABY POUND PUPPIES MEET THE RAINBOW GANG!

I'VE SAT THROUGH SO MUCH OF THIS DRECK OVER THE YEARS, AND IT IS ONLY BY A CONSTANT, QUIETLY MOCKING DIALOGUE/COMMENTARY, THAT I HAVE MAINTAINED SANITY.

PAPA SMURF IS SUCH A FASCIST.

THE KIDS WERE ALWAYS TOO YOUNG TO COMPREHEND THE SARCASM. IT'S LIKE WHEN YOU SING A HORRIBLE SONG TO A BABY THAT IS DRIVING YOU MAD AND YOU SING THE TERRIBLE WORDS TO A LOVELY, FAMILIAR, UNTHREATENING TUNE.

IF YOU DON'T GO TO SLEEP I'LL SMOTHER YOU, ALL YOU CAN DO IS SCREAM AND POO...

TO THE TUNE OF HUSH LITTLE BABY.

THESE ARE THE TRICKS A FATHER USES TO SURVIVE. WHATEVER. ASK WARD CLEAVER, ASK BIL KEANE...

IT'S TRUE.

WHAT'S THIS? "SHERRI SMALLS AND HER..."

SHERRI SMALLS AND HER BIG BAND: COMPLETELY BANANAS!

WOW, WHERE DID THIS EVEN COME FROM?

HEY, I THOUGHT YOU MIGHT WANT THIS FOR YOUR KID. I DOUBT WE'RE GONNA REVIEW IT HERE AT THE MAGAZINE.

THE CHICK LOOKS PRETTY HOT...

HMMM...

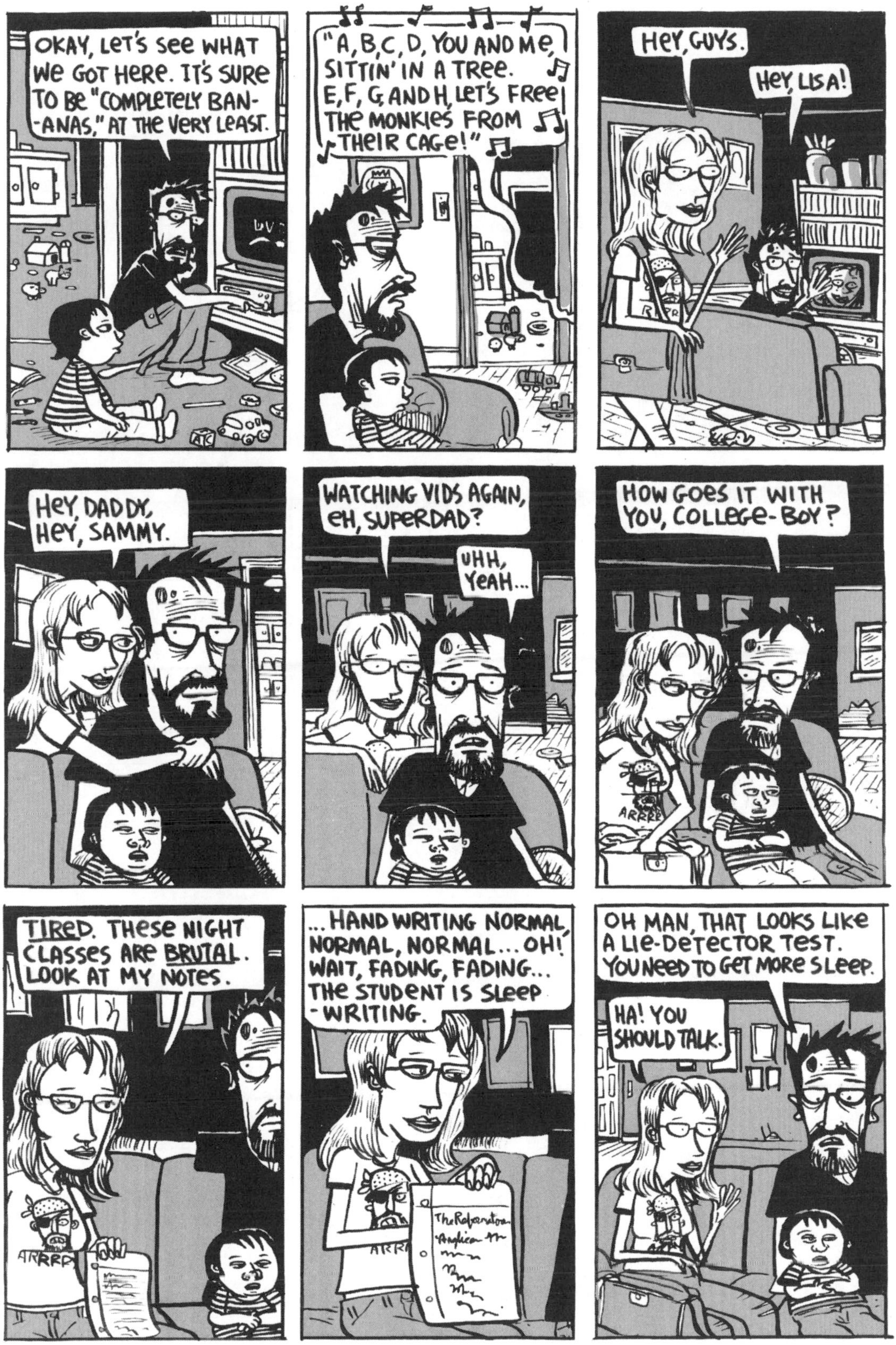
OKAY, LET'S SEE WHAT WE GOT HERE. IT'S SURE TO BE "COMPLETELY BAN--ANAS," AT THE VERY LEAST.
"A, B, C, D, YOU AND ME, SITTIN' IN A TREE. E, F, G, AND H, LET'S FREE THE MONKIES FROM THEIR CAGE!"
HEY, GUYS.
HEY, LISA!
HEY, DADDY, HEY, SAMMY.
WATCHING VIDS AGAIN, EH, SUPERDAD?
UHH, YEAH...
HOW GOES IT WITH YOU, COLLEGE-BOY?
TIRED. THESE NIGHT CLASSES ARE BRUTAL. LOOK AT MY NOTES.
...HAND WRITING NORMAL, NORMAL, NORMAL... OH! WAIT, FADING, FADING... THE STUDENT IS SLEEP-WRITING.
OH MAN, THAT LOOKS LIKE A LIE-DETECTOR TEST. YOU NEED TO GET MORE SLEEP.
HA! YOU SHOULD TALK.

WHAT'S THIS INSANE THING YOU'RE WATCHING?

MAN, CHILDREN'S PROGRAMMING HAS GONE TO HELL. DON'T THESE LITTLE DOUCHES WATCH RAFFI OR SHARON, LOIS & BRAM?

NO OFFENCE, SAM.

SAM WATCHES RAFFI! GOOD LORD, I'VE MEMORIZED EVERY RAFFI VIDEO. I CAN DO ALL HIS MOVES.

THIS DVD IS NEW. IT'S PRETTY GOOD, ACTUALLY.

M-HMM.

SERIOUSLY, THIS CHICK HAS THAT SAME QUALITY RAFFI AND THOSE OTHERS HAVE, WHATEVER THE HELL IT IS THAT KIDS LOVE. KIDS ARE HOT-WIRED FROM CONSCIOUSNESS ONWARD TO REACT TO CERTAIN THINGS: TELE-TUBBIES, RAFFI. THEY'RE CRACK FOR KIDS...

...THIS GIRL IS LIKE THAT TOO. HER SONGS ARE SOPHISTICATED AND HER MONKEY SIDEKICK HAS A KIND OF "BUSTER KEATON-Y" QUALITY TO HIM.

THIS MARSHMALLOW AIN'T A-BIG ENOUGH FOR THE BOTH OF US...

ALL I'M SAYIN' IS, IT'S NOT EASY KEEPIN' IT REAL WEARING A MONKEY SUIT OR SINGING SONGS FOR KIDS, BUT THIS SHERRI SMALLS DOES IT. SHE'S GENUINE. I'VE WATCHED THIS THREE TIMES TONIGHT AND I'M STILL DIG-GIN' IT...

SOUNDS LIKE GREAT COPY FOR A CD COVER — ALSO SOUNDS LIKE DADDY'S GOT THE HOTS FOR THE CHILDREN'S PERFORMER.

I DO NOT.

CHAPTER THREE:

ONE ANGRY MONKEY

I ACTUALLY USED TO FALL FOR THIS SHIT, THE SMOLDER-ING BAD-BOY ROUTINE.

THIS BULLSHIT POUTING AND SEETHING RAGE USED TO ACTUALLY WORK ON ME. DISTRACTING ME FROM HIS MISCONDUCT SO WELL THAT I WAS THE ONE WALKING ON EGGSHELLS, THE ONE APOLOGIZING.

JESUS, THIS SHIT IS AMATEUR. THIS COULD ONLY APPEAL TO A TWISTED, IMMATURE LITTLE GIRL. IT DOES NOT WORK ON ME TONIGHT.

THE MONKEY COSTUME DOESN'T HELP.

I HOPE YOU'RE HAPPY.

YEAH SHERRI, I'M FUCKING ECSTATIC...

WHAT IS THE MATTER WITH YOU?

LOOK SHERRI, THERE IS ALWAYS ONE KID IN EVERY CROWD WHO THINKS THEY'RE TOO OLD OR TOO COOL TO BE AT ONE OF OUR CONCERTS.

YOU KNOW, SOME LITTLE PECKER-HEAD WHO'S JUST STARTED GETTING BONERS, OR HE'S LISTENING TO HIS BROTHER'S RAP CD S. MAYBE HE'S BABYSITTING A SMALLER KID OR MAYBE HIS PARENTS ARE JUST CLUELESS, OR THEY BOUGHT THE TICKETS BEFORE HE GOT ALL COOL...

THE POINT IS, HE DOESN'T WANT TO BE AT A KIDDIE CONCERT, AND HE'S PISSED AND THEY ALWAYS TAKE IT OUT ON ME THE ASS-CLOWN IN THE APE SUIT...

YOU GET OFF EASY; THE KIDS ADORE YOU, AND THE OLDER ONES JUST OGGLE YOUR TITS LIKE THEIR FATHERS DO.

OH, GROSS.

IT'S TRUE: THEY LOVE YOU. I'M THE ONE SWEATING MY BAG OFF IN A FORTY-FIVE-POUND MON-KEY SUIT, AND SOME PISSANT TWELVE-YEAR-OLD PRETENDS TO GO IN FOR A HUG, THEN PUNCHES ME IN THE BALLS.

WELL, I'M SORRY SHERRI, I'M HUMAN. MY NUTS ARE HUMAN. I REACTED...

YOU PUSHED A TWELVE-YEAR-OLD BOY OFF THE STAGE!!

I WAS ASSAULTED!!

GODAMNIT, RIC! YOU HAVE MADE ALL OF US ACCOUNTABLE AGAIN BY YOUR BOLLSHIT ANTICS. THE PROMOTERS; THE BAND; THE RECORD LABEL; ME. THEY COULD SUE! THEY COULD PRESS CHARGES!

WHAT ABOUT ME?!? I COULD PRESS CHARGES!

NO, RIC, YOU COULDN'T. YOU CAN'T PROSECUTE A PRE-TEENAGER...

GUG GUG GUG

AND CAN YOU STOP DOING THAT?

WHAT!?

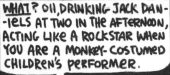

WHAT? OH, DRINKING JACK DAN--IELS AT TWO IN THE AFTERNOON, ACTING LIKE A ROCKSTAR WHEN YOU ARE A MONKEY- COSTUMED CHILDREN'S PERFORMER.

THIS IS HOW WE MAKE A LIVING, RIC: WE ENTERTAIN CHILDREN. THERE ARE MINIMUM STANDARDS WE HAVE TO UPHOLD. THIS IS THE MOST MONEY YOU AND I HAVE EVER MADE IN OUR LIVES AND YOU'RE ENDANGERING THAT FOR ALL OF US.

ESPECIALLY NOW WITH THE NETWORK WATCHING OUR EVERY MOVE.

OH YEAH, " THE NETWORK, THE NETWORK," THE PRECIOUS FUCK-ING NETWORK! - JESUS, SHERRI, YOU'VE CHANGED, MAN...

- 17 -

POOR RIC; MORE ROCK AND ROLL CLICHE'S.

I DON'T BITE THE HAND THAT FEEDS ME. THE NETWORK WANTS ME TO DO A SATURDAY MORNING KIDS' SHOW. I WANT TO DO THAT SHOW, SO I DON'T PUNCH CHILDREN.

I HAVEN'T CHANGED, RIC, I'M BEING REALISTIC, AS ALWAYS. YOU'RE COMMITTING CAREER SUICIDE, AS USUAL...

AND WHO EVEN WANTS A "CAREER" LIKE THIS?

YEAH, WELL, TOUCHÉ RIC... I'M ACTUALLY HAVING A HARD TIME ARGUING AGAINST ANY OF THIS. I FEEL ALL THE SAME THINGS I JUST DON'T HAVE RIC'S IMMATURITY, AND DRUG AND ALCOHOL ISSUES TO CLOUD IT OVER. HIS ACCUSATIONS OF "SELLOUT" STING BECAUSE I'VE CONDEMNED MYSELF OF THE SAME THINGS.

THIS IS MY CONSTANT BATTLE: HEY SHERRI, HOW'D YOU END UP BEING A CHILDREN'S PERFORMER? TRUE, YES, A LUCRATIVELY PAID CHILDREN'S PERFORMER, ONE OF THE "TOP" CHILDREN'S PERFORMERS, WITH A MANAGER, AND A TOUR BUS, AND A HOUSE ALMOST PAID FOR.

I MEAN, I CAN LAUGH AT RIC LIVIN' THE ROCK AND ROLL DREAM: MORE COKE THAN HE CAN HANDLE, JACK DANIELS TWENTY-FOUR/SEVEN, ELABORATE CONDITIONS IN BACK-STAGE RIDERS, AND ALL OF IT PAID FOR BY WEARING A MONKEY-SUIT AND CAPERING FOR AN AUDIENCE OF SIX-YEAR-OLDS.

BUT HOW AM I DIFFERENT? I USED TO BE A SINGER/SONGWRITER FOR GROWN-UPS, I RECOIL IN HORROR MYSELF WHEN I LOOK OUT AT AN AUDIENCE OF SPOILED KIDDIES AND THEIR YUPPIE PARENTS. I KNOW I'VE SOLD OUT.

BUT I KNOW I'M GOOD AT IT TOO. SO...

RIC, I KNOW THIS ISN'T WHAT WE IMAGINED DOING WHEN WE WERE TWENTY-ONE... I KNOW IT'S NOT "COOL" OR WHATEVER... BUT IT PAYS THE BILLS AND WE'RE <u>NOT</u> TWENTY-ONE ANY MORE.

OH, FUCK PAYING THE BILLS, SHERRI.

VERY TELLING THAT HE ONLY COMMENTS ON THE FIRST PART OF THE STATEMENT...

WELL, THAT'S <u>YOUR</u> DECISION, BUT YOU DON'T HAVE THE RIGHT TO COCK IT UP FOR THE REST OF US.

ARE YOU THREATENING TO KICK ME OUT OF THE "BAND" AGAIN?

OH, PLEASE SHERRI! DON'T KICK ME OUT OF THE "BAND," HOW WILL I "PAY THE BILLS?"

I SHOULD SAVE YOU THE TROUBLE AND JUST QUIT...

<u>AGAIN</u>, THAT'S YOUR DECISION.

FINE.

RIC... YOU KNOW I WANT YOU IN THE BAND. WE'VE BEEN THROUGH A LOT TOGETHER, NON? I STUCK BY YOU THROUGH YOUR DRUNK-DRIVING CHARGES AND ALL OF YOUR OTHER FUCK-UPS BECAUSE I KNOW YOU'RE WORTH IT.

I KNOW IT'S NOT JUST A MONKEY SUIT. I KNOW HOW GOOD YOU ARE WITH THE KIDS. I <u>NEED</u> YOU. WE STAND TO MAKE SOME SERIOUS MONEY WITH THE NET-WORK DEAL. YOU CAN TAKE THE MONEY AND RUN - WE CAN BE SET FOR LIFE...

RIGHT, WE JUST HAVE TO LIVE WITH OURSELVES...

OH, COME ON MAN, YOU'VE LIVED WITH WAY WORSE THAN THAT... JUST TAKE IT EASY WITH THE BOOZE AND DECIDE IF YOU WANT TO BE PART OF THIS OR NOT, OKAY?

BECAUSE YOU NEED TO REMEM-BER WHAT IS PAYING FOR YOUR KEITH MOON ANTICS IS WHAT WE'RE DOING: ENTER-TAINING LITTLE CHILDREN.

HEY, SHERRI...

...THANKS.

THANKS FOR TALKING, MAN... I'M... UH...

...SORRY IF I'VE BEEN A DICK...

AH... THIS IS HOW THE MAT-URE ME KEEPS GETTING REELED BACK IN...

...THE SURLY MAN-BOY, ex-BOYFRIEND TOSSES ME A TINY RAY OF HOPE AND IMMEDIATELY I'M ALL: "OH LOOK, HE'S CONTRITE! HE'S REALLY SINCERE THIS TIME."

I SHOULD KICK HIM OUTTA THE BAND LIKE I KICKED HIM OUTTA THE RELATIONSHIP...

"IF" YOU'VE BEEN A DICK?

LATER, RIC.

CHAPTER FOUR:
CRUSHES ON OLDER MEN

I KNOW
I KNO
WE'V

We've done everything we can do here damage control -wise... The kid's parents were great, really. By the end, they were blaming THEIR KID.

Ever the lawyer, Harvey... No, I did not get them to sign something to that effect. I'm reasonably convinced that Sherri and all of us are safe here.

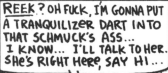

REEK? OH FUCK, I'M GONNA PUT A TRANQUILIZER DART INTO THAT SCHMUCK'S ASS... I KNOW... I'LL TALK TO HER. SHE'S RIGHT HERE, SAY HI...

HI HARVEY! SORRY FOR ALL THE TROUBLE...

OKAY HARVEY, I'LL LET YOU KNOW IF ANYTHING CHANGES HERE... OKAY, BYE.

SHERRI! THAT WAS A GREAT SHOW UP TO WHERE THE ASS IN THE MONKEY SUIT ATTACKED THE KID...

SNAP!

THANKS FOR TALKING TO THE PARENTS, SWEETY. THAT HELPED A LOT.

THANKS TO **YOU**, KARL, FOR HANDLING ALL OF THIS!

MEH, IT'S IN THE JOB DESCRIP-TION. IF I'M NOT CONTINUALLY HANDLING SHIT, YOU'RE PAYING ME TOO MUCH, SHERRI.

IT'S LITTLE WONDER THAT I KEEP DEVELOPING CRUSHES ON THE OLDER MEN THAT SUR-ROUND ME AND TAKE CARE OF ALL MY TROUBLES. THEY'RE CAPABLE AND THOUGHTFUL AND DON'T ACT LIKE PETULANT CHILDREN ALL THE TIME.

A BOY LIKE RIC DOESN'T STAND A CHANCE WITH STUDS LIKE KARL AND HARVEY AROUND.

SHERRI, WE NEED TO TALK ABOUT REEK...

BACK WHEN WE WERE IN A PUNK COVER BAND, "RICK" CHANGED HIS NAME TO THE MORE ROCK-AND-ROLL "RIC." UNFORTUNATELY, MOST PEOPLE TEND TO READ AND PRONOUNCE IT AS "REEK." VERB: SMELL STRONGLY AND UNPLEASANTLY; STINK.

I KNOW, I KNOW...

SHERRI, NOT TO BE A PUSHER—AND, I'LL BACK ANY DECISION YOU MAKE — BUT THAT BOY IS NOT GOING TO CHANGE.

HE'S CONSTANTLY PUTTING YOU IN A PLACE OF LIABILITY AND WITH THE NETWORK WATCHING OUR EVERY MOVE, IT COULD SCREW UP THE SATURDAY MORNING SHOW DEAL.

I'M PRAYING, FUCKING PRAYING I TELL YOU, THAT THEY DON'T GET WIND OF THIS LATEST FIASCO. I'M HOPING NOBODY GOT THAT ON A CELL PHONE VIDEO THAT WILL COME UP ON YOUTUBE AND BITE US ON THE ASS.

THE GUY FROM DEVELOPMENT AT PLAYTIME IS WAY ON TO REEK. HE ASKED A LOT OF QUESTIONS, KNEW ABOUT THE DRUNK DRIVING ARREST, HINTED POLITELY ABOUT DRUG USE...

THEY ARE ON TO HIM AND THEY ARE EXTREMELY NERVOUS. PLAYTIME IS THE SECOND BIGGEST CHILDREN'S CABLE NETWORK AND THEIR BIGGEST BACKER IS A CONSORTIUM OF CHRISTIAN-RIGHT MILLIONAIRES. THEY DON'T DIG DRUG-ADDLED ALCOHOLICS AS THE CHILDRENS TALENT.

WELL, THAT SOUNDS HORRIBLE, KARL. I DON'T EVEN KNOW IF I CAN STAND BEING IN CAHOOTS WITH SUCH PEOPLE.

MAR
JUIN.

WELL, SUCH PEOPLE ARE OFFERING YOU COMPLETE CREATIVE CONTROL TO DEVELOP A CHILDREN'S SHOW AND THEY HAVE SHITLOADS OF MONEY. CHRISTIAN-RIGHT AMERICAN MONEY, YES, BUT WITH A GUARANTEE OF COMPLETE CREATIVE CONTROL.

NOT TO BE THE DEVIL IN YOUR EAR, BUT THIS IS PROBABLY THE BEST OFFER YOU WILL EVER GET AND YOUR ON-AGAIN, OFF-AGAIN BOYFRIEND IN THE MONKEY SUIT MIGHT WELL JEOPARDIZE ALL OF THAT.

I KNOW YOU'RE NOT THE MERCENARY TYPE, I KNOW YOU'RE AN ARTIST, BUT I ALSO KNOW THAT REEK IS NOT THE TYPE TO DO THE RIGHT THING. YOU ARE GOING TO HAVE TO MAKE THE DECISION HERE...

He's **NOT** MY ON-AGAIN, OFF-AGAIN BOYFRIEND...

WELL, THAT WASN'T THE MAIN THRUST OF MY SPEECH, SHERRI...

AH KARL, IT'S A LOT TO THINK ABOUT... I'M ALSO NERVOUS ABOUT RIC FLUBBING UP THIS DEAL AND THEN I'M NOT EVEN SURE I WANT IT MYSELF...

I DON'T KNOW WHAT TO TELL YOU, BABY. I'M A MONEY-GRUB-BING OLD MAN, PLUS I GET TEN PERCENT, SO **MY** FEELING IS, PROTECT THE NETWORK DEAL WITH EVERYTHING YOU GOT.

SHERRI, THE THING ABOUT DEALS WITH THE DEVIL IS THE DEVIL DOESN'T WANT TO DEAL WITH JUST ANYBODY...

IF YOU REALLY ARE NOT SURE THAT THIS IS WHAT YOU WANT TO DO, THEN YOU SHOULD FOLLOW YOUR HEART AND WALK AWAY AS FAST AS YOU CAN...

I GOTTA GO. WE HAVE A ONE-THIRTY SOUND CHECK FOR TOMORROW'S SHOW. YOU WANT ME TO PICK YOU UP?

NAW, I'LL SEE YOU THERE.

KARL, YOU'RE A GOOD KID, YOU KNOW THAT?

YEAH, WELL, FOR THE RECORD, THE MONEY-GRUBBING MAN-AGER PART OF ME SAYS **NOT** TO FOLLOW YOUR HEART.

HEY, STEVIE!

HEY SHERRI BABY, WHAT'S HAPPENING?

OH, JUST WONDERING WHICH DIRECTION TO TAKE FOR THE REST OF MY LIFE... NO BIGGIE... YOU EVER WONDER WHAT THE HELL YOU'RE DOING WITH YOUR LIFE, STEVIE?

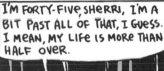

I'M FORTY-FIVE, SHERRI, I'M A BIT PAST ALL OF THAT, I GUESS. I MEAN, MY LIFE IS MORE THAN HALF OVER.

JESUS, STEVIE, NO IT ISN'T!

IT'S TRUE...

WELL, THANKS FOR GETTING RIC OUT OF THERE AFTER THE "INCIDENT" WITH THE KID.

SHERRI, YOU KNOW I'M ALWAYS A HAIR'S BREADTH AWAY FROM THUMPING THAT GUY. I DON'T WANNA BE A PRICK HERE, BUT YOU'VE GOT TO GET WISE AND KICK HIM OUT OF THE BAND AND GET HIM OUT OF YOUR LIFE. HE'S BAD NEWS.

I'M GIVING HIM ONE LAST CHANCE...

STEVIE, WHO'S BEEN WITH ME AS LONG AS RIC HAS, AND KNOWS OUR HIST-ORY, DOESN'T EVEN SNORT AT THE THOUGHT OF "ONE MORE CHANCE" THAT RIC CAN ADD TO HIS STOCK PILE OF CHANCES THROWN AWAY THAT HE MUST KEEP SOMEWHERE IN HIS CLOSET.

CHAPTER FIVE:
THE OLD GRIND

MEEP MEEP MEEP
MEEP MEEP

400

IT'S MY MORNING TO GET UP EARLY WITH SAM AND AM I THINKING: "HOW NICE FOR MY TIRED WIFE TO BE SLEEPING IN AND HOW SHE'LL BE DOING THE SAME FOR ME TOMORROW?"

NO, I AM INTENTLY, RESENT-FULLY COUNTING THE MINUTES. WHEN THERE IS A FAMINE, IT RARELY BRINGS OUT GOOD BEHAVIOR; A MOTHER KILLS A SON FOR A HANDFUL OF GRAIN.

WE HAVE A FAMINE OF TIME AND SLEEP IN OUR HOUSE AND IT INEVITABLY MAKES US PETTY INSTEAD OF NOBLE.

HEY, TIME'S UP.

GOOD MORNING TO YOU TOO...

I GOTTA GO. I'M GONNA BE LATE FOR WORK.

OKAY, OKAY.

LOOK, YOU'VE ALREADY HAD SEVEN MINUTES LONGER THAN YOU'RE SUPPOSED TO...

UH, THERE'S THE PETTINESS I WAS TALKING ABOUT...

(*APOLOGIES TO FIGHT CLUB.)

OH JOHN, I'VE GOT CROSBY LITTLETON'S AGENT ON THE LINE. WANNA GET YOUR COAT OFF AND CALL HIM BACK?

NO, I NEED TO TAKE IT. THANKS, SALLY.

JOHN SPEAKING...HEY, MARIO. HOW ARE YOU?

"FUCKING EXCELLENT?"

...OH, THAT'S GREAT... NO I HEARD THE SHOOT WENT WELL. I GET THE CONTACT SHEETS TODAY. I'LL SEND YOU OVER SOME JPEGS. WHAT'S THAT? YEAH, I HEARD...

LOOK MARIO, IT'S NEVER OUR POLICY TO PAY A SUBJECT FOR A PHOTO SHOOT. MY EDITOR ASSURED ME SHE MADE THIS VERY CLEAR TO CROSBY DURING THE INTERVIEW...

< THANKS, SALLY... >

YEAH, YEAH, I KNOW...

...BUT WE DID DISCUSS IT WITH HIM... MARIO, IT'S ALL QUID PRO QUO. THE PIECE ON YOUR GUY IS GREAT PUBLICITY...

YEAH, YEAH, I KNOW.

THIS GOES ON FOR ALMOST AN HOUR. BY THE END, I'M CHECKING EMAILS, SIGNING MEMOS, PAYING BILLS ONLINE, AND SAYING, "YEAH, YEAH, I KNOW," WHENEVER NECESSARY.

...OKAY, MARIO... GOOD TALKING TO YOU... —OKAY, I WILL.

BYE.

PHEW.

CLICK*

HEEEEY, JOHN. GOT A MINUTE?

HEY SARAH, COME ON IN. I WANTED TO SEE YOU.

OH, WHAT ABOUT?

THAT KID'S DVD YOU GAVE ME... UH... SHERRI... OR JERRI SOMETHING...

I'M BEING COY. THE DVD IS ENTITLED "SHERRI SMALLS AND HER BIG BAND." THE SUBTITLE AFTER THE COLON IS "COMPLETELY BANANAS." THIS DISK IS RATHER A FAVOURITE OF SAM AND I.

OH RIGHT, SHERRI SMALLS. SHE'S LIKE THE NEW RAFFIOR SOMETHING. SHE'S "THE SHIT" IN KID'S MUSIC.

OH, WELL IT WAS PRETTY GOOD. IF YOU GET ANYTHING ELSE OF HERS FOR REVIEW, I'D TAKE THEM. UH, WAS THERE A PRESS KIT ATTACHED TO THAT DVD?

PROBABLY, YOU WANT IT?

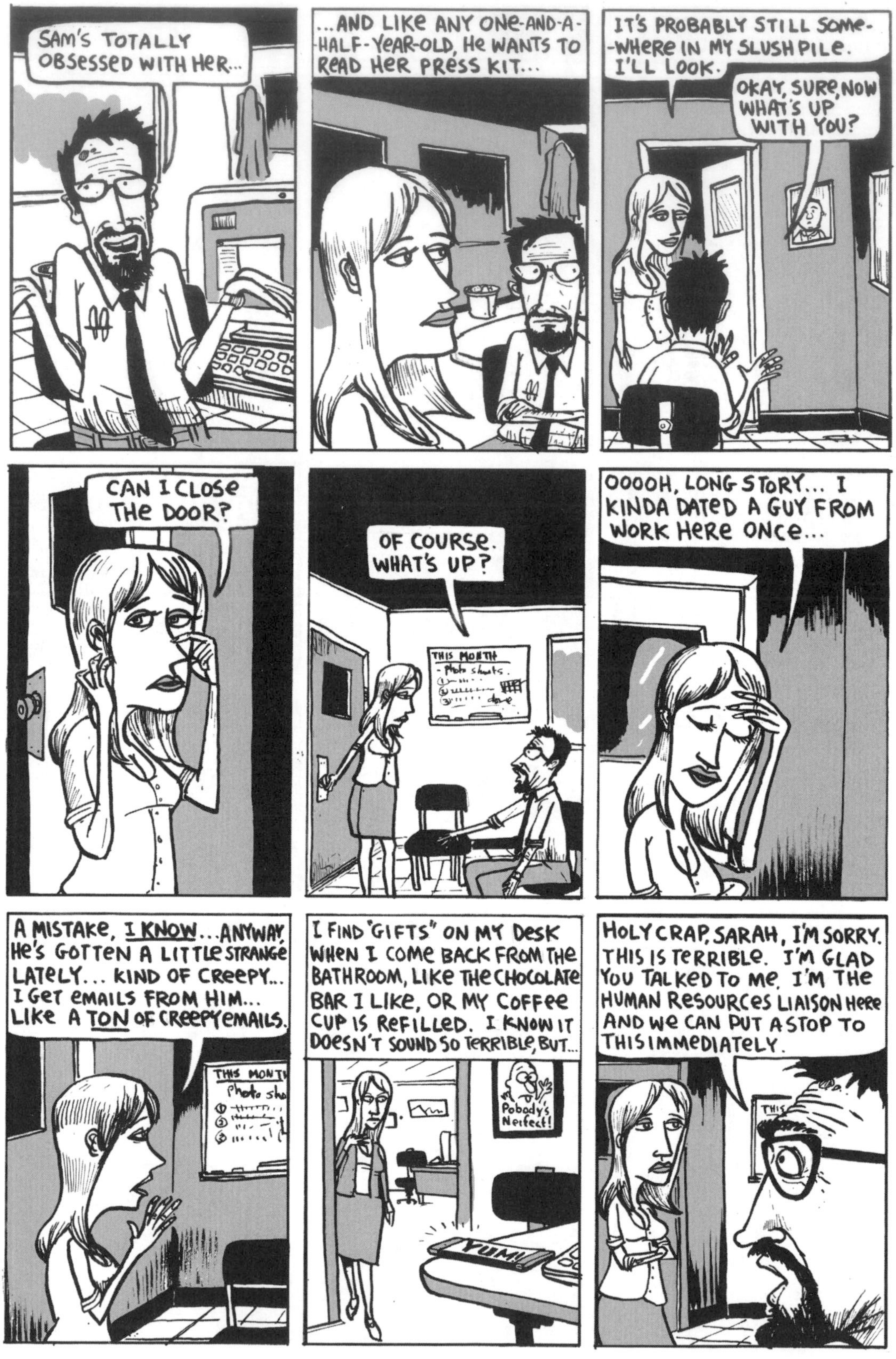
SAM'S TOTALLY OBSESSED WITH HER...
...AND LIKE ANY ONE-AND-A-HALF-YEAR-OLD, HE WANTS TO READ HER PRESS KIT...
IT'S PROBABLY STILL SOMEWHERE IN MY SLUSH PILE. I'LL LOOK.
OKAY, SURE, NOW WHAT'S UP WITH YOU?
CAN I CLOSE THE DOOR?
OF COURSE. WHAT'S UP?
THIS MONTH
OOOOH, LONG STORY... I KINDA DATED A GUY FROM WORK HERE ONCE...
A MISTAKE, I KNOW... ANYWAY, HE'S GOTTEN A LITTLE STRANGE LATELY... KIND OF CREEPY... I GET EMAILS FROM HIM... LIKE A TON OF CREEPY EMAILS.
I FIND "GIFTS" ON MY DESK WHEN I COME BACK FROM THE BATHROOM, LIKE THE CHOCOLATE BAR I LIKE, OR MY COFFEE CUP IS REFILLED. I KNOW IT DOESN'T SOUND SO TERRIBLE, BUT...
Pobody's Neifect!
YUM!
HOLY CRAP, SARAH, I'M SORRY. THIS IS TERRIBLE. I'M GLAD YOU TALKED TO ME. I'M THE HUMAN RESOURCES LIAISON HERE AND WE CAN PUT A STOP TO THIS IMMEDIATELY.

WELL, I CAME TO YOU 'CAUSE YOU'RE MY FRIEND, NOT 'CAUSE YOU'RE THE H.R.-GUY. I'D LIKE TO KEEP IT UNOFFICIAL AT THIS POINT. I WAS HOPING YOU COULD TALK TO HIM OFF THE RECORD OR WHAT-EVER. HE WON'T LISTEN TO ME. HE DENIES THAT HE IS DOING IT, WHICH IS EVEN SCARIER.

YEAH, THAT'S NUTS. - LOOK, WE CAN DO THIS BY THE BOOK. WHAT HE'S DOING IS ILLEGAL, AND

I REALLY DON'T WANT ANYONE TO LOSE THEIR JOB OR ANY-THING, I JUST WANT HIM TO LEAVE ME ALONE. IF YOU CAN JUST TALK TO HIM...

SURE, OKAY, DONE. WHO ARE WE TALKING ABOUT?

OOOH... GOD... LOOK, IT WAS A ONE-TIME THING. WE WENT OUT FOR DRINKS AFTER THE LAST WORK EVENT.

WHO? IT'S MARK, ISN'T IT?

NO WORSE IT'S JEFF IN ACCOUNTING.

OH.

I KNOW: DILBERT. HE'S ACTUALLY CUTE AND HE SEEMED NICE, ES-PECIALLY AFTER FOUR BEERS. GOD: YOU REALLY SHOULDN'T SHIT WHERE YOU SLEEP, EH?

WELL, AS HR LIAISON OFFICER, I WOULD AGREE... DON'T WORRY, I'LL TALK TO HIM AND WE'LL KEEP IT QUIET AS LONG AS HE COOPERATES, OKAY?

THANKS, JOHN. YOU'RE THE GREATEST.

UH, TECH-NICALLY AGAINST HR-POLICY...

CHAPTER SIX:

YOU KNOW YOU'RE A GROWN-UP WHEN...

YOU COULD LOSE YOUR JOB. SO, YOU NEED TO CALM DOWN AND LISTEN TO ME. I'M TALKING TO YOU AS... AS A FRIEND...

YEAH, WELL, THE HESITATION, THE ELLIPSIS IN THERE AND THE REP-EPITION OF "AS" MAY HAVE RUINED THE AUTHENTICITY OF THAT...

THERE'S NOTHING TO LISTEN TO. I HAVEN'T DONE ANYTHING.

JEFF, YOU'RE ACTING SCARY. YOU'RE SCARING ME RIGHT NOW. I'M THE COMPANY'S HR REP. I'M HERE UNOFFICIALLY, BUT I'M TELLING YOU IF YOU SEND ONE MORE EMAIL TO SARAH, OR EVEN TALK TO HER OR LEAVE ANY--THING ON HER DESK...

...IF YOU HAVE ANY CONTACT WITH HER AT ALL, I WILL WRITE YOU UP WITH AN OFFICIAL WARNING. THE COMPANY WILL NOT TOLERATE THIS KIND OF BEHAVIOUR AND AS SOMEONE WHO WORKS WITH YOU, I GOTTA SAY, YOU ARE ACTING REALLY CREEPY, JEFF.

LIKE YOU'VE NEVER DONE ANYTHING WRONG... MISTER PERFECT.

HEY JEFF, YOU NEED TO CALM THE HECK DOWN. GO TAKE A WALK, WASH YOUR FACE AND THEN GO BACK TO WORK. LEAVE SARAH ALONE. I DON'T KNOW WHY YOU'RE PISSED AT ME. I'M KEEPING THIS OFF THE RECORD...

BUT I'LL BE WATCHING YOU AND IF ANYTHING HAPPENS, THIS WILL BECOME HARDCORE OFFICIAL. SO SLOW DOWN AND LOOK AT THIS RATIONALLY, OKAY?

OKAY. FINE.

MAYBE I'LL BE WATCHING YOU.

OKAY, WHATEVER. YOU DO THAT, JEFF. JUST STAY AWAY FROM SARAH, UNDERSTAND?

WOW, THAT WAS BORDERLINE INSANE.

RANDY?

JOHN, CHECK THIS OUT! CHECK THIS OUT! PALM PILOT HAS JUST RELEASED AN EXTENDED FULL-SIZE KEYBOARD YOU CAN SNAP ON AND A TWELVE--INCH ADD-ON SCREEN. OH MY GOD, IT'S SO COOL!

RIGHT, BUT, WELL, IT'S NOT VERY PORTABLE... ISN'T THAT THE POINT OF THESE DEVICES?

IT'S FOR AT HOME, JOHN.

OH, WELL, IT IS COOL THEN.

WHAT'S UP, IS YOUR FONT PROBLEM BACK?

OH MY GOODNESS, NO! NO, IT'S ALL GOOD THERE! NO, NO, NO... WHEW!

LIKE ALL TECHNICIANS, MECHANICS, DOCTORS, OR ANY PROFESSION THAT HAS AN EXPERTISE THAT YOU DO NOT, RANDY IS ABUSIVE, SARCASTIC AND MAKES ONE FEEL LIKE A PURPOSELY DULL-WITTED INFANT THAT THEY ARE VERY ANGRY AT.

...TOLD YOU BEFORE, TPD-TYPE FONTS WILL CORRUPT IF YOU'RE RUNNING A DMP-V.2 OPERATING SYSTEM. END OF STORY.

I'M SO VERY GLAD TO REPORT THAT MY FONT PROBLEM IS NOT BACK.

NO, NO, I...I WANT YOU TO KEEP AN EYE ON SOME--ONE, UNOFFICIALLY.

I KEEP AN EYE ON EVERYONE AND I DO SO OFFICIALLY.

YEAH, I KNOW, LOOK, IT'S A HUMAN RESOURCES THING, A BORDERLINE HARASSMENT THING, AND THE COMPLAINANT WANTS TO KEEP IT UNOFFICIAL AT THIS POINT. I'VE TALKED TO THE OTHER PARTY AND THEY WERE KIND OF CRAZY TO PUT IT LIGHTLY...

I SHOULDN'T HAVE TO TELL YOU THAT YOU'RE BREAKING LIKE FOUR HUNDRED LEVELS OF COMPANY PROTOCOL BY EVEN SUGGESTING THIS BECAUSE YOU'RE THE "HR MANAGER". -SNORT.

RIGHT, I DO KNOW, BUT I'M ASKING YOU AS A FRIEND TO HELP ANOTHER FRIEND...

I NEED TO KNOW WHO IS INVOLVED AND WHAT THEY ARE INVOLVED IN BEFORE I CAN TELL YOU ANY--THING ABOUT ANYTHING. AND, I'M NOT BREAKING ANY COMPANY POLICIES.

It's Jeff Pool in Accounts and Sarah, the review editor.

Eww, gross, Sarah and "Dilbert." Pool spends much of his day surfing porn and looking for a new job, which puts him in the same league as about 97% of the drones here...

Hmm, well, all I need is a heads up if he tries to send Sarah any more emails, if you can do that?

SKEITCH.

Dude, I can program it so that the Eiffel Tower lights up if he sends her an email.

"If you can do that." Jeez!

Well, okay, I guess you know that just the heads up will be enough... As usual, I am in awe of your giant brain. Thanks man.

Done.

TYPE TYPE TYPE TYPE

So, it's after one o'clock and I have no work done. Which I have recently discovered puts me in league with 97% of my co-workers, minus the porn and the job search. My exchange with the crazed Dilbert has left me pretty shook up, I confess.

When I was younger, I would have handled that so differently. I would have been thinking of all the ways I could kick the shit out of that mouthy, psycho account-ant. Now, I just think that a crazy dude like that could have a gun, could kill my kids, burn my house down, go on an office shooting spree, etc., etc...

My dad told me once that the biggest part of growing up is learning of the good sense in being afraid of things. I guess I'm grown up now, 'cause I'm afraid all the time now of almost everything.

CHAPTER SEVEN:
CHECK ONE, TWO, (BUCKLE MY SHOE)

SETTING UP FOR A SHOW IS THE ONE TIME THAT ALL OF US CAN ALLOW OURSELVES THE LUXURY OF PRETENDING WE'RE ALL ROCK AND ROLL.

ROADIES CARRYING AMPS TRAILING WIRES, THE DRUMMER SETTING UP HIS KIT, GUITARS COMING OUT OF CASES WITH EXAGGERATED SNAPPING OF LOCKS. THE SOUND GUY INTONING "SIBILANCE, SIBILANCE, CHECK..."

CHECK ONE... CHECK...

OH, IT ALL TENDS TO FALL APART A BIT WHEN WE LAUNCH INTO A SONG LIKE "YOUR ELEPHANT IS ASLEEP ON MY FOOT."

OPENING NOTES OF PURPLE HAZE

SHERRI! ARE YOU GOOD THIS MORNING, MY DEAR GIRL? YOU LOOK SMASHING.

HEY KARL, HOW ARE YOU? I'M ACTUALLY A BIT ROUGH. I DROWNED MY SORROWS IN RED WINE AND DORITOS LAST NIGHT.

WELL, SUCK IT UP GIRL. GARY FRIED-KIN, JUNIOR DIRECTOR OF PROG--RAMMING AT PLAYTIME IS STOPPING BY TODAY. I'M HOPING TO CHRIST HE HASN'T HEARD ABOUT REEK'S LAT-EST ANTICS BUT I SUSPECT THAT'S THE REASON FOR A "FRIENDLY" SURPRISE VISIT.

OH, NO, NO, NO, KARL! NOT BEFORE A SHOW, I ALREADY FEEL LIKE BARFING...

COME ON, SHERRI SWEETIE, WE ALL GOTTA PLAY NICE. I HAVE TO KEEP A MUZZLE ON THE MONKEY SUIT AND YOU WILL DAZZLE THE EXECUTIVE, BARFING OR NOT.

SMEK!

THE MORE I HAVE TIME TO THINK ABOUT THIS DEAL, THE LESS I WANT IT.

PART OF ME WANTS TO REJECT IT BECAUSE THIS DEAL MEANS ACCEPTING THAT I ENTERTAIN CHILDREN FOR A LIVING. NOT AS A TEMPORARY GIG, OR A LARK, BUT AS A CAREER.

THAT I DO NOT WRITE WRY, CLEVER, SAD SONGS ABOUT BREAKUPS, DRINKING TOO MUCH, OR FUCKING, FOR ADULT AUDIENCES, AND A BIG PART OF ME HATES THAT AS MUCH AS RIC DOES.

SELL OUT...

THE NETWORK GUY IS COMING AND I CAN ALREADY SMELL HIS COLOGNE. WE'LL HAVE TO HAVE LUNCH—PROBABLY EXPENSIVE SUSHI—AND I'LL HAVE TO EXPLAIN THAT FISH AREN'T VEGET- ABLES TO ME, THAT I'M THAT KIND OF VEGETARIAN, AND HE'LL SAY HORRIBLE STUFF AND THEN FAKE STUFF TO APPEASE ME AND HE WILL UNDOUB- TEDLY KEEP CHECKING THAT MY TITS ARE STILL THERE.

OUT- STANDING! HA HA HA!

KARL, YOU MEET THE NETWORK GUY, PLEASE?

RECYC YOUR CUP?

DEAR GIRL, I'D LOVE TO HAVE A FREE LUNCH WITH THE HANDSOME YOUNG MAN IN QUESTION, BUT I'M MEET- ING WITH YOUR RECORD LABEL SO THAT UNCLE KARL CAN TEAR THEM A NICE, NEW A-HOLE FOR HOW INEPTLY THEY DISTRIBUTED YOUR LAST C D. THAT'S WHAT I'M HAVING FOR LUNCH.

EXIT.

UH, SHERRI, THE SOUND- GUY NEEDS YOU AT THE MIC.

TINY TIME CAPSULES.

THE OTHER THING IS: WHY DO I HAVE TO MAKE THE GOOD CAREER MOVE? WE'RE ALL TRAINED, LIKE GLUTTONS AT A BUFFET, TO KEEP GOBBLING UP EVERY "OPPORTUNITY" THAT PRESENTS ITSELF LIKE IT WERE POPCORN SHRIMP OR CHICKEN NUGGETS OR SOMETHING.

SHERRI, CAN YOU JUST SING SOMETHING, ANYTHING, SO I CAN GET SOME LEVELS?

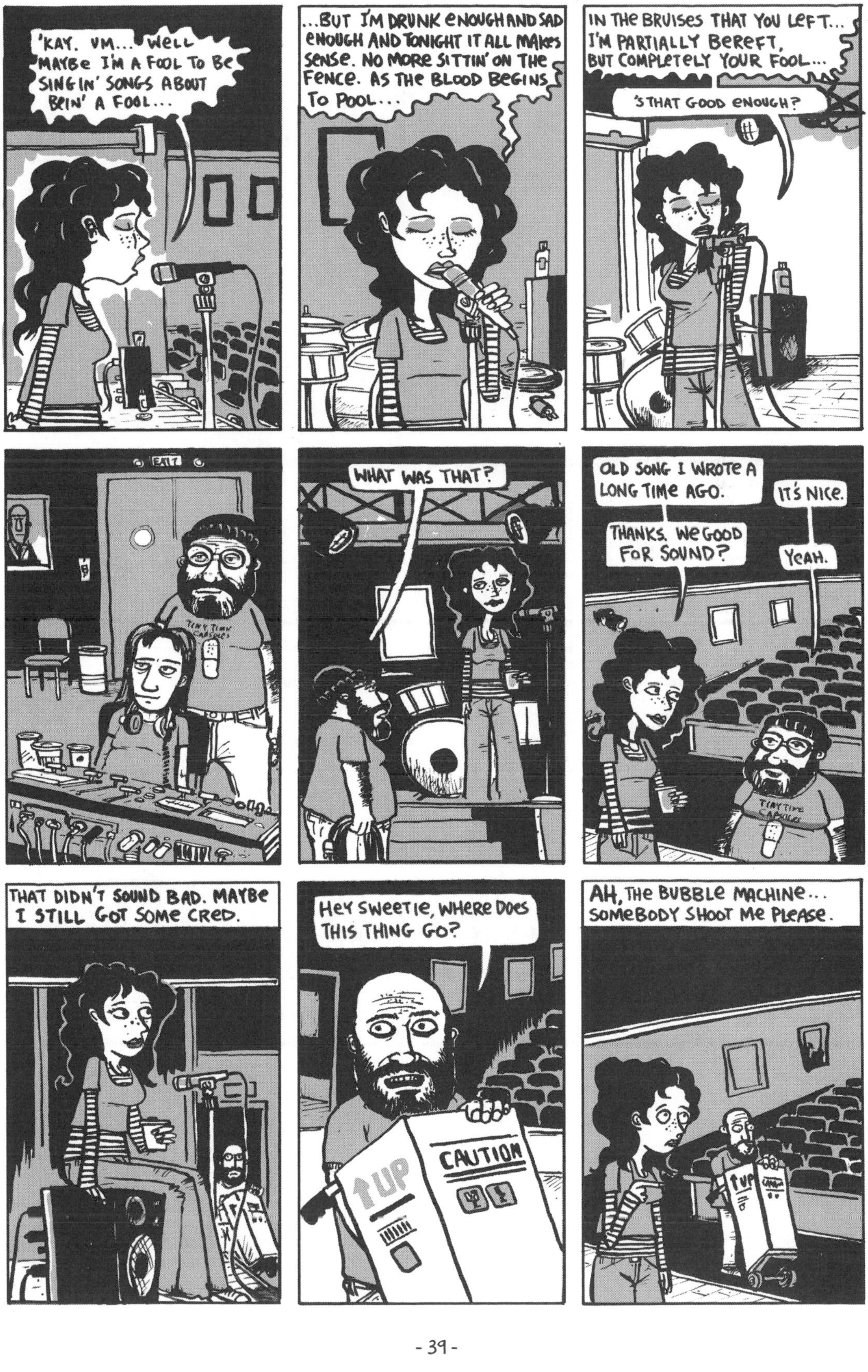
'KAY. UM... WELL MAYBE I'M A FOOL TO BE SINGIN' SONGS ABOUT BEIN' A FOOL...
...BUT I'M DRUNK ENOUGH AND SAD ENOUGH AND TONIGHT IT ALL MAKES SENSE. NO MORE SITTIN' ON THE FENCE. AS THE BLOOD BEGINS TO POOL...
IN THE BRUISES THAT YOU LEFT... I'M PARTIALLY BEREFT, BUT COMPLETELY YOUR FOOL...
'S THAT GOOD ENOUGH?
EXIT
WHAT WAS THAT?
OLD SONG I WROTE A LONG TIME AGO.
IT'S NICE.
THANKS. WE GOOD FOR SOUND?
YEAH.
THAT DIDN'T SOUND BAD. MAYBE I STILL GOT SOME CRED.
HEY SWEETIE, WHERE DOES THIS THING GO?
UP
CAUTION
AH, THE BUBBLE MACHINE... SOMEBODY SHOOT ME PLEASE.

CHAPTER EIGHT:

THE EYE, AND HOW THE OCULAR MUSCLES DEVELOP A TENDENCY TO WANDER

YEAH, SO...

...THE SHOTS OF THE BASKETBALL PLAYER ARE IN AND, AT A GLANCE, THEY ARE MEDIOCRE. LIKE NOTH-ING STANDS OUT. LOOKS LIKE I'LL BE PULLING THE OLD "ENLARGE THE BAD PHOTO AND MAKE IT ART" TRICK. NO WORRIES.

OKAY... THAT GUY'S A JERK... WHAT ABOUT THE ILLUSTRATIONS FOR THE BEHIND THE SCENES IN RESTAURANT KITCHENS PIECE?

RIGHT, WELL, A FINISHED ARTICLE WOULD HELP ME AND THE ILLUSTRATOR... MS. DOR-MAN, YOU'RE BREAKIN' MY BALLS.

I KNOW, I KNOW, I'M SORRY... MY BALLS ARE AS BROKEN AS YOUR OWN. BUT I'M PROMISED A NEW DRAFT TODAY. I'LL SEND IT TO YOU IMMEDIATELY. SO, WE'RE LOOKING PRETTY GOOD THIS ISSUE.

YEAH, PRETTY GOOD, I GUESS. WE DON'T HAVE A COVER OF COURSE. BUT I'M COUNTING ON THE PHOTO SHOOT OF THAT WRITER LADY TO KNOCK OUR SOCKS OFF.

I GOTTA REMEMBER TO COM-MISSION A PHOTOGRAPHER FOR THAT, IT'S COMING UP SOON. OR, WE COULD TRY FOR A RE-SHOOT OF THE BASKETBALL PRICK. HE'D DO IT IF WE PAY.

I DON'T WANT THAT CREEP ON MY COVER. KEEP ME INFORMED ON THE WRITER-LADY PHOTO SHOOT...

ANYTHING ELSE?

NOPE, THE COLUMNISTS LOOK OKAY. SAME OL' SAME OL'. THE FINISHED SPREADS LOOK OKAY.

I DON'T KNOW, JOHNNY... IT ALL LOOKS OKAY...

OKAAAAAAY... THANKS. I KNOW THINGS ARE KIND OF LAME AT THIS POINT, BUT I'M GOING OVER ALL THE LAYOUTS AGAIN AND I PROMISE YOU WILL BE DAZZLED, DAZZLED BEYOND THREE "OKAYS," AT LEAST.

I'M SORRY, BUDDY. I JUST THINK WE NEED TO "JAZZ IT UP" A BIT...

'KAY. "JAZZ IT UP" I SHALL. THERE'S A "JAZZ IT UP" FILTER IN PHOTOSHOP, I THINK. — WHAT ARE YOU DOING FOR LUNCH?

EATING A CAN OF SALMON.

GROSS. OKAY, SEE YOU.

WHERE'S THE GOD--DAMN WAITRESS?

-41-

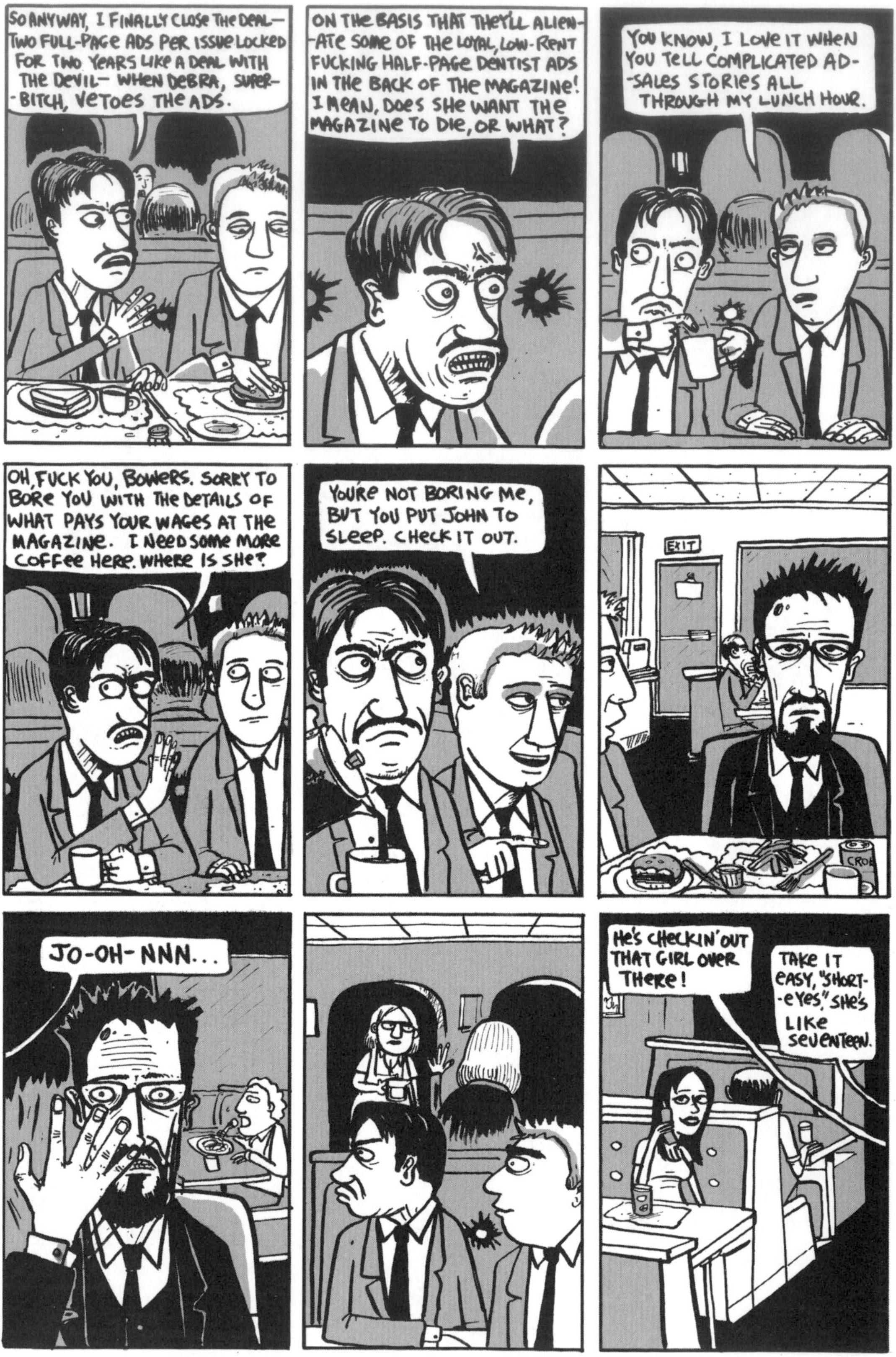
SO ANYWAY, I FINALLY CLOSE THE DEAL— TWO FULL-PAGE ADS PER ISSUE LOCKED FOR TWO YEARS LIKE A DEAL WITH THE DEVIL— WHEN DEBRA, SUPER--BITCH, VETOES THE ADS.
ON THE BASIS THAT THEY'LL ALIEN--ATE SOME OF THE LOYAL, LOW-RENT FUCKING HALF-PAGE DENTIST ADS IN THE BACK OF THE MAGAZINE! I MEAN, DOES SHE WANT THE MAGAZINE TO DIE, OR WHAT?
YOU KNOW, I LOVE IT WHEN YOU TELL COMPLICATED AD--SALES STORIES ALL THROUGH MY LUNCH HOUR.
OH, FUCK YOU, BOWERS. SORRY TO BORE YOU WITH THE DETAILS OF WHAT PAYS YOUR WAGES AT THE MAGAZINE. I NEED SOME MORE COFFEE HERE. WHERE IS SHE?
YOU'RE NOT BORING ME, BUT YOU PUT JOHN TO SLEEP. CHECK IT OUT.
EXIT
JO-OH-NNN...
HE'S CHECKIN' OUT THAT GIRL OVER THERE!
TAKE IT EASY, "SHORT--EYES," SHE'S LIKE SEVENTEEN.

I WAS NOT. I WAS STARING INTO SPACE. JESUS, TELL ME MORE ABOUT THE ADS, MARK. THAT SHIT IS FASCINATING.

BUT I WAS...

OGLING A GIRL WHO MIGHT BE THE SAME AGE AS MY DAUGHTERS. NOT COOL. IT'S LIKE AS I'VE BECOME SEXLESS AND UNNATTRACTIVE TO PRETTY YOUNG WOMEN, INVISIBLE TO THEM REALLY, THEY HAVE BECOME INFINITELY MORE INTERESTING TO ME.

SO I'M AN OGLER. REDUCING WOMEN TO A SERIES OF PARTS AND ANALYSING THE MERITS OF THOSE BITS IN SECRET, SEXIST DIATRIBES IN MY HEAD THAT SHOCK EVEN ME.

HUH HUH HUH HUH.

OUTWARDLY, I'M STILL A SENSITIVE NEW-AGE GUY WHILE ALL OF THIS IS GOING ON. I KNOW ALL OF THE RIGHT THINGS TO SAY AND FEEL BECAUSE I USED TO SAY AND FEEL THEM. I MEAN, I GOT MORE RESPECT FOR THE GUY WHO OPENLY GOES TO STRIP JOINTS AND IS HONEST ABOUT HIS SEXIST SHIT THAN A CLOSET SCUMBAG LIKE MYSELF.

HUH H. HUH HUH

IT'S NOT LIKE IT'S ABOUT SEX ANYWAY. I'M NEVER GOING TO FLIRT OR MAKE ANY KIND OF MOVES ON ANYONE. ALL THIS IS CONCURRENT TO MY RABID SEX-DRIVE ACTUALLY BEGINNING TO DECLINE.

I DON'T WANT TO EUPHEMISTICALLY "SLEEP" WITH ANY OF THESE WOMEN, I GUESS I'D JUST LIKE IT IF ONE OF THEM WOULD ACTUALLY CONSIDER EUPHEMISTICALLY SLEEPING WITH ME. OH YEAH, PLUS, I'M HAPPILY MARRIED. SHEESH, WHAT A KOOK!

WE GOTTA GO. I GOT LOYAL ADVERTISERS TO ALIENATE.

OKAY, LET'S GO. HOW MUCH DO I OWE?

CHAPTER NINE:
SYMPATICO WITH THE DEVIL

SO, GARY FRIEDKIN, JUNIOR DIRECTOR OF PROGRAMMING AND DEVELOPMENT AT PLAYTIME, IS YOUNG AND HANDSOME, NOT AN UGLY OLD GOON. HE'S SINCERE AND NOT SMARMY OR FALSE. WHO KNEW?

HE REMEMBERS MY NAME, AND NOT IN A SCARY, ROBOTIC SALES-GUY WAY, BUT AS IF HE LIKES SAYING IT. HE'S FAMILIAR WITH THE BAND'S RECORD-INGS AND SEEMS GENUINELY EXCITED TO BE DOING THE JOB HE'S DOING. IF HE'S A PHONY, HE'S A GOOD ONE. IF HE'S THE DEVIL, I SAY, "HAIL SATAN!"

HE'S A JACK RUSSEL. I-UH... RESCUED HIM FROM A TEST--ING LAB.

I'M SORRY, I KEEP BLATHERING ON ABOUT ME. I WANT TO TALK ABOUT YOU AND YOUR SHOW!

HERE'S THE WAY I ENVISION IT... STOP ME ANYTIME I'M OFF TRACK. YOU AND YOUR SONGS DON'T TALK DOWN TO THE KIDS. YOU TREAT THEM WITH RESPECT; SOMETIMES THEY WANNA LAUGH, SOMETIMES THEY WANNA FEEL SAD. JUST LIKE "REAL" PEOPLE, NO?

OH, WELL, I ... TRY AND COME UP WITH STUFF I'M NOT COM--PLETELY ASHAMED TO STAND BEHIND.

WELL, IT SHOWS. SO THE SHOW OPER-ATES UNDER THE SAME PRINCIPLES. WE RESPECT THE KIDS' INTELLI-GENCE. WITHIN REASON. I MEAN, KIDS ARE PRETTY DENSE SOMETIMES.

SHERRI, I'VE GOT THIS PRODUCTION DESIGNER WHO DID SOME ASSIST-TANT WORK ON PEE WEE'S PLAYHOUSE WHEN HE WAS LIKE TWELVE...

OH MY GOD, I LOVED THAT SHOW. THAT'S THE KIND OF SHOW I WANNA DO. GENUINE, NO CUTESY CRAP.

I'M SO GLAD WE'RE ON THE SAME TRACK. THIS GUY—HIS NAME'S PETE—HE LOVED YOUR DVD AND HE'S GOT A MILLION IDEAS. LOOK, I DON'T WANNA BE A COMPLETE CORPORATE DORK, BUT I DO HAVE A POWERPOINT PRESENTATION TO SHOW YOU...

SO, I'VE KNOWN THIS GUY FOR LIKE TEN MINUTES, PLUS HE REPRESENTS A CORPORATION THAT WANTS ME TO SIGN A CONTRACT WITH THEM, BUT I'M SERIOUSLY SITTING HERE THINKING: "COULD HE BE THE ONE?"

ANYWAY, I GOT SOME SKETCHES YOU CAN LOOK AT. SHERRI, I'M NOT SURE HOW YOU FEEL ABOUT PUPPETS?

LOVE 'EM.

OH, GREAT!

AND LATELY, I'M WONDERING MORE AND MORE IF SOME GUY IS THE "ONE." AQUAINTANCES, WAITERS, HOBOES, EVERYONE'S THE "ONE" WITH ME OF LATE. I'M NOT EVEN HALF-HEARING WHAT HANDSOME-GARY IS SAYING. I'M JUST ADMIRING WHAT A KID OF OUR COMBINED GENES WOULD LOOK LIKE.

HE'S THINKING PUPPETS, PUPPETS, PUPPETS AND MORE LIKE

OH, SHERRI, I LOVE YOU AND OUR BABY.

I HAVE SO MUCH STUFF I WANT TO TALK TO YOU ABOUT REGARDING THE SHOW... THIS IS SO "SHOW-BIZ" BUT ARE YOU FREE FOR LUNCH? I KNOW YOU HAVE A SHOW TONIGHT AND YOU'RE SETTING UP AND ALL.

...BUT YOU GOTTA EAT, RIGHT?

RIGHT, I MEAN, I DO GOTTA EAT...

GREAT, WHAT DO YOU FEEL LIKE?

UH, CAN YOU TAKE ME TO MY DRESSING ROOM AND IMPREGNATE ME?

I'M UP FOR SUGGESTIONS.

WELL, UH, YOU KNOW THE TOWN BETTER THAN I DO. IS THERE A PLACE THAT HAS SOMETHING FOR VEGETARIANS? I CONFESS, I'M A CRAZY VEGETARIAN.

NO SHIT...

CHAPTER TEN:

I'M A GIRL WATCHER (AND ALL THE CREEP- -INESS THAT SONG TITLE IMPLIES)

AFTER LUNCH, FEELING SICK FROM FRENCH FRIES AND FROM BEING A DIRTY OLD MAN, I FIND THAT SARAH HAS LEFT THAT SHERRI SMALLS PRESS KIT ON MY DESK. YOU KNOW, FOR SAM...

I'M STARING AT THE INCLUDED HEADSHOT FOR WHAT IS, EVEN TO ME, A LONG, CREEPY LOOKING TIME. SHE'S A STUNNING LOOKING GIRL AND THERE'S SUCH INTELLIGENCE IN HER EYES.

YEAH, THAT'S IT OLD MAN, YOU'RE STARING AT HER INTELLIGENCE.

I PUT THE FOLDER ASIDE AND GET TO WORK. I HAVE A PRO- -DUCTIVE AFTERNOON, ANSWER A TON OF EMAILS, CHECK OVER THE INTERN'S WORK (THEY'RE ONE THIRD MY AGE AND WAY MORE TALENTED -SIGH AND FUCK IT.) I LOOK OVER THE BASKETBALL SHOOT CONTACTS AND MARK THE FEW LAME POSSIBILITIES WITH A CHINA MARKER.

IT'S LIKE AT LEAST TWO HOURS LATER BEFORE I'M BACK AT THE PHOTO OF SHERRI SMALLS AND FLIPPING THROUGH HER C.V.

SHE LEFT HOME AT SEVENTEEN. WORKED AS A WAITRESS AND DID SOME BUSKING ON HER DAYS OFF. SHE WAS NEVER ACTUALLY "HOME- -LESS" AS IS OFTEN QUOTED IN THE PRESS.

THOUGH SHE DID LIVE IN A HOSTEL FOR SEVERAL WEEKS UNTIL SHE GOT ON HER FEET. SHE AND TWO FRIENDS FORMED AN ALL-GIRL PUNK BAND, "LABIA MINORITY," WHICH PLAYED TWO GIGS IN TOTAL.

SHE BEGAN PLAYING SOLO GIGS IN SMALL VENUES IN THE 90'S, GARNERING INCREASING ATTEN- -TION AS A SINGER/SONGWRITER IN THE INDIE MUSIC PRESS, CUL- -MINATING IN THE RELEASE OF HER ONLY (AS OF YET!) ALBUM FOR ADULTS, "ASHTRAY," (ASTERIX, 1999).

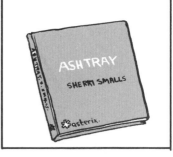

PITCH FORK DESCRIBED ASHTRAY AS: "(SHERRI SMALLS) SINGS LIKE A REALLY GOOD FRIEND SCRATCHING YOUR BACK AND WHISPERING ALL THE SECRETS OF THEIR LIFE AND ALL THE SECRETS OF YOUR LIFE WHILE YOU BOTH STARE AT A LAVA LAMP."

AHH...

WHILE TOURING FOR THE CD, ASHTRAY, SHERRI GOT THE OPPORTUNITY TO SING BACK-UP VOCALS FOR LEGENDARY CHILDREN'S PERFORMER HENRY "CHICK" BROWN.

SHE SOON MOVED FROM BACK-UP SINGER TO MULTI-INSTRUMENTALIST, TO FEATURED PERFORMER, TO CHICK'S SIDEKKK AND COSTAR. WHEN CHICK BROWN ENTERED INTO SEMI-RETIREMENT, SHERRI STRUCK OUT ON HER OWN, FORMING THE SHERRI SMALLS BIG BAND AND HAS SINCE BUILT A LOYAL FOLLOWING OF KIDS AND PARENTS WHO APPRECIATE HER UNPATRONIZING BRAND OF... BLAH, BLAH...

WHOAH.

THERE'S A PICTURE OF THE YOUNG SHERRI SMALLS, MAYBE TWENTY, PLAYING HER GUITAR. SHE'S THE EMBRYONIC VERSION OF THE KNOCKOUT SHE IS TODAY. THERE'S A DISCOGRAPHY; FOUR KIDS CDS. I ORDER THEM ONLINE. FOR SAM.

"SONGS ABOUT BANANAS"? OOOKAY.

CLICK!

THEN I GOOGLE "SHERRI SMALLS". THE FIRST HIT IS A METHODIST ORGANIST IN THE NETHERLANDS.

BUT THE NEXT 70,000 OR SO PURPORT TO BE LINKS ABOUT THE CHILDREN'S PERFORMER. I SWITCH TO IMAGE SEARCH AND SIFT THROUGH THUMBNAILS OF CONCERT PHOTOS, PUBLICITY STILLS...

Google

SHERRI PERFORMING WITH CHICK BROWN, (A RAFFI-LITE PERFORMER I RECALL FROM THE GIRLS' CHILDHOOD), SHERRI HUGGING FANS, VISITING SICK KIDS...

GET WELL

HOLY SHIT, SHE'S WEARING A BATHING SUIT HERE.

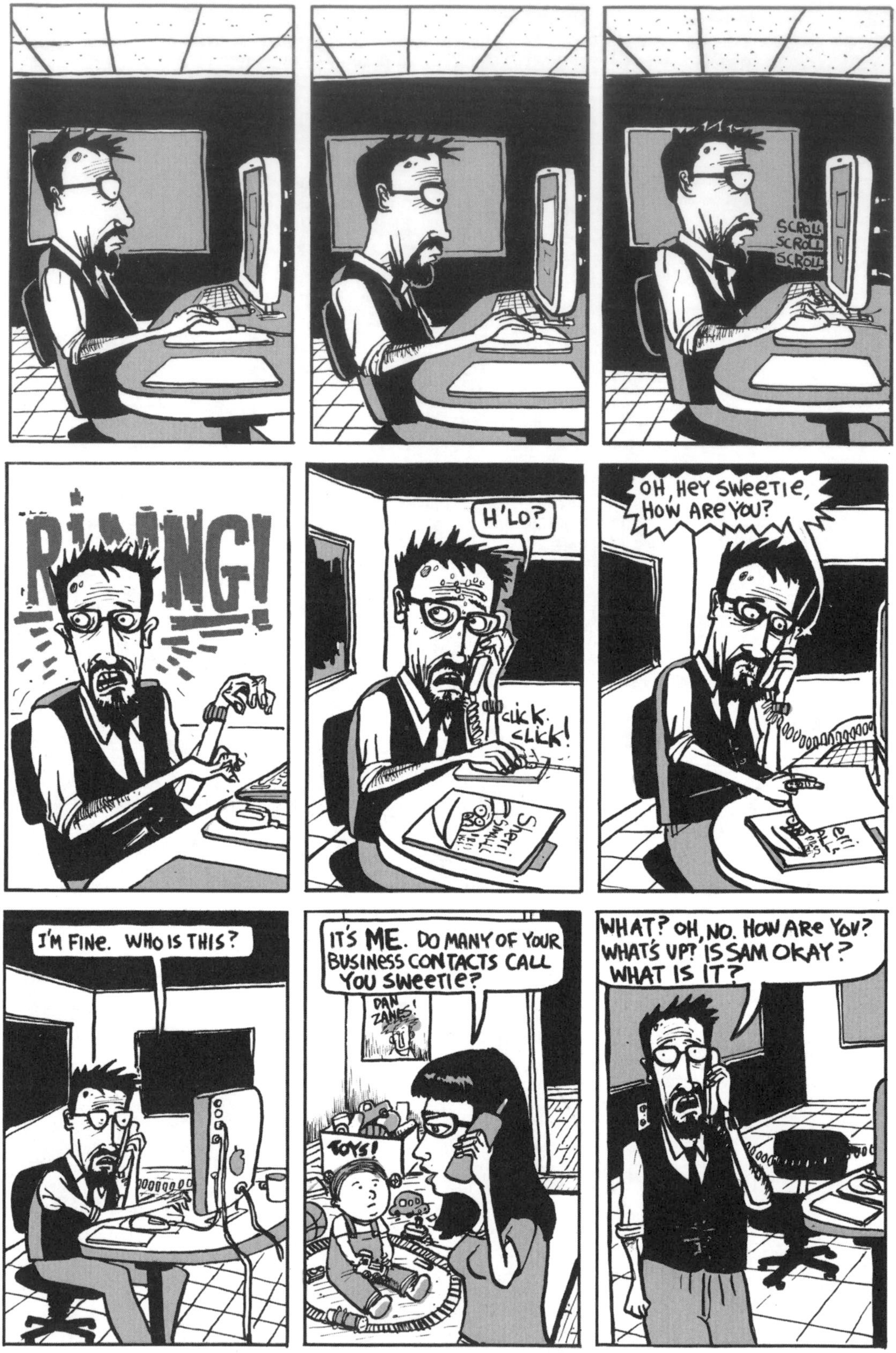

SCROLL SCROLL SCROLL
RING!
H'LO?
CLICK CLICK!
OH, HEY SWEETIE, HOW ARE YOU?
I'M FINE. WHO IS THIS?
IT'S ME. DO MANY OF YOUR BUSINESS CONTACTS CALL YOU SWEETIE?
DAN ZANES!
TOYS!
WHAT? OH, NO. HOW ARE YOU? WHAT'S UP? IS SAM OKAY? WHAT IS IT?

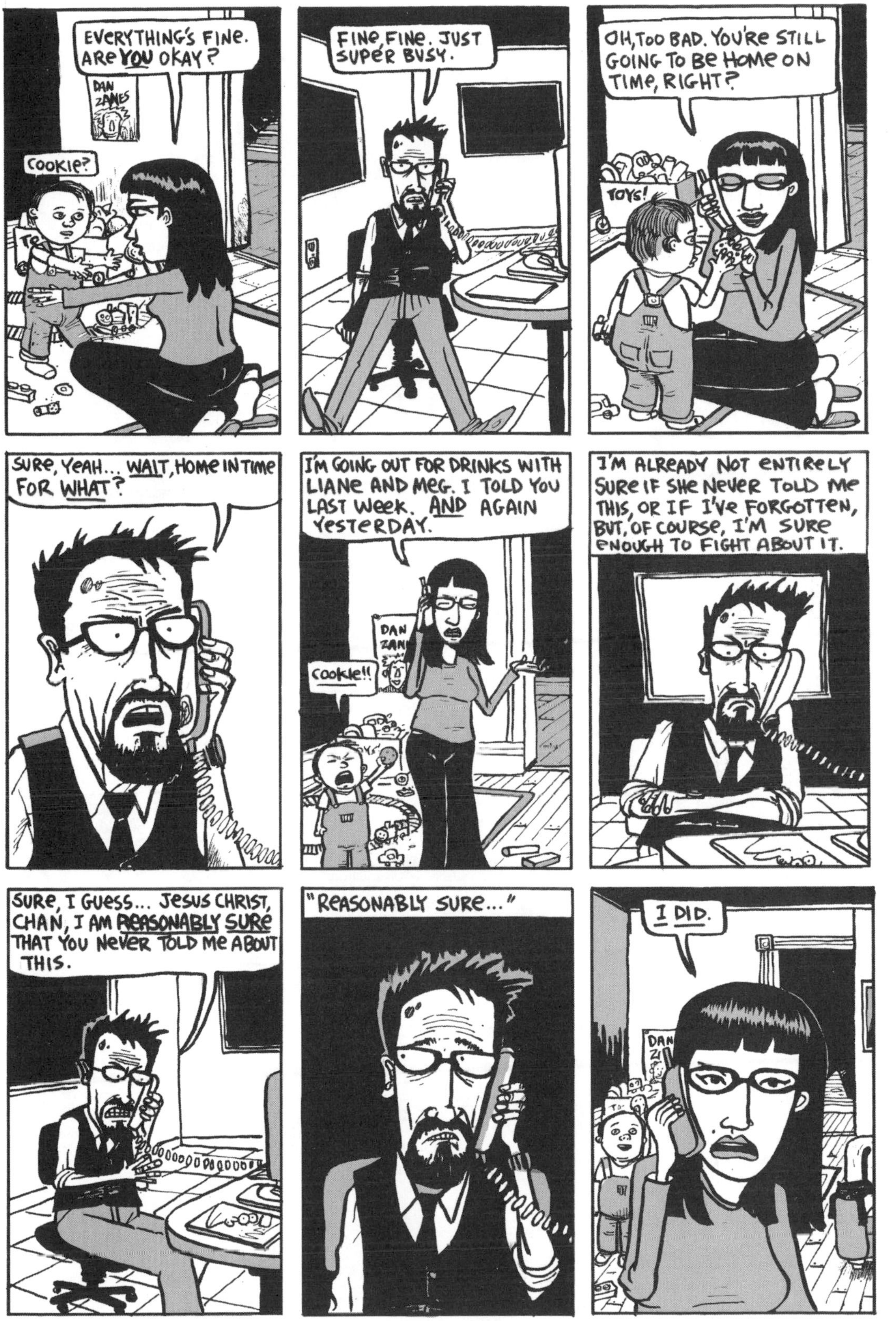
EVERYTHING'S FINE. ARE YOU OKAY?
DAN ZANES
COOKIE?
TOYS!
FINE, FINE. JUST SUPER BUSY.
OH, TOO BAD. YOU'RE STILL GOING TO BE HOME ON TIME, RIGHT?
TOYS!
SURE, YEAH... WAIT, HOME IN TIME FOR WHAT?
I'M GOING OUT FOR DRINKS WITH LIANE AND MEG. I TOLD YOU LAST WEEK. AND AGAIN YESTERDAY.
COOKIE!!
I'M ALREADY NOT ENTIRELY SURE IF SHE NEVER TOLD ME THIS, OR IF I'VE FORGOTTEN, BUT, OF COURSE, I'M SURE ENOUGH TO FIGHT ABOUT IT.
SURE, I GUESS... JESUS CHRIST, CHAN, I AM REASONABLY SURE THAT YOU NEVER TOLD ME ABOUT THIS.
"REASONABLY SURE..."
I DID.

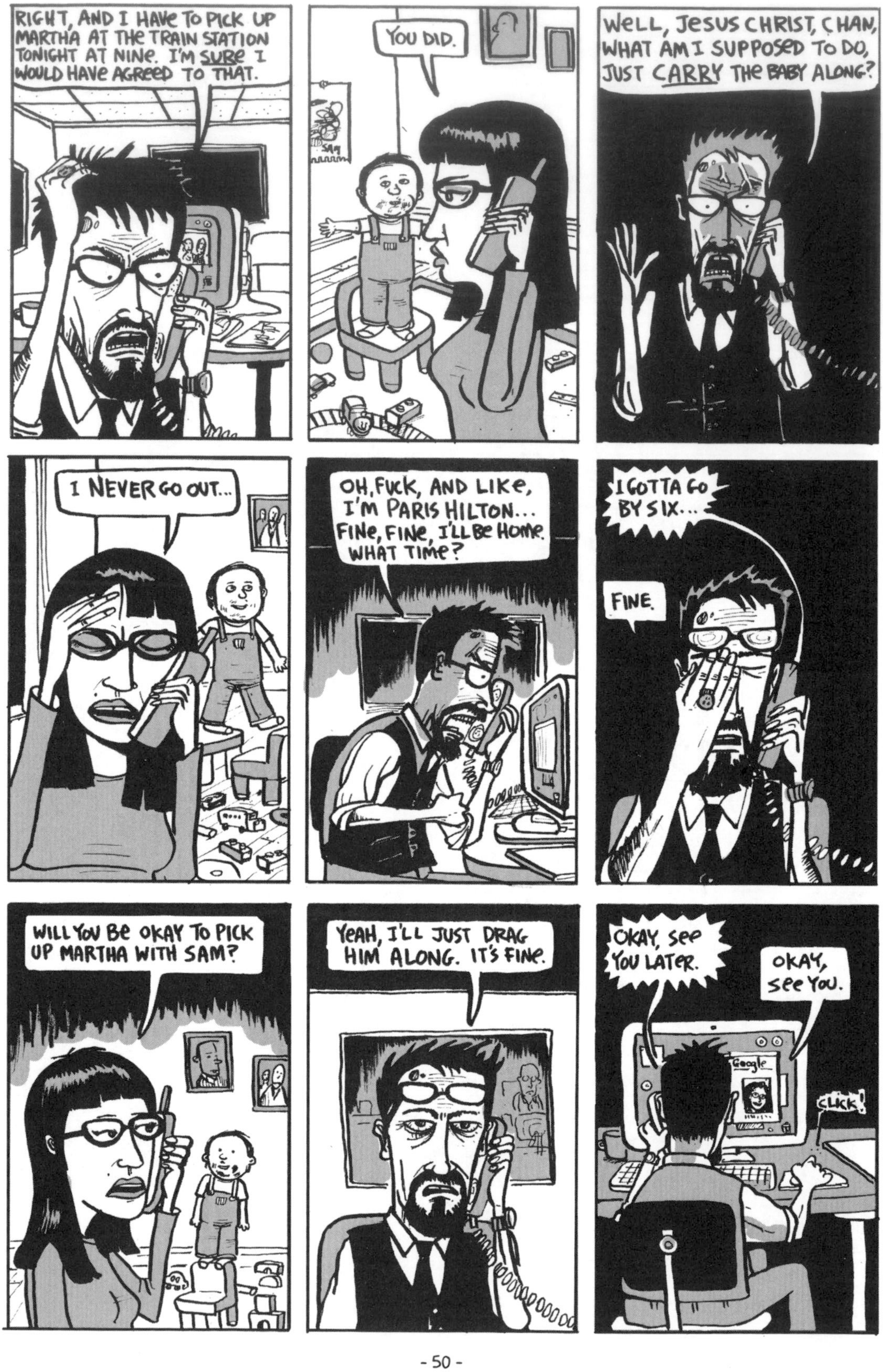
RIGHT, AND I HAVE TO PICK UP MARTHA AT THE TRAIN STATION TONIGHT AT NINE. I'M SURE I WOULD HAVE AGREED TO THAT.
YOU DID.
SAM
WELL, JESUS CHRIST, CHAN, WHAT AM I SUPPOSED TO DO, JUST CARRY THE BABY ALONG?
I NEVER GO OUT...
OH, FUCK, AND LIKE, I'M PARIS HILTON... FINE, FINE, I'LL BE HOME. WHAT TIME?
I GOTTA GO BY SIX...
FINE.
WILL YOU BE OKAY TO PICK UP MARTHA WITH SAM?
YEAH, I'LL JUST DRAG HIM ALONG. IT'S FINE.
OKAY, SEE YOU LATER.
OKAY, SEE YOU.
Google
CLICK!

OH, YOU KNOW, SHE NEVER <u>DOES</u> GO OUT. <u>WE</u> NEVER GO OUT.

IT'S HARDER FOR HER, ACTUALLY. SHE'S HAD LIKE THIRTY YEARS OF COMPLETE FREEDOM. I LIKE TO WHINE TO MYSELF (AND NOT JUST TO MYSELF TO BE COMPLETELY HONEST) THAT I'M ACCUSTOMED TO LITTLE ELSE BUT DRUDGERY AND SACRIFICE SINCE THE AGE OF SEVENTEEN.

I GUESS THAT MAKES ME RESENT IT MORE, AS IF ABSURDLY HOLDING HER RESPONSIBLE FOR THE UNEQUAL DISTRIBUTION OF FUN AND RESPONSIBILITY IN OUR PAST LIVES, WHICH I REALIZE IS LUDICROUS AND POSSIBLY EVEN CHILDISH. POSSIBLY...

DRUDGERY

FUN!

CHAPTER ELEVEN:

Cheque please!

SO, HE'S A VEGETARIAN BECAUSE HE CAN'T STAND THE THOUGHT OF KILLING ANIMALS, NOT FOR HIS BULLSHIT YUPPIE CHOLESTEROL. "SHERRI AND GARY," IS THAT CUTE OR WHAT?

...I THOUGHT OF MAYBE SETTING THE SHOW IN A FICTITIOUS NEIGHBOURHOOD WE INVENT FOR YOU. KINDA STANDARD KIDSHOW FODDER, I KNOW...

...BUT WE CAN DEVELOP A BUNCH OF CHARACTERS TO MAKE IT INTERESTING. I MEAN, ONE OF THEM WILL BE A GUY IN A MONKEY SUIT, SO...

OH, RIGHT, RIC...

OH RIGHT, RIC, HE SHOULD MAKE THINGS... INTERESTING.

I CONFESS WE'VE BEEN MORE THAN A LITTLE BIT NERVOUS ABOUT RIC OVER AT THE NET-WORK, SHERRI.

OH-OH, HERE COMES THE NET-WORK STOOGE, HOUSE-WRECKIN' OUR HAPPY MARRIAGE.

WELL, YEAH... WE'VE ALL TALKED TO RIC. I'M FAIRLY SURE THAT WE WON'T HAVE ANY MORE TROUBLE FROM HIM.

OH, THAT'S GOOD NEWS. I'VE BEEN FIGHTING LIKE CRAZY FOR THE MONKEY! SOME OF THE OLDER GUYS WERE FOR CUTTING HIM OUT OF THE SHOW, BUT I...

WHOAH...

...THERE IS NO "SHOW" IF YOU PEOPLE TRY AND "CUT OUT" ANYONE IN MY CREW.

SHERRI, SHERRI, WAIT, WAIT! THAT CAME OUT ALL WRONG! I LOVE THE MONKEY. I LOVE HIS 'WORK'!

DID HE JUST SAY THAT WITH SARCASTIC SINGLE QUOTES AROUND IT?

SERIOUSLY! I'VE WATCHED THE DVDS; RIC BRINGS A LOT TO YOUR ACT. I'M SERIOUS, I'VE BEEN FIGHTING LIKE HELL WITH THE OLD NETWORK COPROLITES TO STAY OUT OF THINGS AND LET YOU GUYS SORT THIS OUT.

..."COPROLITES," THAT'S FOSSILIZED...

...FOSSILIZED DINOSAUR TURDS, I KNOW. GARY, SIXTY PERCENT OF MY DEMOGRAPHIC ARE SIX--YEAR-OLD BOYS, TWO THINGS I KNOW ARE DINOSAURS AND POOP.

OKAY. SHERRI... ARE WE COOL HERE?

WE'RE FINE, I JUST DON'T TAKE KINDLY TO PEOPLE TRYING TO FORCE MY FRIENDS OUT.

SHERRI, NO ONE IS FORCING ANYONE ANYWHERE. THE NETWORK BELIEVES IN YOU AND ARE SET TO INVEST A LOT OF MONEY. THEY WANT TO PROTECT THEIR INTER--ESTS, I WANT TO PROTECT YOUR INTERESTS.

IF SOMETHING WERE TO HAPPEN LIKE WHAT HAPPENED LAST NIGHT WHILE YOU WERE REPRESENTING THE NETWORK, YOU WOULD BE LIABLE FOR RIC'S ACTIONS.

MY OWN WORDS SOUND SO ANNOY--ING COMING FROM SOMEONE ELSE.

THESE NETWORK GUYS ARE IN--TERESTED IN GOD AND IN PRO--TECTING THEIR INVESTMENTS. AND NOT ALWAYS IN THAT ORDER.

WELL, STOP RIGHT THERE. I DON'T WANNA DEAL WITH PEOPLE LIKE THAT.

WAIT, WAIT, I WILL DEAL WITH THESE GUYS. THEY'RE A SMALL PART OF THE PEOPLE AT PLAYTIME, EVERYONE ELSE ARE DEDICATED CREATIVE PEOPLE.

I CAN HANDLE THE MONEY GUYS AND I'M ON YOUR SIDE. I WANT RIC ON YOUR SHOW; WE AREN'T AT ODDS HERE. I FEEL LIKE WE NEED TO MAKE THE EXECS FEEL SAFE AND PUT THE ONUS ON RIC TO BE A GOOD CITIZEN WHO DOESN'T ASSAULT PRE-TEEN FANS AND ENDANGER CO-WORKERS.

JUST HEAR ME OUT...

FIRSTLY, WE CREATE A SPECIAL CONTRACT FOR RIC. HE'S ON THE SHOW, A COSTAR, A MAJOR PARTICIPANT. PROMINENT ELEMENTS OF THAT CONTRACT ARE SEVERAL EXIT CLAUSES.

RIC IS A WELCOME MEMBER OF THE SHOW AS LONG AS HE DECIDES TO KEEP HIS NEGATIVE BEHAVIOUR IN CHECK. IF HE FUCKS UP, HE FUCKS UP, IT'S IN THE CONTRACT HE AGREED TO. YOU'RE NOT THE BAD GUY. I'M NOT THE BAD GUY. IT'S RIC'S DECISION. NO GUILTY FEELINGS FOR ANYONE AND IT MAY INSPIRE RESPONSIBILITY IF THE OBLIGATION IS ON HIM.

NO GUILT. I'M LIKING THIS AND HATING MYSELF FOR HOW MUCH I LIKE IT.

BUT YOU MUST HAVE STUFF LIKE THAT IN ALL OF OUR CONTRACTS, NO?

'COURSE, BUT RIC'S WOULD BE MORE STRENUOUS AND SPECIFIC.

THE MODERN INTERPRETATION OF THE DEVIL AS A HANDSOME BUSINESSMAN IS NOT FOR NO REASON; PEOPLE MANIFEST EVIL IN A WAY THEY CAN RELATE TO. GARY'S SLEAZY, BACKDOOR PLAN TO GET RID OF RIC IS SO MUCH MORE EVIL THAN ME SIMPLY FIRING HIM. AND I'M EMBARRASSED AT HOW MUCH I WANT TO TAKE THIS ROUTE.

AH, GARY, OUR HOUSE IN THE SUBURBS, DRINKS ON THE DECK, AND THE HANDSOME CHILDREN ... IT'S ALL GONE. BURST LIKE BULLSHIT BUBBLES.

WELL, SEND THE CONTRACTS TO MY LAWYER AND HE'LL TELL ME WHAT I THINK OF THEM. THANKS FOR LUNCH...

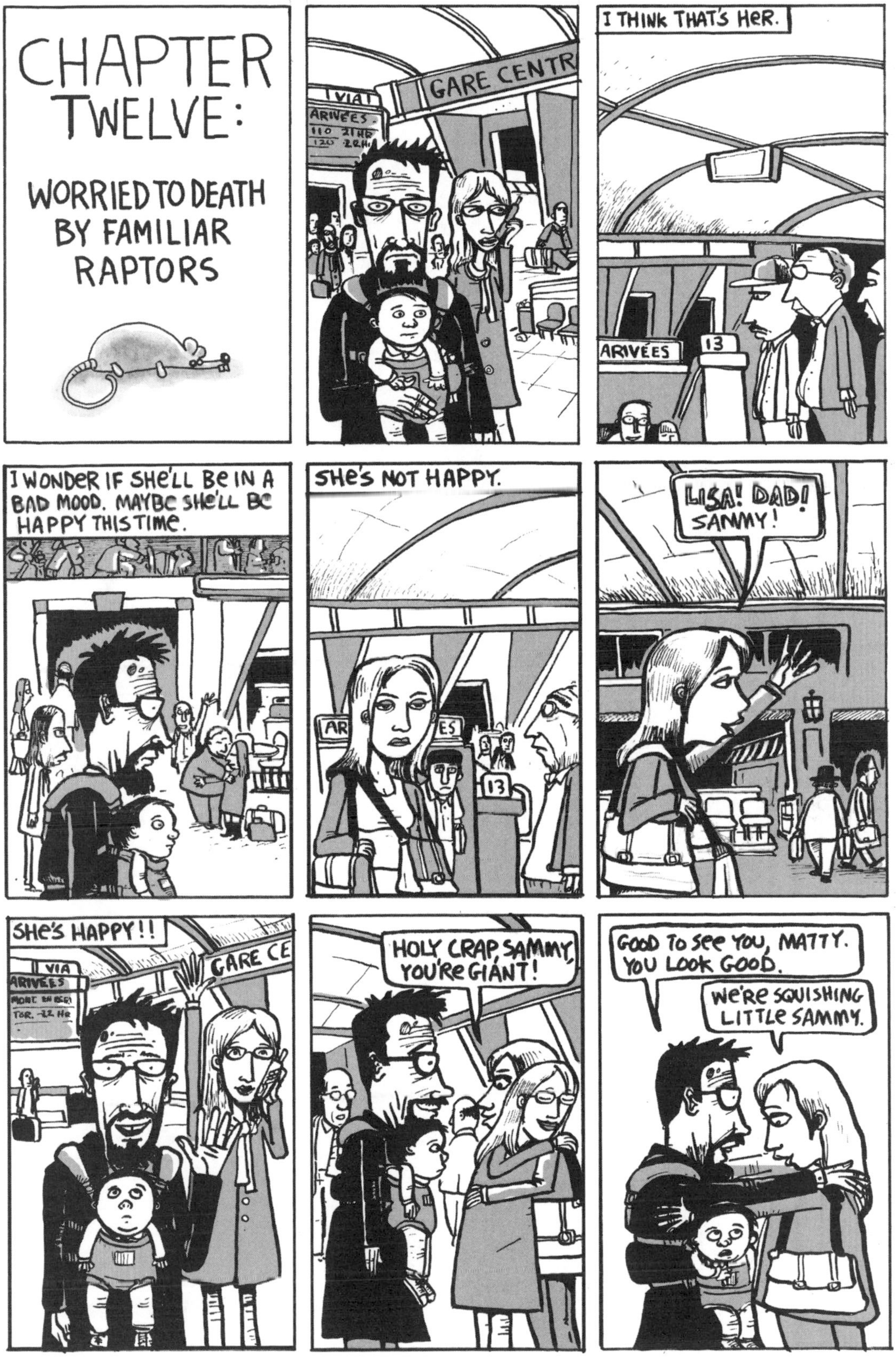
CHAPTER TWELVE:
WORRIED TO DEATH BY FAMILIAR RAPTORS
GARE CENTR
VIA
ARIVÉES
I THINK THAT'S HER.
ARIVÉES
13
I WONDER IF SHE'LL BE IN A BAD MOOD. MAYBE SHE'LL BE HAPPY THIS TIME.
SHE'S NOT HAPPY.
13
LISA! DAD! SAMMY!
SHE'S HAPPY!!
VIA
ARIVÉES
GARE CE
HOLY CRAP, SAMMY, YOU'RE GIANT!
GOOD TO SEE YOU, MATTY. YOU LOOK GOOD.
WE'RE SQUISHING LITTLE SAMMY.

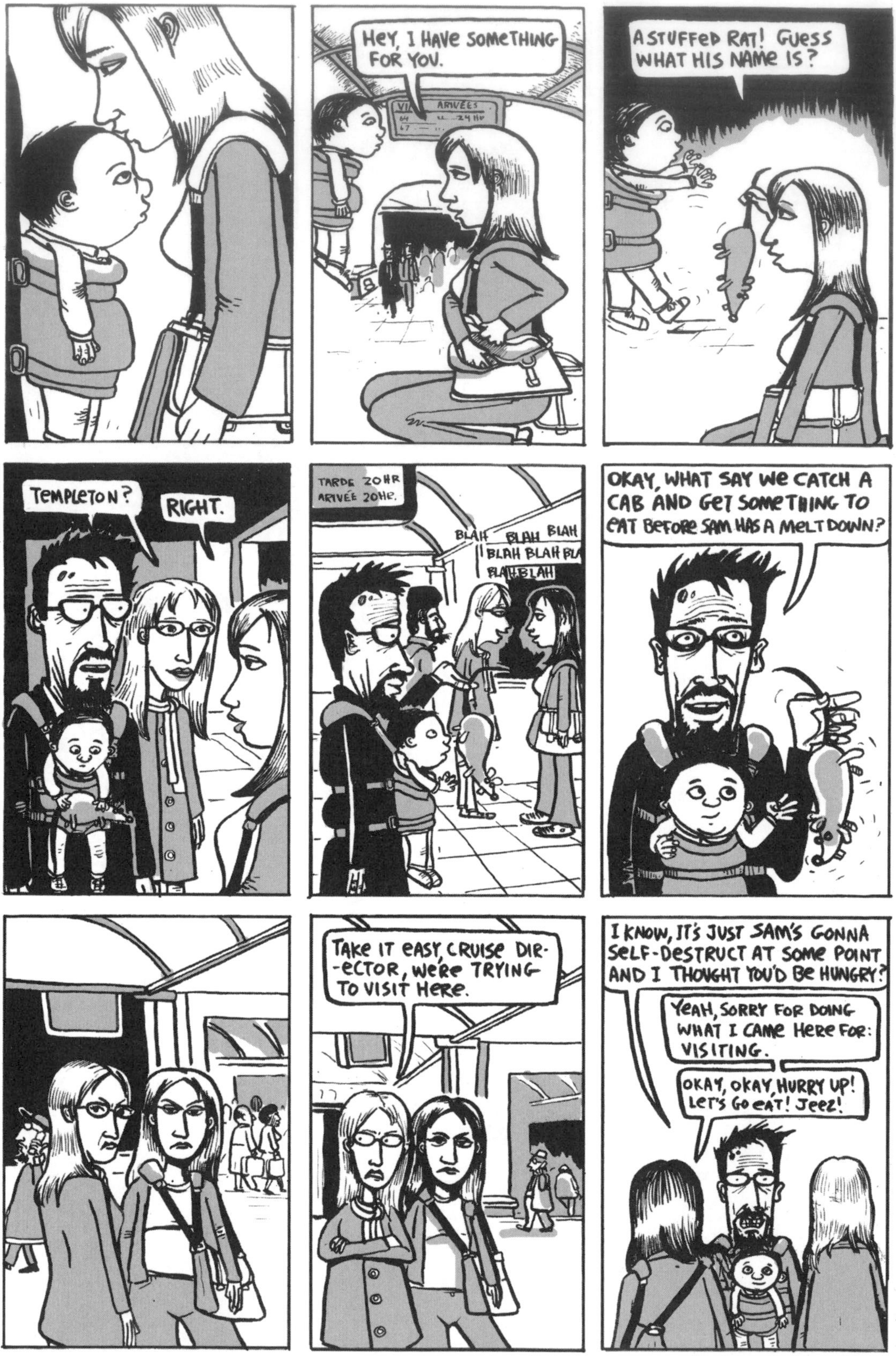
HEY, I HAVE SOMETHING FOR YOU.
ARIVÉES
A STUFFED RAT! GUESS WHAT HIS NAME IS?
TEMPLETON?
RIGHT.
TARDE 20HR
ARIVÉE 20HR.
BLAH BLAH BLAH
BLAH BLAH BLA
BLAH BLAH
OKAY, WHAT SAY WE CATCH A CAB AND GET SOMETHING TO EAT BEFORE SAM HAS A MELTDOWN?
TAKE IT EASY, CRUISE DIR- -ECTOR, WE'RE TRYING TO VISIT HERE.
I KNOW, IT'S JUST SAM'S GONNA SELF-DESTRUCT AT SOME POINT AND I THOUGHT YOU'D BE HUNGRY?
YEAH, SORRY FOR DOING WHAT I CAME HERE FOR: VISITING.
OKAY, OKAY, HURRY UP! LET'S GO EAT! JEEZ!

These two girls who both used to coerce me to be their ally against the other in their constant battles are now always united against me. Since the divorce, since they live apart in different cities.

I AM glad they are working together on a project, though. I guess I have mixed emotions about it really.

They gang up on me when they're together like those intelligent raptors in Jurassic Park, you know?

I feel like I'm some hapless scientist around them, being hunted and worried to death.

Oh my god, I try and be patient with their anger; they're so pissed at the divorce, at our more-than-perfect domesticity — family meals and weekend excursions — all torn asunder.

KOOL AID

COOL WHIP

JELLO PUDDING

MASH AND GRAVY

MEAT LOAF

FROZEN CORN

GUM

The poor things, my dear baby girls. I wish I could have sheltered them more, but my head was pretty far up my own ass during the divorce and the hair on my head was dyed mid-life-crisis-blonde.

LOREAL MIDLIFE CRISIS BLONDE #22

NEWLY BUFF AND WEARING GIRLFRIEND T-SHIRT

GOD, WHAT A DOUCHE.

CALVIN JUNIOR

SEXY... FOR KIDS!

BUY IT NOW.

I know, what an advertisement for non-consensual sex.

CALVIN JUNIOR

SEXY...

My heart sometimes feels like it may burst with the love I feel for these two girls.

THE THREE OF US WATCHING CAR-TOONS UNDER A BLANKET TENT, EATING SUGAR CEREAL TOGETHER, CHRISTMAS, READING TREASURE ISLAND OUT LOUD (THEY HATED IT).

DON'T LOOK, SAM.

SEXY... FOR KIDS BUT...

"the dirk, where it had pinned my shoulder to the mast, seemed to burn like a hot iron; yet it was not so much these real sufferings that caused me distress... it was the horror I had upon my mind falling, from the cross-trees into that still green water beside the body of the coxswain I clung..."

WHAT'S A DIRK AGAIN?

...AND A COXSWAIN?

WRITE IT DOWN, GIRLS. THAT'S WHAT THE CLIPBOARDS ARE FOR. DEFINITIONS AT THE END OF CHAPTERS.

IT'S ONLY EVER THE THREE OF US IN MEMORY.

FOR ME, THEIR MOTHER ONLY APPEARS AS COMIC FOIL OR AS A VILLAIN. CHILDISH, I KNOW. I'M SO DETERMINED THAT SAM WILL NEVER GO THROUGH ANY OF THIS, THAT I'LL DO EVERYTHING RIGHT THIS TIME...

CADEUX

TWO MOMENTS THAT ARE TRANSCENDENT TO ME, THAT LITERALLY SUPER-HEAT MY HEART AND LIQUIFY IT, ARE COMING UPON MY YOUNG DAUGHTERS AT PLAY, ABSENTLY SINGING SOME SONG IN A TINY VOICE.

JACK WAS A LONELY COWBOY, WITH A HEART SO BRAVE AND TRUE...

A COWBOY SONG, PERHAPS. SUNG FOR THEMSELVES AND UNWITTINGLY SUNG FOR ME, AN EAVESDROPPER, HIDING BEHIND A DOOR-FRAME, STIFLING A SOB. SEEING THEIR LIVES PASS BEFORE ME IN THAT MOMENT, SEEING THE ELATION, THE PAIN AND SADNESS, AND ALL THE BULLSHIT WE ALL OF US EVENTUALLY KNOW, GOOD AND BAD.

DO YOU REMEMBER SWEET BETSY FROM PIKE...

I CAN'T WAIT 'TIL SAM CAN SING SO I CAN HEAR THAT INNOCENCE AGAIN FIRST-HAND.

MY GOD, THE GIRLS AND I, WE ARE ALL OF US SO STUCK IN THE PAST IN A WAY. WE NEED TO FIND A WAY TO DEAL WITH EACH OTHER IN THE PRESENT SOME HOW.

DAD, WE WANT PITAS...

...AND FRIES.

SHRIES.

SURE, WHATEVER YOU GUYS WANT.

IN THAT EMOTIONAL MOMENT, THEY COULD HAVE HAD ANYTHING IN THE WORLD FROM ME, BUT THEY CHOSE PITAS. HA.

KIDS' BREATH ALWAYS SMELLS SWEET. THEY DON'T HAVE BAD BREATH FOR THE FIRST FEW YEARS.

I WAS ALWAYS AMAZED BY THAT. EVEN WHEN THEY START EATING THE SAME STUFF AS YOU DO, THEIR BREATH SMELLS LIKE NOTHING OR MAYBE LIKE MILK. IT'S LIKE THERE'S NO STINK OF DECAY ABOUT THEM YET.

SHRIES?

THE GIRLS WERE LIKE THAT AND THEN ONE DAY THEY COME UP AND TALK AT YOU, AND IT'S ALL LIKE: "WHOA! YOU'RE ALL GROWN-UP, POO-BREATH." SAM'S EATING TZATZIKI AND YET HIS BREATH IS STILL SPRING WATER, BUT FOR HOW LONG?

DAD, WHERE'S CHAN? AT HOME KILLING THE FATTED CALF FOR ME, I HOPE?

OH, SHE'S OUT FOR DRINKS WITH HER FRIENDS. SHE ALREADY HAD PLANS. SHE ALMOST NEVER GOES OUT...

RELAX DUDE, I'M JOKING. HOW ARE THE KITTIES?

OH, THEY'RE GREAT. YOU WANT A FEW?

OH YEAH, MY DOG WOULD LOVE THAT.

OH YEAH, DAD HATES THE CATS NOW.

I DON'T HATE THE CATS. I CAN'T HAVE THREE CATS IN A HOUSE WITH A BABY. IT'S TOO MUCH. THERE'S NOTHING BUT SHIT EVERYWHERE.

LISA ALWAYS SAID THEY WERE HER CATS, SHE WAS THE ONE WITH THE CAT CALENDARS. YOU TWO TALKED ME INTO GETTING THE FIRST TWO CATS AND THEN YOU HAD TO GET ME ANOTHER ONE WHEN I MOVED OUT.

NOW I'M STUCK WITH THREE CATS AND I NEVER WANTED ANY OF THEM!

WOW, NICE VEINS IN YOUR FOREHEAD, MAN...

SEE, SUDDENLY HE HATES THE CATS.

YOU ALWAYS SAID WHEN YOU MOVED OUT YOU WERE TAKING THE CATS. IT'S NOT **ME** THAT HATES THE CATS.

I SAID THAT WHEN I WAS LIKE FIVE YEARS OLD. ANYWAY, I TOLD YOU, **TWO** OF MY ROOM-MATES ARE ALLERGIC TO CATS.

AND WHY IS THAT **MY** PROBLEM? WHY IS THAT MY PROBLEM?

SO NICE TO BE HOME AGAIN. GEEZ.

HEY BABY...

OH! HE'S ASLEEP... SHHH... WHERE ARE THE GIRLS?

THEY WENT OUT CLUBBING.

HOW'S MARTHA?

SHE'S FINE. YOU SMELL LIKE BOOZE.

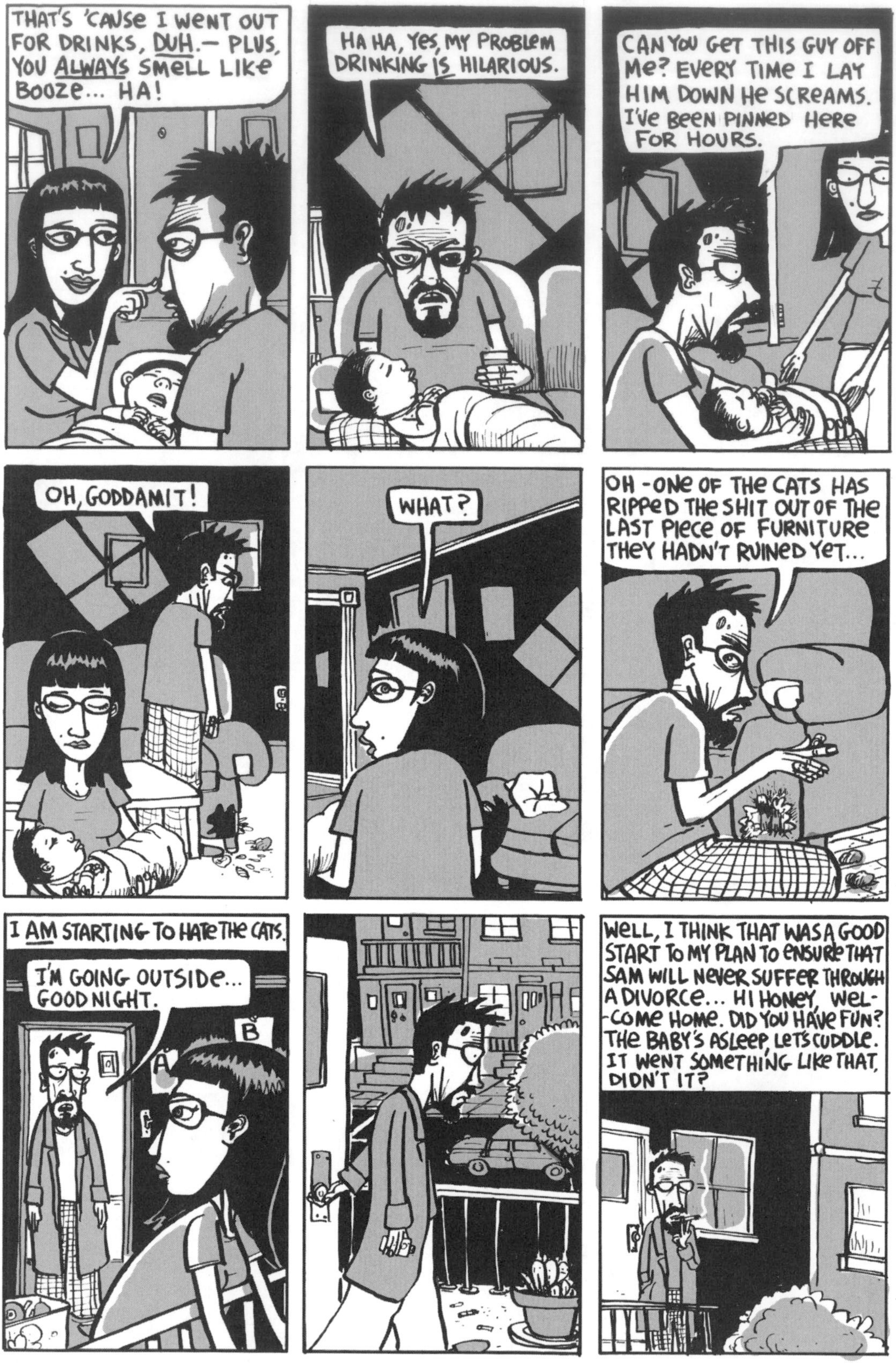
THAT'S 'CAUSE I WENT OUT FOR DRINKS, DUH.— PLUS, YOU ALWAYS SMELL LIKE BOOZE... HA!
HA HA, YES, MY PROBLEM DRINKING IS HILARIOUS.
CAN YOU GET THIS GUY OFF ME? EVERY TIME I LAY HIM DOWN HE SCREAMS. I'VE BEEN PINNED HERE FOR HOURS.
OH, GODDAMIT!
WHAT?
OH - ONE OF THE CATS HAS RIPPED THE SHIT OUT OF THE LAST PIECE OF FURNITURE THEY HADN'T RUINED YET...
I AM STARTING TO HATE THE CATS.
I'M GOING OUTSIDE... GOOD NIGHT.
A
B
WELL, I THINK THAT WAS A GOOD START TO MY PLAN TO ENSURE THAT SAM WILL NEVER SUFFER THROUGH A DIVORCE... HI HONEY, WEL-COME HOME. DID YOU HAVE FUN? THE BABY'S ASLEEP, LET'S CUDDLE. IT WENT SOMETHING LIKE THAT, DIDN'T IT?

CHAPTER THIRTEEN:

THE FINEST OF WINES, THE BEST BRANDS OF POTATO CHIPS

I MEAN IT KARL, I WANT YOU AND HARVEY TO LOOK AT THESE CONTRACTS WITH AN ELECTRON MICROSCOPE AND HI-LITE EVERYTHING THAT I SHOULD BE CONCERNED ABOUT.

SHERRI, DO YOU HONESTLY THINK THAT HARVEY AND I WOULDN'T HAVE DONE THAT WITHOUT YOUR SAY-SO PROMPTING US?

MY DEAR GIRL, THAT IS WHAT OLD FUDDY-DUDDIES LIKE US THRIVE UPON.

YEAH, BUT I WANT YOU TO LOOK FOR EVERY SLIMY, UNDERHANDED CLAUSE THIS NETWORK STOOGE GARY HAS HIDDEN IN THERE.

I INTEND TO MAKE THIS AS DIFFICULT AS POSSIBLE FOR THESE BASTARDS.

OKAY, SHERRI. YOU KNOW...

WHAT?

NO, NOTHING...

NO, WHAT, KARL? GO AHEAD.

WELL, GARY WANTS TO PROTECT THE NETWORK FROM REEK. YOU WANT TO PROTECT YOURSELF FROM REEK. I DON'T KNOW WHY YOU'RE SO ANGRY. AND...

...AND?

AND, I DON'T THINK YOU NEED TO SABOTAGE YOUR WAY OUT OF THIS DEAL. IF YOU WANT OUT, WALK AWAY; IT'S YOUR DECISION. BUT THERE'S NO DEAL WITHOUT YOU, AND YOU'RE ENDANGERING IT FOR EVERYONE.

GRATING TO HAVE YOUR WORDS CAST BACK IN YOUR TEETH TWICE IN ONE DAY. TOUCHÉ, KARL.

ANYWAY, I SHOULDN'T HAVE LET HIM MEET WITH YOU BEFORE A SHOW, BUT YOU TWO WERE GETTING ON LIKE JOANNIE AND CHACHI WHEN I LEFT YOU

ARE YOU GOING TO BE OKAY TO DO THE SHOW?

OF COURSE YOU WILL! THIS WILL BE THE BEST SHOW EVER... JESUS, YOUR SHOULDERS FEEL LIKE A BAG OF WALNUTS!

THANKS SO MUCH BOYS AND GIRLS, MOMS AND DADS, AND ANY MON-KEYS IN THE AUDIENCE, THANKS FOR SINGING WITH US TODAY!

WELL, THAT WAS THE __WORST__ SHOW EVER.

A BUNCH OF SIX-YEAR-OLDS ONLY WANTING ONE ENCORE. AND EVEN THAT SEEMED LIKE POLITE APPLAUSE, LIKE THEY DIDN'T WANT TO OFFEND ME.

I'M SO PISSED OFF AND IT'S REALLY HARD TO CONVINCINGLY ACT LIKE MARY POPPINS FOR AN HOUR AND A HALF IN THAT STATE.

THE BAND ARE ALL SCARED OF ME RIGHT NOW. I HEARD ONE OF THEM WHISPER SOMETHING ABOUT PMS. EVEN RIC-CONTRITE-IS ON HIS BEST BEHAVIOUR. HE'S A REAL PLAYER WHEN IT'S ALL TOO LITTLE, TOO LATE.

AND HOW LONG WILL THIS BELATED GOOD BEHAVIOUR EVEN LAST?

HEY SHERRI, WHAT'S WRONG? YOU RAN OFF SO FAST...

NOT NOW, RIC...

WHY ARE YOU BEING SUCH A FUCKING BITCH?

HA! IT DOESN'T LAST LONG.

HANG IN THERE!

RIC, LEAVE ME ALONE. THAT WAS A SHITTY SHOW AND I WANT TO BE LEFT ALONE.

YOU NEVER APPRECIATE ANYTHING.

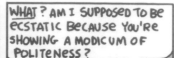

WHAT? AM I SUPPOSED TO BE ECSTATIC BECAUSE YOU'RE SHOWING A MODICUM OF POLITENESS?

SHOULD I BE AGOG THAT YOU ARE DOING YOUR JOB AND THAT YOU AREN'T DRUNK AND SHOVING LITTLE KIDS AROUND? 'CAUSE I AM RIC. I'M SOOO GRATEFUL. THANK YOU.

YOU KNOW, THE NETWORK WANTS YOU OFF THE SHOW. THEY'RE MAKING YOU A SPECIAL CONTRACT TO GIVE YOU ENOUGH ROPE AND SEE IF YOU HANG YOURSELF.

HOW LONG YOU THINK THAT'LL TAKE YOU, RIC?

THANKS FOR THE VOTE OF CONFIDENCE, SHERRI.

I'M NOT YOUR PERSONAL TRAINER, RIC...

FUCK YOU.

UH-HUH, SAME AS IT EVER WAS...

SO, IT APPEARS THEN THAT THIS IS MY FUTURE.

CHIPS AND A BEER GLASS FULL OF WINE ALONE EVERY NIGHT. BUT, WITH THE NETWORK DEAL, I'LL BE ABLE TO AFFORD A BETTER BRAND OF CHIPS. THOSE OLIVE OIL KIND. COVERED IN DEAD SEA SALT.

I WOULD IMAGINE BETTER WINES COULD BE AFFORDED AS WELL.

TO THE FUTURE: CHEERS.

OH, SHERRI SMALLS, WHAT ARE YOU GONNA DO? TAKE THE MONEY, GIVE UP YOUR DREAM?

COULD YOU EVEN MAKE IT AS A "STRAIGHT" ACT ANYMORE? YOU'RE REALLY NOTHING WITH-OUT YOUR BUBBLE-MACHINE GIRL.

OH, WHY WON'T SOMEONE LOVE ME?

...AND TAKE THESE CHIPS AWAY FROM ME?

WHY ISN'T KARL LIKE TWENTY-SEVEN YEARS YOUNGER, STRAIGHT, AND ATTRACTED TO ME?

SIGH...

THOSE OLIVE OIL CHIPS ARE GONNA BE SO GOOD THOUGH.

CRUNCH CRUNCH

CHAPTER FOURTEEN

DIGGING A DEEPER HOLE, AND EVER MORE EFFICIENTLY SO

YOU'RE SURE YOU DON'T WANT ME TO BUY YOU A SANDWICH? THERE'S STILL TIME...

I'M FINE, DAD, JUST RELAX. OH, THEY'RE LETTING US BOARD.

WELL, IT WAS GOOD SEEING YOU ALL. SAM IS SUCH A LITTLE WEIRDO. HE'S GREAT.

YEAH, IT WAS GOOD SEEING YOU TOO. YOU DOING GOOD THESE DAYS?

TICKETS PLEASE, BILLETS, S.V.P.

OKAY MISS, GO AHEAD.

YOU GOING WITH YOUR GIRLFRIEND, SON?

UH, NO.

EWWWWW!

BYE. LOVE YOU. CALL ME WHEN YOU GET HOME.

MY DAUGHTERS AND I, WE TALK AND TALK AND THEY NEVER REALLY TELL ME ANYTHING.

I'M ALL LIKE, HOW "ARE" YOU — EYEBROWS RAISED — WINK WINK, HOW "ARE" YOU REALLY? BUT THEY NEVER SAY ANYTHING BUT "FINE," LIKE THEY WOULD SAY TO ANY STRANGER WHO PUT THE QUESTION TO THEM.

AH WELL, TEN MINUTES LATER, SUPER-DAD REMEMBERS THAT THERE IS A SHERRI SMALLS CD FOR ADULTS THAT HE STILL DOESN'T HAVE.

IT'S OUT OF PRINT BUT ONE OF THE USED-RECORD STORES MIGHT HAVE IT.

I FIND IT AT THE SECOND STORE. THERE'S NO PICTURE OF HER, JUST A PLAIN BLACK COVER WITH THE TITLE "ASH TRAY" EMBOSSED IN EIGHTEEN-POINT HELVETICA.

FIFTEEN-NINETY-FIVE.

I'M SO GLAD IT DOESN'T SUCK.

IT'S ACTUALLY REALLY GOOD. HER SONGS DELIVER THE PROMISE I SAW IN HER KIDS' MUSIC.

THIS GIRL SHOULD HAVE BEEN BIG. WHY IS SHE SINGING FOR CHILD-REN AND DANCING WITH MONKEYS?

HE'S FINALLY ASLEEP! YOU WANNA WATCH FIFTEEN MINUTES OF A MOVIE?

UH, I'M GONNA TRY AND WORK ON THAT SCRIPT FOR THAT NEW STORY. MAYBE WE CAN WORK 'TIL ELEVEN?

SOUNDS GOOD, I'M POOPED. WHAT'S THIS YOU'RE LISTEN--ING TO?

OH, UH, IT'S THAT KID'S PERFORMER SAM LIKES...

SHE DID A GROWN-UPS' ALBUM A LONG TIME AGO. THOUGHT I'D GIVE IT A LISTEN.

SOUNDS PRETTY DEPRESSING.

A LITTLE VOICE IN MY HEAD IS SO PISSED AT THIS. THAT SAME VOICE IS DEFENDING SHERRI AND TEAR--ING DOWN CHAN. CHAN, THE LADY I'M MARRIED TO...

ME, I REMAIN NEUTRAL.

JESUS, IT IS NOT DEPRESSING. YOU'VE LISTENED FOR LIKE TWO SECONDS. WAY TO BE JUDGEMENTAL...

GIANT ROBOT

OKAAAY, I'LL SEE YOU LATER THEN.

NEXT DAY.

HMM...

NEW! SHERRI SMALLS!
FUN
MUSIC

PEOPLE NEVER UPDATE THEIR WEBSITES. AND SHERRI'S FAN-SITES ARE RUN BY SIX-YEAR-OLDS AND THEIR OVER-ANXIOUS, YUPPIE PARENTS.

SIGH.

KLAK!

I KNOW, I KNOW, I'M SULLYING THINGS...

Google

Sherri smalls Nude

Google Search   I'm feel

advertising.   Merchandi

AND, I ALSO KNOW I MAY GET A TON OF NUDE PICTURES OF THAT BAPTIST ORGAN-PLAYER OF THE SAME NAME, BUT THIS IS WHAT PEOPLE DO ON THE INTER-NET. I WANT NEW CONTENT.

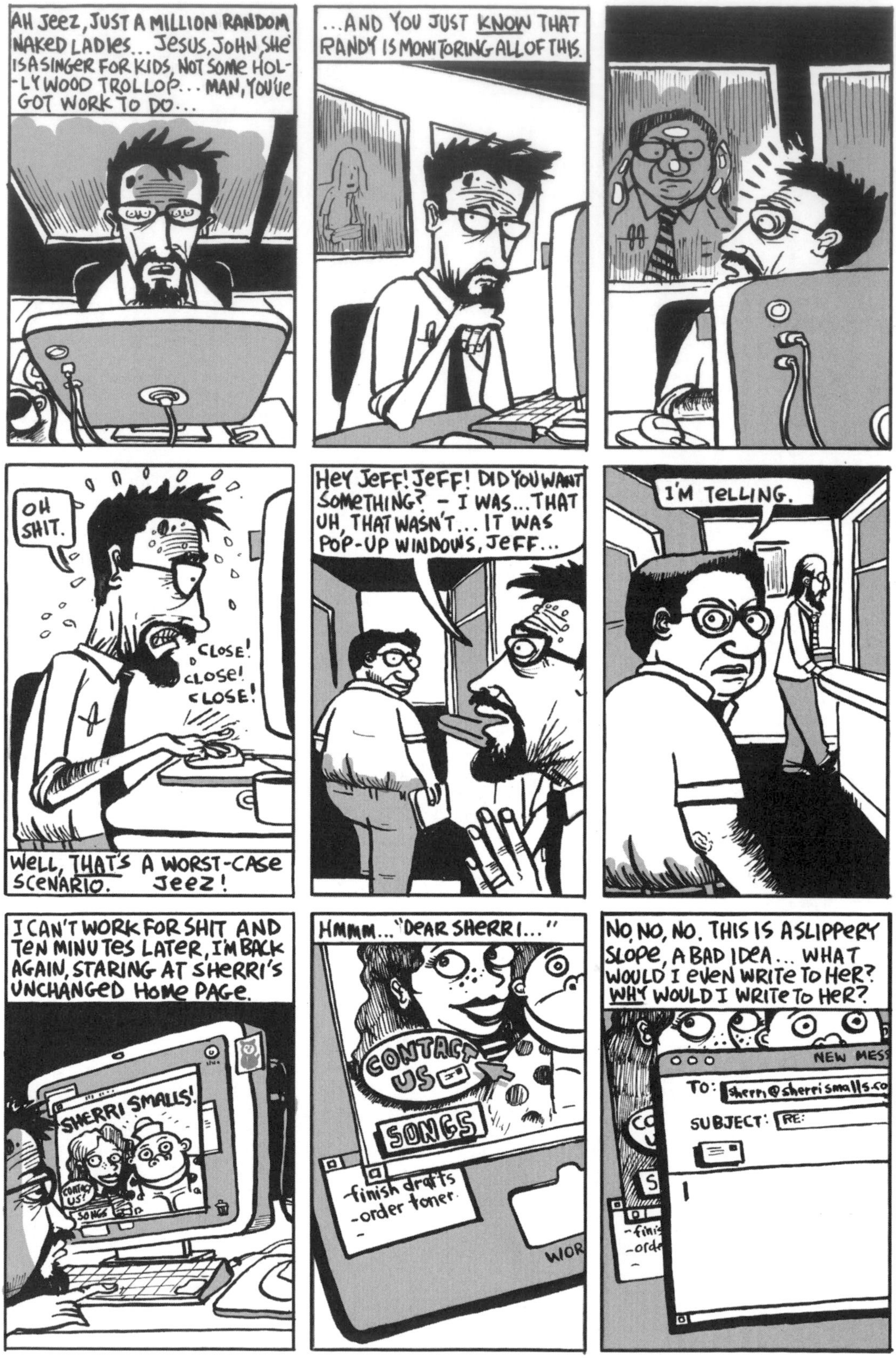
AH JEEZ, JUST A MILLION RANDOM NAKED LADIES... JESUS, JOHN, SHE IS A SINGER FOR KIDS, NOT SOME HOL-LYWOOD TROLLOP... MAN, YOU'VE GOT WORK TO DO...
...AND YOU JUST KNOW THAT RANDY IS MONITORING ALL OF THIS.
OH SHIT.
CLOSE! CLOSE! CLOSE!
WELL, THAT'S A WORST-CASE SCENARIO. JEEZ!
HEY JEFF! JEFF! DID YOU WANT SOMETHING? - I WAS... THAT UH, THAT WASN'T... IT WAS POP-UP WINDOWS, JEFF...
I'M TELLING.
I CAN'T WORK FOR SHIT AND TEN MINUTES LATER, I'M BACK AGAIN, STARING AT SHERRI'S UNCHANGED HOME PAGE.
SHERRI SMALLS!
CONTACT US!
SONGS
HMMM... "DEAR SHERRI..."
CONTACT US
SONGS
-finish drafts
-order toner
-
NO, NO, NO. THIS IS A SLIPPERY SLOPE, A BAD IDEA... WHAT WOULD I EVEN WRITE TO HER? WHY WOULD I WRITE TO HER?
NEW MESS
TO: sherri@sherrismalls.co
SUBJECT: RE:

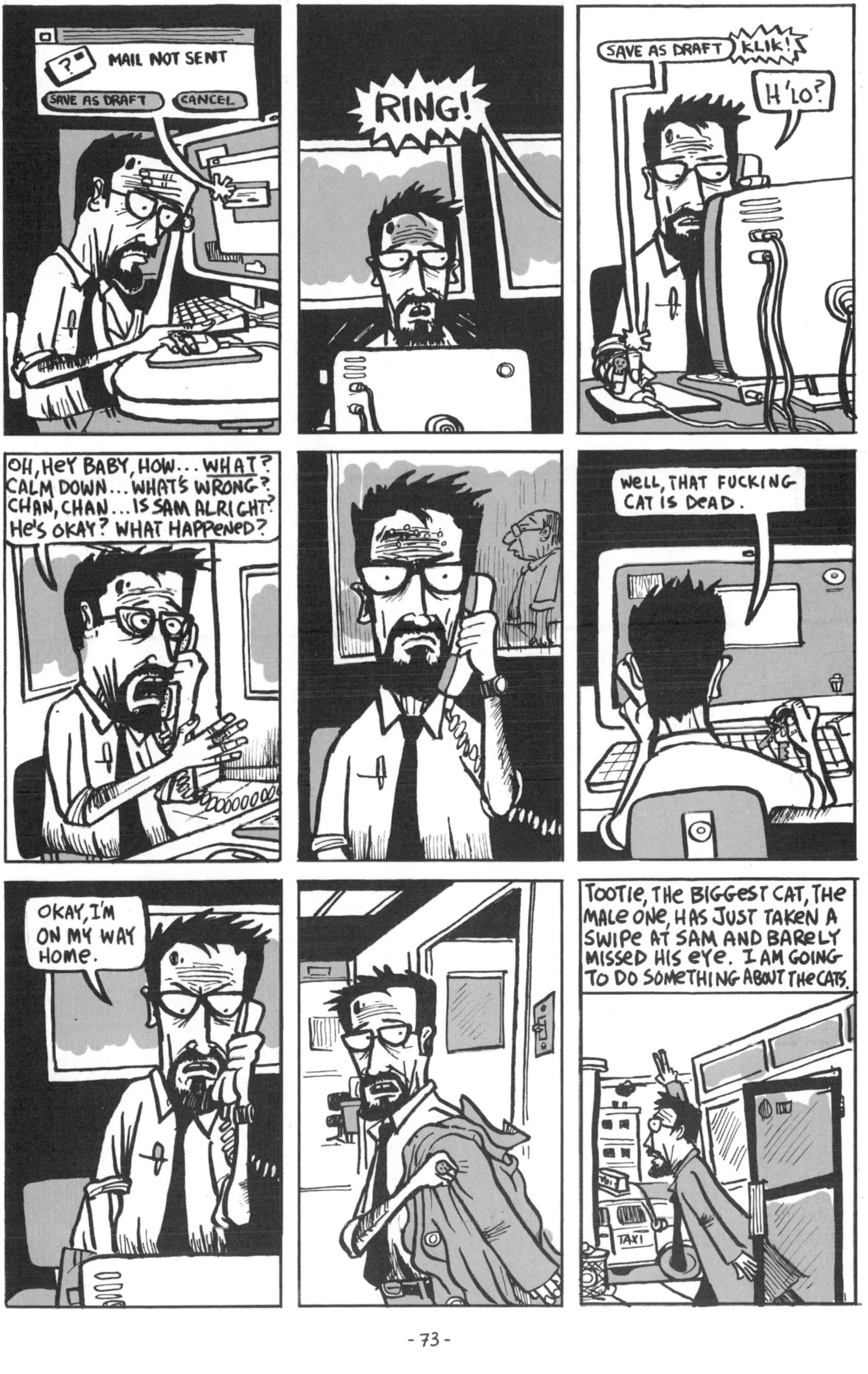
MAIL NOT SENT
SAVE AS DRAFT
CANCEL
RING!
SAVE AS DRAFT
KLIK!
H'LO?
OH, HEY BABY, HOW... WHAT? CALM DOWN... WHAT'S WRONG? CHAN, CHAN... IS SAM ALRIGHT? HE'S OKAY? WHAT HAPPENED?
WELL, THAT FUCKING CAT IS DEAD.
OKAY, I'M ON MY WAY HOME.
TOOTIE, THE BIGGEST CAT, THE MALE ONE, HAS JUST TAKEN A SWIPE AT SAM AND BARELY MISSED HIS EYE. I AM GOING TO DO SOMETHING ABOUT THE CATS.
TAXI

IN THE MIDDLE OF CHAN TELLING ME THIS— AND I'M ALREADY CLOSE TO HAVING A HEART ATTACK, SEEING SAM EYELESS, BLEEDING, SCREAMING IN PAIN, AND ALL OF IT MY FAULT—

CENSORED

— BUT AT THAT SAME MOMENT— I ALSO REMEMBER THAT I NEVER ASSIGNED A PHOTOGRAPHER FOR THE COVER SHOOT THAT WAS TO HAVE TAKEN PLACE THIS MORNING AND THE SUBJECT OF THE PHOTO SHOOT IN QUESTION, A FAMOUS BRIT-ISH AUTHOR, IS NOW ON A PLANE BACK TO ENGLAND, PROBABLY PISSED AT ME, AND I NEED TO SHOW THE PROPOSED COVER NEXT WEEK...

GAH!

AND THERE IS NO WAY WE CAN GET A RE-SHOOT DONE IN TIME, EVEN IF THE AUTHOR WOULD AGREE AND I DON'T KNOW HOW I LET THIS HAPPEN AND I'M SWEATING WAVES OF SWEAT THAT FEEL LIKE HOT WORMS COMING OUT OF MY PORES.

AND I FEEL LIKE I MAY SHIT MY PANTS AND I FEEL GUILTY THAT I'M THINK-ING OF THIS WHEN MY SON MAY BE BLINDED AND THERE'S A VEIN IN MY NECK THAT SEEMS AS IF IT MAY BURST AND I FEEL...

LIKE A LITTLE KID WHO HAS JUST DONE SOMETHING REALLY BAD THAT THEY KNOW CAN'T BE FIXED AND I KNOW I SHOULD TRY AND FIGURE OUT THIS PROBLEM...

UH, JUST MAKE IT TWELVE DOLLARS.

OR TELL SOMEONE, BUT I JUST RAN OUT THE DOOR TO TRY AND DEAL WITH THIS OTHER PROBLEM I'M RESPONSIBLE FOR.

SALUT, JOHN, ÇA...

OUI, ÇA VA, MERCI...

I CAN'T BELIEVE YOU! YOUR BROTHER IS NEARLY BLINDED AND YOU ARE BABBLING TO ME ABOUT YOUR GODDAMN ROOMATES' FRIGGING ALLERGIES?!?

I'M WARNING YOU, LISA, YOU ARE GOING TO TAKE AT LEAST THIS ONE FUCKING MURDEROUS CAT OR I'M GONNA DEAL WITH HIM.

WHY DO I HAVE TO BE THE ONE TO DEAL WITH EVERYTHING? WHY IS THIS ALL MY RESPONSIBILITY?

WELL, THAT'S JUST BULLSHIT, LISA! BYE!!

HER RESPONSE, "BECAUSE YOU'RE THE ADULT HERE," BESIDES REALLY PISSING ME OFF, EVENT--UALLY MAKES ME STOP AND THINK.

SLAM!

EVENTUALLY. BUT RIGHT NOW, PISSED OFF IS THE OVERWHELM--ING EMOTION AND I GO WITH IT. THE CAT IS LOCKED IN THE GUEST ROOM, WHERE WE PUT HIM TO PUNISH HIM.

THE ROOM HAS A LOFT BED WITH A DUVET, A LITTER BOX, FOOD AND WATER. THAT I SHOULD HAVE SUCH PUNISHMENT.

AND, S.P.C.A. BE FUCKED, I'M GO--ING TO YELL AT A CAT.

ROW?

YOU UNGRATEFUL LITTLE FUCKER!!! I RESCUED YOU FROM THE WILDERNESS. I FEED YOU AND KEEP A ROOF OVER YOUR HEAD...

NGROOOOWWW

OH, WHAT? YOU'RE GONNA ATTACK ME NOW? YOU... YOU... INGRATE, YOU...

HE DOES ATTACK. WHILE I SEARCH FOR STRONGER, MORE INSULTING IN--VECTIVES, HE BITES CLEAN THROUGH THE WEBBING BETWEEN MY THUMB AND FOREFINGER.

AUGH!!!

CHOMP!

AND **THAT'S** WHEN I THINK ABOUT WHAT LISA SAID: "BECAUSE YOU'RE THE ADULT HERE." AND WHAT IT MEANS IN THE LARGER SENSE AND WHAT IT MEANS IN CONJUNCTION WITH THE "CONVERSATION" I JUST HAD WITH THE CAT IN THERE.

IF THIS WERE A SCENE IN A BOOK, THE CATS WOULD BE A CENTRAL METAPHOR OF PARENTAL RESPONSIBILITY. NO, WAIT, REALLY — IN THE PAIN OF THE CAT-BITE, IT'S ALL REALLY CLEAR TO ME. WHEN LISA SAYS I HAVE TO TAKE CARE OF CATS "BECAUSE I'M THE ADULT," IT'S A COMMENTARY ON OUR FAMILY'S DESCENT FROM NUCLEAR FAMILY TO NUCLEAR WASTE. POST-DIVORCE.

I FAILED THE GIRLS THEN; I WAS NOT "THERE," SO ABSORBED IN THE PAIN OF MY CUCKOLDING BY THEIR MOTHER. I KNOW I WAS NOT THE ADULT THERE. AND MY SPEECH TO THE CAT, THE METAPHOR, ALL "YOU INGRATE, I FEED YOU, I GAVE YOU A PLACE TO LIVE," IS MY RESPONSE TO THAT CRITICISM.

OH YEAH, THE CATS! IT'S TRUE! I DID FEED AND CLOTHE THE GIRLS. I PAID SHIT-LOADS OF SUPPORT MONEY WHILE I LIVED LIKE A MONK. WELL, A DRINK-DRUG-AND-SEX-ADDLED MONK. BUT STILL, MONEY WAS SHORT FOR ME...

← DAD, GETTING HIS GROOVE ON. (AHEM.)

"YOU'VE GOT FOOD AND WATER, GIRLS. THE LITTER BOX IS CLEAN. YOU'VE GOT EVERYTHING YOU REQUIRE AND NOTHING YOU NEED.

H2O   Food.

OH, WE NEVER SPEAK OF THESE THINGS; WE HIDE BEHIND CAT METAPHORS. I'M TOO ASHAMED OF THE THINGS I DIDN'T DO, AND MAYBE THE GIRLS ARE EQUALLY ASHAMED OF ME. OH MAN, I'VE MADE A MESS OF THINGS...

I'LL BE KIND OF GLAD WHEN THE CLARITY OF THIS CAT BITE SUBSIDES.

...AGAIN, SORRY FOR BEING SUCH A TURD. I ALWAYS KNOW THAT THE DAD ON "FULL HOUSE" WOULD HAVE HANDLED THINGS BETTER. THANKS, BOB SAGET.

SERIOUSLY SORRY FOR YELLING AND BEING OBNOXIOUS, I WAS WORRIED ABOUT SAM. TOOTIE BIT MY HAND! I REALLY DON'T KNOW WHAT TO DO WITH HIM.

PART OF ME STILL LOVES THAT OLD CAT. LIKE YOU'VE SAID, HIS FUR IS SALTED WITH ALL OF OUR TEARS... -SEE YOU, LOVE DAD.

WELL, A HALF-ASSED APOLOGY— NOTHING ADDRESSED, NOTHING RESOLVED; A GOOD NIGHT'S WORK, MR. OLSEN. YOU'VE EARNED YOURSELF A DRINK.

OH FUCK— THE PHOTOGRAPHER!

CHAPTER FIFTEEN:
TROUBLES BEGIN TO STACK UP LIKE WEIGHTS IN A MEDIEVAL TORTURE DEVICE.

I WISH TODAY WAS FRIDAY. MAYBE I SHOULD QUIT AND START THE WEEKEND EARLY.

OKAY, MISS DORMAN, YOU'VE GOT SOME SOLID BACK UP PLANS. YOU'RE A REAL POLLYANNA. SERIOUSLY, THANKS. NOW, GO GET TO IT...

NICE MATCHING OUTFITS, BY THE WAY.

JOHN, CAN I SEE YOU FOR A MINUTE?

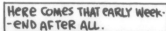

HERE COMES THAT EARLY WEEK--END AFTER ALL.

JOHN, YOU KNOW I HAVE TO REAM YOU OUT HERE, DON'T YOU?

IT'S NOT JUST THIS MISSED PHOTO SHOOT, EITHER. WHAT IS GOING ON WITH YOU? IS IT THE KID?

JESUS, THEY SHOULD OUTLAW EMPLOYEES HAVING BABIES. THINGS ARE SLIPPING LIKE CRAZY IN YOUR DEPARTMENT. PEOPLE ARE TALKING. THE OWNERS ARE TALKING. IS THERE SOMETHING I CAN DO?

OH, I WISH IT WERE THE KID. I WISH IT WERE AS NICE AS THAT- THE PLOT OF A THOUSAND SHLOCKY MOVIES: THE WORKAHOLIC WHOSE WORK SLIPS WHEN HE LEARNS THE VALUE OF SPENDING TIME WITH HIS KID. I WISH I WERE THAT GUY.

IT SOUNDS WAY BETTER THAN MY MIND IS OFF MY WORK 'CAUSE I FEEL OLD AND I'M GUILTY OVER MY DIVORCE AND MY ADULT KIDS AND MY INFANT SON DRIVES ME CRAZY AND THE WOMAN WHO IS THE LOVE OF MY LIFE AND I ARE DRIFTING APART WITH ALL THE DRUDGERY OF OUR LIVES.

AND IT'S ALSO TRUE I'M BECOMING UNHEALTHILY OBSESSED WITH A CHILDREN'S SINGER AND ALL OF THIS MAKES MY WORK SUFFER. YOU KNOW, I MEAN THAT MAKES A LOUSY MOVIE PLOT.

I HAVE NOTHING TO SAY IN MY DEFENCE. I... DROPPED THE BALL...

"DROPPED THE BALL?" JESUS, YOU SOUND LIKE TONY ROBBINS NOW.

JUST GET BACK TO WORK AND PULL A MAGAZINE COVER OUT OF YOUR ASS BY THURSDAY, OKAY?

THANKS, WALTER.

MOVE CAUTIOUSLY, JOHN, PEOPLE ARE WATCHING YOU...

WELL, NO PRESSURE THERE.

I GO INTO SURVIVAL MODE; I'M PISSED AT FUCKING UP AND THAT ACTS AS A MOTIVATOR. I CON-CENTRATE, WORK MY ASS TO THE BONE, AND GET TWO FAIRLY DEC-ENT COVER OPTIONS TOGETHER.

I WRITE AN APOLOGY TO THE AUTHOR OF THE MISSED PHOTO-SHOOT AND BEG FOR THE USE OF ANY PUBLICITY STILLS TO AC-COMPANY HER INTERVIEW.

I START AT THE BEGINNING AND REWORK ALL OF THE LAYOUTS OF THE MAIN ARTICLES, AND BY LATE THAT EVENING, I SEND NEW PDFs TO THE EDITOR AND I'M EVEN HAPPY WITH SOME OF THEM.

EVERYONE'S ASLEEP WHEN I GET HOME. I GET A DRINK AND CHECK ON OUR PRISONER CAT, OUR MAD FELINE, MRS. ROCHESTER.

ROW?

MER?

HEY GUYS. IS THIS IN SOLIDARITY OR ARE YOU GLOATING THAT YOU'RE FREE? DON'T FEEL BAD FOR 'OL TOOTIE, HE'S A BABY-SCRATCHER.

MAO?

GROW.

ROW?

HEY MAN, HOW YOU DOING? YOU'VE REALLY DONE IT THIS TIME. I'M SORRY MAN. YOU KNOW I LOVE YOU. YOU WERE MY ONLY CON-FIDANT AFTER THINGS WENT TO HELL WITH THE FIRST MARRIAGE. BOY, WHAT TIMES WE HAD, EH?

YOU AND ME WANDERING AROUND THE APARTMENT DRUNK AS HELL 'TIL ALL HOURS OF THE NIGHT. I KNOW I OWE YOU, BUT YOU'RE EN-DANGERING A LITTLE KID. I DON'T KNOW WHY YOU ATTACKED SAM; SOME EXTENSION OF THE METAPHOR I'VE STUMBLED ONTO? I DON'T KNOW WHAT TO DO, BUT I HAVE TO DO SOMETHING.

OKAY, SO APPARENTLY HE'S NOT AS AFFECTED BY MY SPEECH AS I AM.

ZZZZ

I JUST REMEMBER—AND THIS IS THE TOPPER TO A RARE GENUINELY GOOD DAY—THAT IT IS MY DAY TO SLEEP IN TOMORROW. I FALL ASLEEP IN MINUTES. I CAN FEEL MYSELF SLEEP-SMILING.

I WAKE UP TO THE SOUND OF SCREAMING.

OH MY GOD, JOHN, GET OUT HERE. IT'S ZOOEY! I THINK SHE MIGHT BE DEAD!

ZOOEY? OH NO. OH NO. POOR LITTLE... OH JESUS... PLEASE, I... I THINK SHE'S...

...SHE'S DEAD. I'LL GET A TOWEL. OH SHIT, POOR LITTLE ZOOEY, WHAT HAPPENED?

FIRST THERE'S JUST THE PHY--SICAL: OH GROSS, THE POOL OF CLEAR, GELID PUKE, THE LOOK OF PAIN- WAS SHE POISONED? WAS SHE SICK? DID I LEAVE POISON OUT? SAM COULD HAVE BEEN POISONED.

SHE'S STILL FLOPPY AND FROM A MILLION COP SHOWS, I ASSUME THIS MEANS SHE HASN'T BEEN DEAD LONG. THE WEIGHT, OR LACK OF WEIGHT, OF HER TINY BODY IN THE TOWEL SEEMS IM--POSSIBLE, LIKE A STUFFED ANIMAL WITH BONES.

I MECHANICALLY CLEAN THINGS UP AND PLACE HER GENTLY IN A SMALL, PADDED BOX. I REMEM--BER THE LAST THING I SAID TO HER WAS "GET OUT, SHOO!" AND A GROAN SPONTANEOUSLY ESCAPES MY THROAT.

I CALL THE GIRLS AND THEY BOTH TAKE IT HARD. MAYBE MY BLUBBERING ON THE PHONE, SOMETHING I THINK THEY'VE NEVER HEARD BEFORE, IS THE DISQUIETING ASPECT, BUT I CAN'T HELP MYSELF.

THE DEATH OF THIS LITTLE CAT THAT MY DAUGHTERS GAVE ME AFTER THE DIVORCE IS KICK-ING ME HARD IN THE GUTS.

SAM'S NAPPING. I DON'T THINK HE KNOWS WHAT'S GOING ON.

OH, POOR LITTLE ZOOEY. SHE WAS MY FAVOURITE. I DON'T KNOW WHAT COULD HAVE HAPPENED.

ARE YOU OKAY?

I CAN'T STOP BLUBBERING. IT'S SO HYPOCRITICAL; I'VE DONE NOTHING BUT BITCH ABOUT THE CATS. I HAVE NO RIGHT TO BE ACTING LIKE THIS.

AH, POOR LITTLE ZOOEY. AW... UGHH...

DO YOU WANT TO LOOK AT HER?

POOOT!

YEAH, SHE DOESN'T EVEN LOOK DEAD NOW.

SNURF

SWEATERS

↑ UP

OH...

BROCOLLI

OH ZOOEY, YOU HAD THE SOFT--EST FUR IN THE WORLD. YOU LOVED US AND HATED EVERYONE ELSE.

SWEATERS

BROCOLLI

CHAN TAKES CHARGE AND ACTS LIKE A KINDLY FUNERAL DIR--ECTOR. I'M REMINDED WHY I FELL IN LOVE WITH THIS GIRL.

SWEATERS

BROCOLLI

YOU WERE A FIESTY LITTLE THING. I'M SORRY I YELLED AT YOU, ZOOEY.

IS SHE IN THERE?

YEAH.

BROCO

AW, LISA ...

BROC

YOU WANT TO SEE HER? SHE LOOKS PEACEFUL.

YEAH.

LISA, WHO USUALLY THINKS EVERYTHING IS GROSS, PLACES A HAND ON ZOOEY'S DEAD BODY AND SAYS SOMETHING I CAN'T HEAR.

BROCOLLI

YOU ONLY GET ONE CHANCE WITH DEATH AND A LIFETIME TO REGRET THINGS UNDONE, I GUESS.

ROCOLLI

- 83 -

THE VETS AREN'T OPEN 'TIL MONDAY.

IT'S A LITTLE LATE FOR THE VETS, DAD.

YEAH, UH, THEY HAVE TO... WHAT ARE WE GONNA DO WITH THE BODY? THE VETS HAVE A...SERVICE. I'LL TAKE HER ON MONDAY.

I WANT TO COME WITH YOU.

I HAVE NO EXPERIENCE WITH DEATH, NO TRADITIONS OF MY OWN, SO I APPROPRIATE SOME. WE COVER THE MIRRORS WITH SHEETS AND SIT A LOW-RENT, GOYISH VERSION OF SHIVA.

ON MONDAY, LISA AND I TAKE TURNS CARRYING THE BOX— BARELY WEIGHTED IT SEEMS— TO THE VETS AND I CAN ONLY THINK THAT I SHOULD BE BRING-ING THE CAT THERE FOR A CHECK-UP OR SHOTS INSTEAD OF THIS.

BROCOLLI

I THINK OF ALL MY COMPLAINTS AGAINST THE CATS AND I FEEL LIKE I'M ONE OF THE PARENTS IN THE STORY "THE MONKEY'S PAW." BE CAREFUL WHAT YOU WISH FOR, INDEED.

BROCOLLI

I'M TOO CLOSE TO BREAKING DOWN TO DO ANYTHING MORE THAN EXPLAIN THE BOX IN A CHOKING VOICE AND HAND OVER MY CREDIT CARD.

EXIT

BROCOLLI

ERINARIAN
DR. P. SAUL

- 84 -

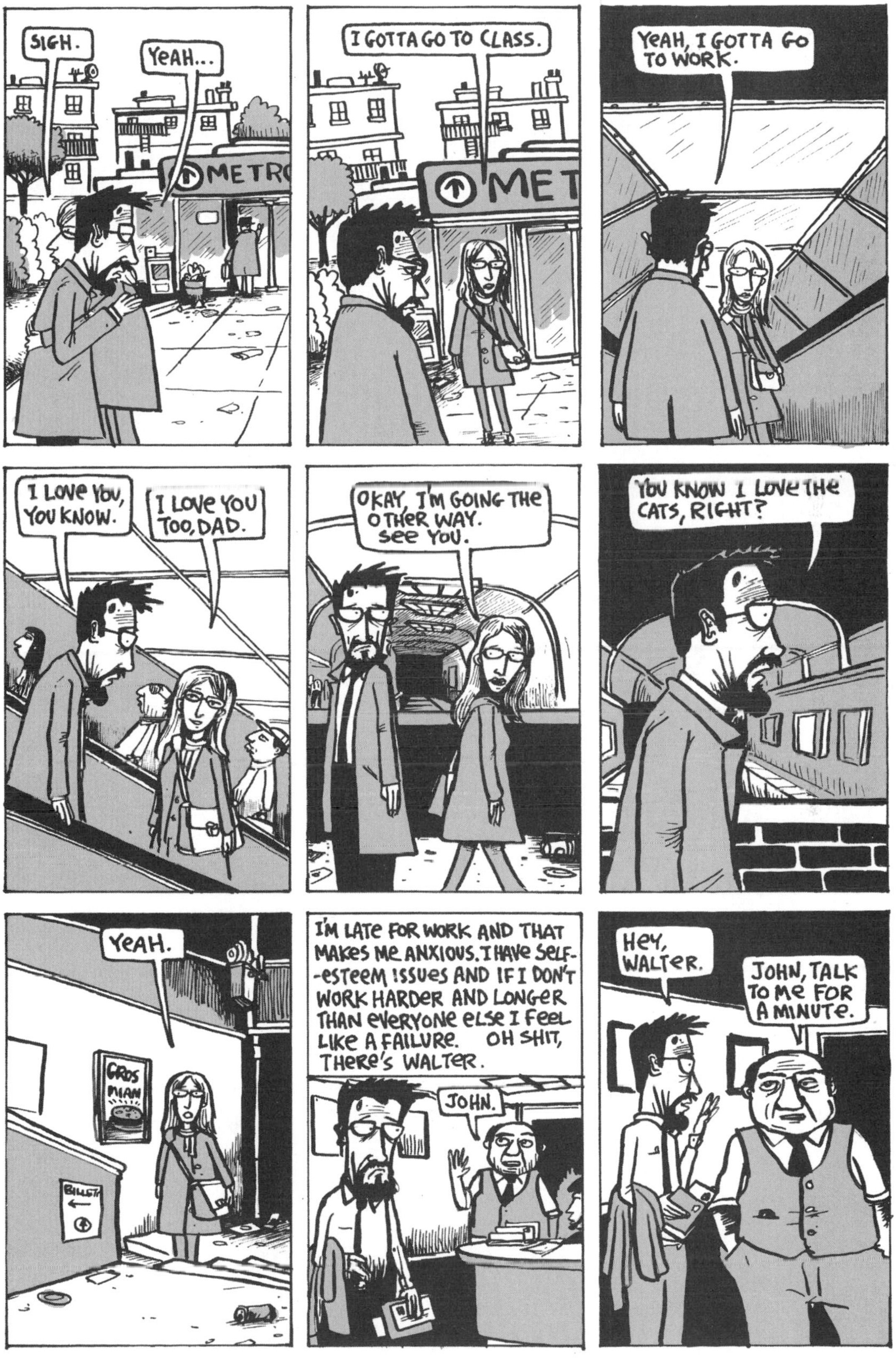
SIGH.
YEAH...
METRO
I GOTTA GO TO CLASS.
MET
YEAH, I GOTTA GO TO WORK.
I LOVE YOU, YOU KNOW.
I LOVE YOU TOO, DAD.
OKAY, I'M GOING THE OTHER WAY. SEE YOU.
YOU KNOW I LOVE THE CATS, RIGHT?
YEAH.
I'M LATE FOR WORK AND THAT MAKES ME ANXIOUS. I HAVE SELF-ESTEEM ISSUES AND IF I DON'T WORK HARDER AND LONGER THAN EVERYONE ELSE I FEEL LIKE A FAILURE. OH SHIT, THERE'S WALTER.
JOHN.
HEY, WALTER.
JOHN, TALK TO ME FOR A MINUTE.

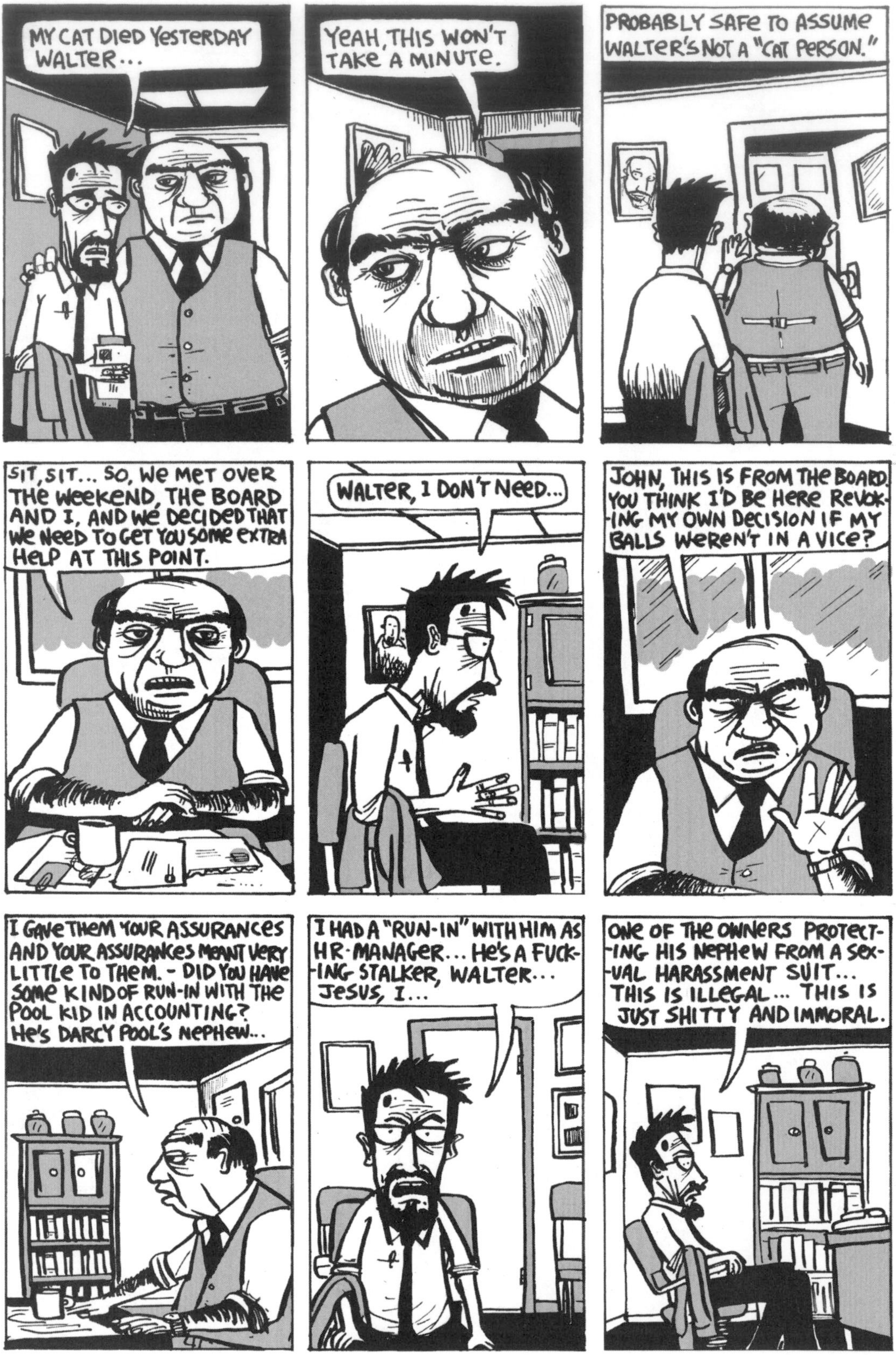
MY CAT DIED YESTERDAY WALTER...
YEAH, THIS WON'T TAKE A MINUTE.
PROBABLY SAFE TO ASSUME WALTER'S NOT A "CAT PERSON."
SIT, SIT... SO, WE MET OVER THE WEEKEND, THE BOARD AND I, AND WE DECIDED THAT WE NEED TO GET YOU SOME EXTRA HELP AT THIS POINT.
WALTER, I DON'T NEED...
JOHN, THIS IS FROM THE BOARD. YOU THINK I'D BE HERE REVOK-ING MY OWN DECISION IF MY BALLS WEREN'T IN A VICE?
I GAVE THEM YOUR ASSURANCES AND YOUR ASSURANCES MEANT VERY LITTLE TO THEM. - DID YOU HAVE SOME KIND OF RUN-IN WITH THE POOL KID IN ACCOUNTING? HE'S DARCY POOL'S NEPHEW...
I HAD A "RUN-IN" WITH HIM AS HR MANAGER... HE'S A FUCK-ING STALKER, WALTER... JESUS, I...
ONE OF THE OWNERS PROTECT-ING HIS NEPHEW FROM A SEX-UAL HARASSMENT SUIT... THIS IS ILLEGAL... THIS IS JUST SHITTY AND IMMORAL.

COME ON JOHN, WE'RE NOT A COUPLE OF LITTLE GIRLS HERE, SO DON'T TALK SHIT TO ME. IT'S NOT JUST POOL'S NEPHEW EITHER, YOU'VE BEEN FUCKING UP FOR QUITE SOME TIME. PEOPLE NOTICED.

NO ONE DIES, NO ONE LOSES A JOB, IT'S NOTHING, SO RELAX. WE'RE GONNA MAKE THAT JUNIOR DESIGNER, TAMMY, YOUR EXECUTIVE ASSISTANT. SHE'S A TALENTED KID AND IT'LL TAKE A LOAD OFF OF YOU.

THEY WANTED ME TO FIRE YOU, JOHN, SO CONSIDER THIS PURE GRAVY...

IN THE ASS-SNIFFING, TERRITORIAL-PISSING, ALPHA-MALE DESIGN WORLD, A DISGUISED DEMOTION LIKE THIS IS DEATH. BETTER THEY SHOULD SHOOT ME IN THE BACK OF THE HEAD.

OF COURSE, I SHOULD RESIGN IMMEDIATELY TO SAVE FACE, BUT I'M FORTY YEARS OLD AND THAT IS OLD FOR AN ART DIRECTOR... I GOTTA MOVE CAREFULLY HERE.

WELL SHIT, WALTER, I THINK I GOTTA QUIT.

RIGHT, CAREFULLY.

I HOPE YOU WON'T DO THAT.

I HOPE YOU'LL BUCK UP, GET YOUR SHIT TOGETHER, GET TO WORK, AND WIN US SOME DESIGN-AWARDS AND MAKE THIS TAMMY KID LOOK LIKE THE CANDY-ASS SHE IS. THAT'S WHAT I HOPE.

HEYYY JOHN...

... UMM, WALTER JUST TALKED TO ME AND HE WANTS US ALL TO MEET AND...

TAMMY, THE CORPSE ISN'T EVEN COLD YET. I HAVEN'T EVEN DE--CIDED IF I'M QUITTING YET. CAN YOU GIVE ME A MINUTE?

WHEN IN DOUBT, CHECK THE EMAIL.

KLAK.

JOHN, TAMMY'S BAWL--ING HER FACE OFF. IS SOMETHING GOING ON?

CAN'T TALK SALLY, CHECKING EMAIL.

ALRIGHT! MY BEGGING LETTER TO THE MISSED PHOTO-SHOOT AUTHOR HAS PRODUCED SERIOUS RESULTS.

SHE'S GOT AN UNEXPECTED STOP OVER IN NEW YORK CITY IN TWO DAYS AND IS WILLING TO DO A PHOTO SHOOT AT THE AIR PORT IF I CAN ARRANGE IT. WILL THIS WORK? UH, HALF OF HER LAST BOOK IS SET IN AN AIR PORT. IT WILL WORK!

I WRITE A GRATEFUL EMAIL SAYING I'LL ARRANGE EVERYTHING AND CONFIRM BY THE END OF DAY.

THEN I FIND TAMMY, APOLOG-IZE: —"I'M AN OLD CRANK!"—AND ASK HER TO RESEARCH NEW YORK PHOTOGRAPHERS. I HAVE, LIKE TWENTY GOOD PEOPLE I KNOW IN N.Y.C., BUT I FEEL BAD, SO I THROW TAMMY A BONE. WE'RE ALL FRIENDS AGAIN.

ISPAIN

I TELL WALTER THE GOOD NEWS AND THAT I'M GOING TO FLY OUT AND SUPERVISE THE SHOOT SO THERE ARE NO SURPRISES AND HE SAYS OKAY.

EVERYTHING IS SET BY 6:30 IN THE AFTERNOON. I CONFIRM WITH ROWINA, THE AUTHOR, IN A LONG, FAWNING EMAIL.

BYE, JOHN.

SEE YOU.

I'M ALONE IN THE OFFICE AND A SHERRI SMALLS SONG COMES ON THE SHUFFLE ON MY COMPUTER. SHERRI SMALLS LIVES IN NEW YORK.

I REMEMBER THAT DRAFT EMAIL SAVED ON MY COMPUTER.

WHAT ARE YOU GONNA DO, WRITE A FAN LETTER TO A CHILDREN'S PERFORMER?

YAHOO mail.

SHE'LL THINK YOU'RE A HALF-WIT MAN-CHILD OR A CHILD MOLESTER.

YAHOO

EXIT

- 89 -

I'LL JUST SEND AN EMAIL ABOUT HOW MUCH I LIKED "ASH TRAY." SHE COULD BE A POTENTIAL STORY FOR THE MAGAZINE.

SARAH DID SAY SHE IS "THE SHIT" IN CHILDREN'S PERFORMERS

YOU SHOULD GO HOME... TO YOUR FAMILY... YOUR WIFE.

IT'S HARMLESS, SHE WON'T EVEN ANSWER...

WHAT IF SHE DOES?

I'LL TRY AND SET UP A MEETING... FOR THE MAGAZINE. IT COULD BE A GOOD STORY. I'M IN NEW YORK ANYWAY... MULTI-TASKING...

JESUS, SHOULDN'T YOU JUST GO OUT AND BUY LEATHER PANTS AND DO THIS MIDLIFE CRISIS UP PROPERLY?

YOU NEVER DO ANYTHING FUN. YOU HAVE NEVER DONE ANYTHING FUN. WHILE EVERYONE ELSE WAS GOING TO BUSH PARTIES AND HIGHSCHOOL DANCES, YOU WERE BUYING DIAPERS AND WORKING NIGHT-SHIFTS IN A BOX FACTORY.

BOX
BOITE

BOX

BOX

WRITE AN EMAIL... A HARMLESSLY FLIRTATIOUS EMAIL EVEN... WHAT COULD HAPPEN?

MID-LIFE: PART TWO

CHAPTER SIXTEEN:
SHOCK THE MONKEY

HI SHERRI, HI! IT'S OKAY, IT'S OKAY...

OH, THERE'S BLOOD... THIS IS MY FAULT. I WAS MEAN AND SHITTY...

NO, THIS WAS ALWAYS GOING TO HAPPEN TO RIC.

SHERRI, SWEETIE, HE'S OKAY! HE'S FINE. HE WAS A LITTLE BLOODY, BUT HE'S FINE. WE MAY NOT BE FINE, BUT REEK IS...

THERE WAS A PHOTOGRAPHER AT THE ACCIDENT SCENE...

BLOW.

NO: FOUL!

FERF!

THEY KNEW WHO HE WAS... JESUS CHRIST, HONEY, HE WAS TOOLING AROUND WASTED WEARING THE FUCKING MONKEY SUIT! I SWEAR I...

HE HAD A BOTTLE OF JACK DANIELS IN HIS CROTCH AND HE IS BEING BOOKED FOR POSSESSION OF MARIJUANA AND COCAINE, SHERRI...

OH NO.

OH YES. SHERRI, YOU HAVE TO FIRE HIM. I'LL DO IT IF YOU DON'T WANT TO.

I'LL TAKE CARE OF IT.

EXIT

OH...

YEAH, THEY HAD TO CUT THE SUIT OFF ME. THERE WAS A LOT OF BLOOD AND THEY THOUGHT STUFF WAS BROKEN.

JUST THE NOSE AND THE WRIST THOUGH.

WE'LL NEED A NEW SUIT...

YOU'LL NEED A NEW MONKEY.

RIC...

SHERRI... I THINK I'M DONE. I'M SORRY I EMBARRASSED YOU. IT WON'T HAPPEN AGAIN AT LEAST...

I KINDA WISH I HAD DIED, YOU KNOW? WOULD A BEEN MORE DIGNIFIED THAN ALL OF THIS. THE AIR BAG BROKE MY NOSE AND I WAS WEARING MY SEAT BELT. NOT VERY ROCK AND ROLL, EH?

OH RIC.

YEAH — I'M PROBABLY GOING TO JAIL THIS TIME. I'M SORRY I WAS WEARING THE SUIT. IT SEEMED FUNNY AT THE TIME. HA.

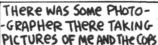

THERE WAS SOME PHOTO- -GRAPHER THERE TAKING PICTURES OF ME AND THE COPS.

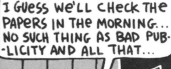

I GUESS WE'LL CHECK THE PAPERS IN THE MORNING... NO SUCH THING AS BAD PUB- -LICITY AND ALL THAT...

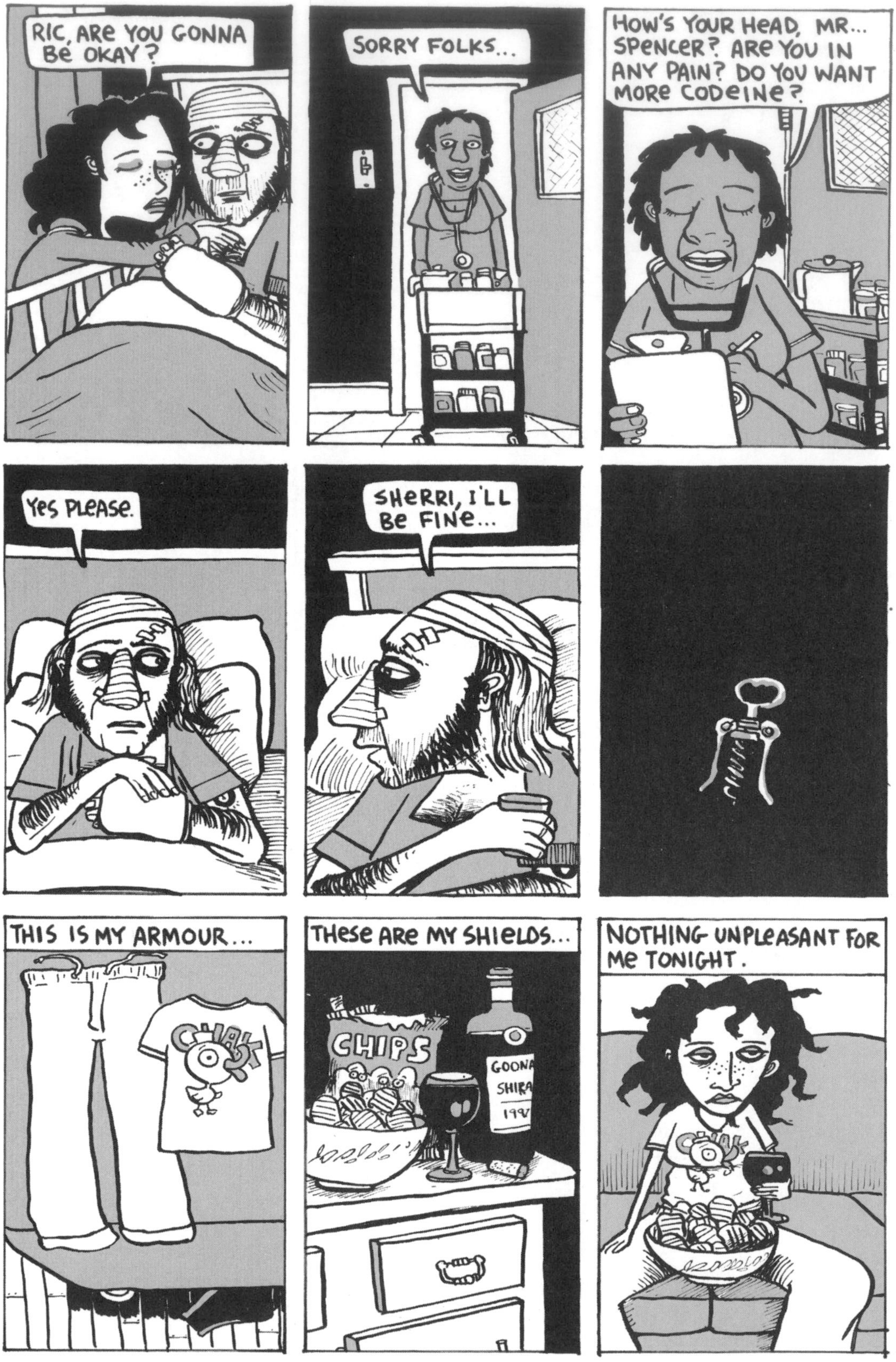
RIC, ARE YOU GONNA BE OKAY?
SORRY FOLKS...
HOW'S YOUR HEAD, MR... SPENCER? ARE YOU IN ANY PAIN? DO YOU WANT MORE CODEINE?
YES PLEASE.
SHERRI, I'LL BE FINE...
THIS IS MY ARMOUR...
THESE ARE MY SHIELDS...
CHIPS
NOTHING UNPLEASANT FOR ME TONIGHT.

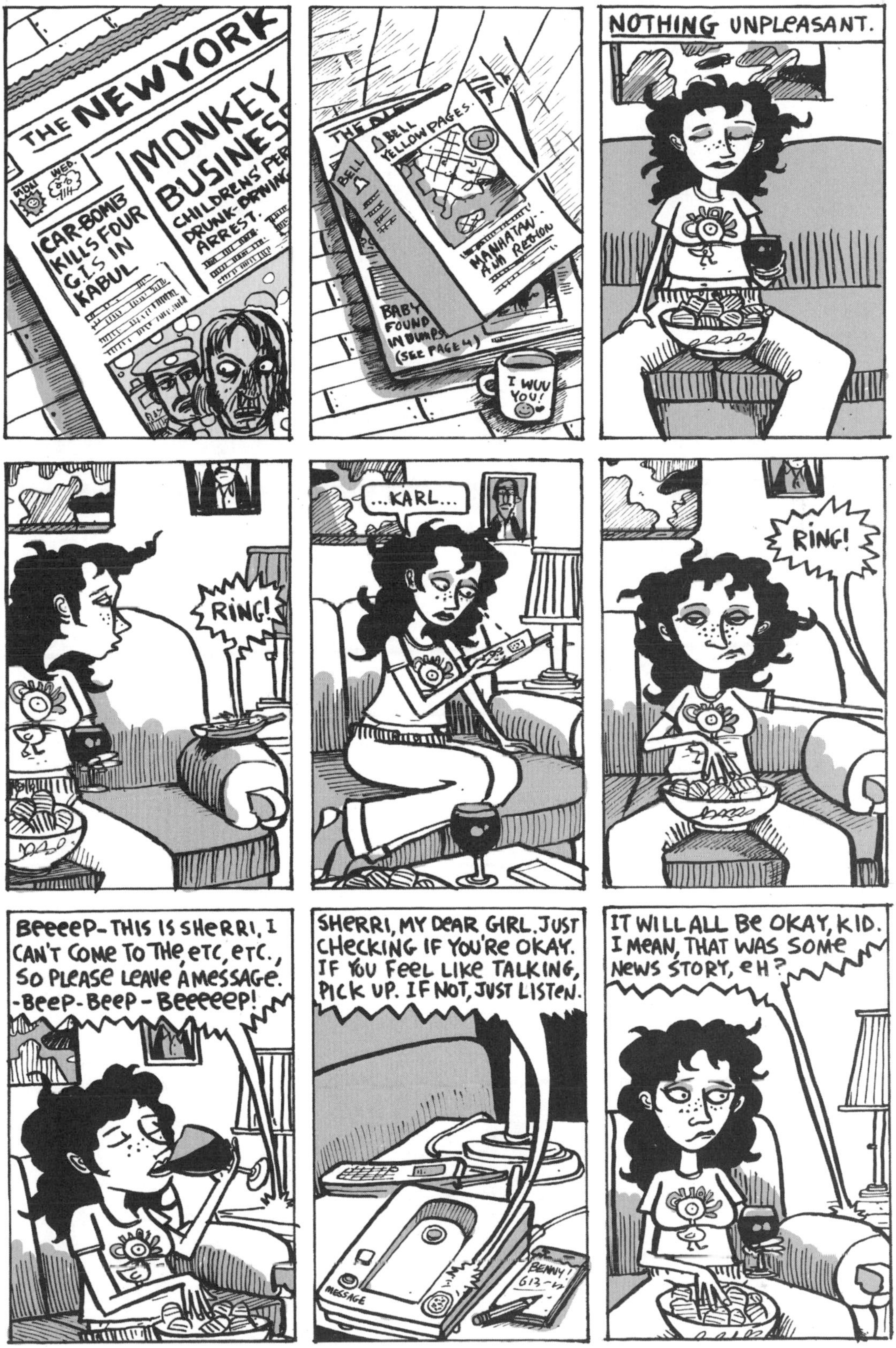
THE NEW YORK
MONKEY BUSINESS
CHILDRENS' PER... DRUNK-DRIVING ARREST.
CAR-BOMB KILLS FOUR G.I.S IN KABUL
BELL YELLOW PAGES.
MANHATTAN AND REGION
BABY FOUND IN DUMPS (SEE PAGE 4)
I WUV YOU!
NOTHING UNPLEASANT.
RING!
...KARL...
RING!
BEEEEP- THIS IS SHERRI. I CAN'T COME TO THE, ETC, ETC., SO PLEASE LEAVE A MESSAGE. -BEEP-BEEP-BEEEEEP!
SHERRI, MY DEAR GIRL. JUST CHECKING IF YOU'RE OKAY. IF YOU FEEL LIKE TALKING, PICK UP. IF NOT, JUST LISTEN.
MESSAGE
BENNY! 613-
IT WILL ALL BE OKAY, KID. I MEAN, THAT WAS SOME NEWS STORY, EH?

I'VE TALKED TO EVERYONE WHO NEEDS TO BE TALKED TO AT THE LABEL AND AT THE NETWORK. I'VE TOLD THEM THAT REEK IS ON "HIATUS". THAT'S WHAT I'M CALLING IT.

I TUCKED HIM IN AT THE HOSPITAL. HE'S HAPPY AS HELL, FULL OF MORPHINE, ETC. SO...

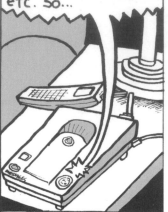

ALSO, I'M FOLLOWING YOUR EXAMPLE. I'VE GOT A BAG OF CHIPS, AND I ASSUMED AN ARGENTINIAN PLONK WOULD GO BEST WITH THOSE. SOO...

OKAY, OKAY... LONG, MES--SAGE FROM A TIPSY KARL.

TOMORROW'S ANOTHER DAY...

WHETHER WE LIKE IT OR NOT...

GOOD NIGHT LOVE. HOPE YOU ARE GOOD.

GOOD NIGHT KARL.

- 98 -

I'M BACK WITH MY MOVIE, A HIT COMEDY THAT EVERYONE'S BEEN TELLING ME IS WAY BETTER THAN I WOULD THINK.

IT ISN'T. IT'S HEAVY ON THE SCATOLOGY, WHICH I'M ACTUALLY FINDING WAY MORE ENGAGING THAN ALL OF THE "IRONIC" HOMOPHOBIA AND SEXISM.

...AND THEN YOU CAN DATE-RAPE HER!

I MEAN, I "GET IT" AND I'M EVEN FAIRLY SURE THAT THE WRITER/ DIRECTOR DOES. I ONLY WORRY THAT THE LEGIONS OF TEEN-AGERS WHO WATCH IT MAY TAKE IT ALL AT FACE VALUE.

I'LL DATE-RAPE YOU, FAGGOT...

JEEZ.

IT'S THE CHILDREN'S PERFORMER IN ME TALKING, QUESTIONING...

...QUESTIONING WHY I DIDN'T BRING THE WINE BOTTLE WITH ME. I LEAVE THE MOVIE RUN-NING, CONFIDENT I'LL PICK UP THE "PLOT" ON MY RETURN.

WHICH WOULD BE MORE INDIC-ITIVE OF A PROBLEM, OPENING ANOTHER BOTTLE WITH WINE STILL IN MY GLASS, OR NEEDING TO OPEN ANOTHER BOTTLE AFTER I KILL THE GLASS?

AH RIC, IT FEELS LIKE IT'S OVER FOR REAL THIS TIME AND I'M KINDA GLAD. THIS WINE IS LIKE TRUTH SERUM.

I'M GLAD RIC'S OUT OF THE PIC- -TURE AND I'M PRETTY SURE I ACTUALLY DO WANT THIS NETWORK DEAL. ALSO, I'M THIRTY-THREE YEARS OLD AND I'M A CHILDREN'S ENTERTAINER. THAT'S NOT SO BAD, IS IT?

MY "SINGER/SONGWRITER" "CAREER" FOR GROWN-UPS IS OVER I THINK. LIKE ANY- -ONE EVEN REMEMBERS IT BUT ME ANYWAY.

I MAKE ANOTHER DECISION... I SWITCH FROM WINE TO THE HARDER STUFF.

SHERRI SMALLS, MAN OF ACTION!

I PROMISED MYSELF HEDON- -ISTIC CHIPS AND BOOZE TONIGHT. I'VE COVERED THE CHIPS AND BOOZE, BUT I'M ITCHING TO CHECK MY WORK EMAIL, LIKE A DOG RETURNING TO ITS VOMIT.

SHERRI, YOU MAY BE RETURN- -ING TO YOUR OWN VOMIT IF YOU KEEP DRINKING TONIGHT.

WHAT WILL IT BE? CUTESY FAN-LETTERS WRITTEN IN BABY TALK BY OVER-ZEALOUS PARENTS OF TWO-YEAR-OLDS?

REQUESTS TO SING AT A SICK KID'S BIRTHDAY PARTY? MORE EIGHT-YEAR-OLD GIRLS INVIT-ING ME TO JOIN THEIR INNAP-ROPRIATELY-SOPHISTICATED FACEBOOK GROUPS?

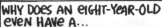
WHY DOES AN EIGHT-YEAR-OLD EVEN HAVE A...

...HELLO... HMM...

DEAR JOHN,
THANKS SO MUCH FOR YOUR EMAIL! IT WAS A MUCH-NEEDED PUNCH IN THE ARM TO HEAR THAT SOMEONE ACTUALLY OWNS AND LIKES MY "BIG PEOPLE" CD. SO, THANKS!

PEOPLE CD. SO, THANKS!
WHAT KIND OF "LIFESTYLE-PROFILE-INTERVIEW-Q+A-PUFF PIECE-PROMO FEATURE" ARE YOU PROPOSING FOR YOUR MAGAZINE? ABOUT MY OLD CAREER, OR THE CHILDREN'S PERFORMER ANGLE?

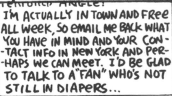

PERFORMER ANGLE!
I'M ACTUALLY IN TOWN AND FREE ALL WEEK, SO EMAIL ME BACK WHAT YOU HAVE IN MIND AND YOUR CON-TACT INFO IN NEW YORK AND PER-HAPS WE CAN MEET. I'D BE GLAD TO TALK TO A "FAN" WHO'S NOT STILL IN DIAPERS...

(NO OFFENCE IF YOU ARE WEARING DIAPERS.)

WEARING DIAPERS.) HA! TALK SOON, SHERRI

THAT IS SO LAME. WHY NOT ADD "L.O.L." AND "EMOTICONS?"

OH WELL.

SEND!

THERE IS ALWAYS THAT MOMENT— AND THIS IS A DISTINCTLY MOD—ERN PHENOMENA—AFTER YOU HIT SEND ON ANY EMAIL AND THEN WONDER DID I HIT REPLY OR REPLY ALL?

DID I REPLY TO THE PERSON I WAS MEANING TO MOCK IN MY FORWARDED EMAIL? IS THE TEXT OF MY EMAIL SOME-HOW VAGUE AND OPEN TO VAR-IOUS KINDS OF INTERPRETATION THAT A PAPER LETTER SOMEHOW WOULDN'T BE?

OR, AS IN TONIGHT'S CASE, IS MY EMAIL TOO FORWARD, SLUTTY, AND DESPERATE 'CAUSE I'M LIKE NINETY PERCENT DRUNK?

URP!

SKRITC

SHERRI SMALLS, YOU ARE BE--COMING RATHER A SLATTERN AND A WINO FOR A CHILDREN'S PERFORMER, I THINK...

BEFORE I DOZE OFF ON THE COUCH, I HAVE TIME TO WONDER IF "DEAR JOHN" COULD BE "THE ONE."

I PLAN ON SCREWIN' ME SOME DRUNK GIRLS!!

THE MOVIE'S STILL RUNNING...

CHAPTER SEVENTEEN:
LIES, LIES, LIES, YEA-EAH!

WHAT'S GOING ON?

KLIK

WHAT?

THAT EMAIL?

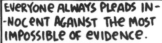

SHE'S READ YOUR YAHOO ACCOUNT ON THE LAPTOP, THE COY COME-ON TO THE CHILDREN'S PERFORMER. YOU ARE DIVORCED, SIR. A TWO-TIME LOSER. YOU'LL BE LIVING ALONE IN A CARDBOARD BOX...

WHAT EMAIL?

EVERYONE ALWAYS PLEADS IN--NOCENT AGAINST THE MOST IMPOSSIBLE OF EVIDENCE.

JOHN, YOU WROTE THIS MORNING THAT YOU WERE ON THE VERGE OF BEING FIRED—THEN I HEAR NOTHING FROM YOU ALL DAY AND YOU COME IN LATE... HELLOO?

OH HEAVENS, **THAT**! HOLY...
IT'S OKAY, IT'S ALL OKAY NOW...
WHEW! I FUCKED UP THE
COVER SHOOT. REALLY! I'M
BECOMING COMPLETELY INCOM-
PETENT! IT'S THE AUTHOR OF "CON-
NECTING FLIGHTS," I COMPLETELY FORGOT!

...BUT IT'S **FINE**!! I AR-
RANGED A NEW PHOTO SHOOT
IN NEW YORK. I HAVE TO GO THERE.

WHAT, NEW YORK **CITY**?

YEAH.

OH, **LUCKY**! CAN
WE COME TOO?

SMOOCH!

NO! I MEAN NO, GOODNESS,
NO. IT'S ALL WORK. I'M
ONLY GONE TWO DAYS...

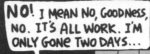

CAN YOU MANAGE THINGS
HERE BY YOURSELF?

WELL, I GUESS I'LL
HAVE TO.

GUILT UPON GUILT. IT'S A LOT
TO HANDLE, EVEN FOR A SEA-
SONED CATHOLIC LIKE MY-
SELF.

I WANT TO BUY HER FLOWERS,
A MAID, A NANNY, A BETTER
HUSBAND...

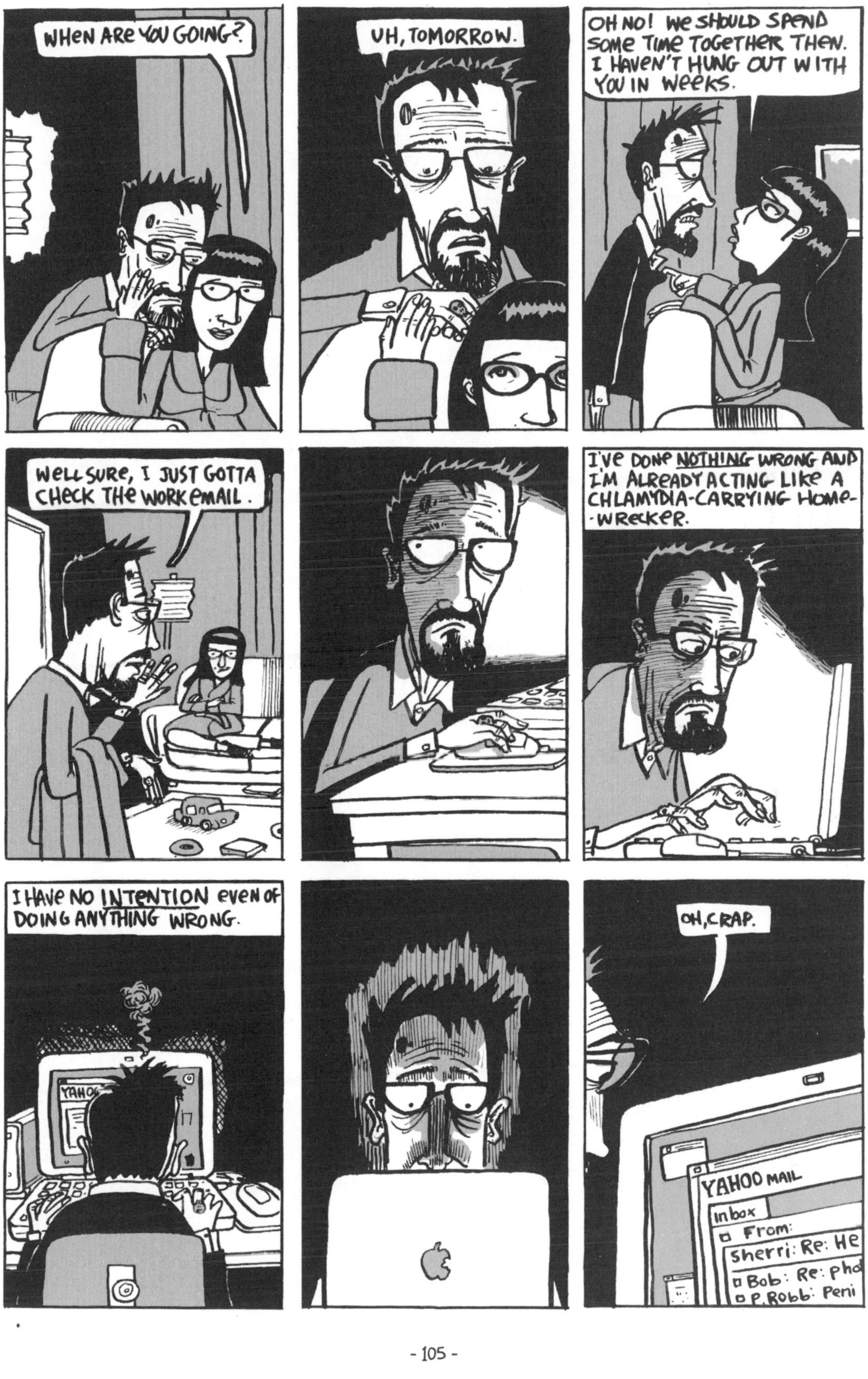

WHEN ARE YOU GOING?
UH, TOMORROW.
OH NO! WE SHOULD SPEND SOME TIME TOGETHER THEN. I HAVEN'T HUNG OUT WITH YOU IN WEEKS.
WELL SURE, I JUST GOTTA CHECK THE WORK EMAIL.
I'VE DONE NOTHING WRONG AND I'M ALREADY ACTING LIKE A CHLAMYDIA-CARRYING HOME-WRECKER.
I HAVE NO INTENTION EVEN OF DOING ANYTHING WRONG.
OH, CRAP.
YAHOO MAIL
inbox
From:
sherri: Re: He
Bob: Re: pho
P. Robb: Peni

AGAIN, MY GUTS FEEL LIKE BOIL-ING WATER IS BEING POURED THROUGH THEM AND THE BLOOD IS POUNDING IN MY EARS LIKE BASS IN THE POROUS PAPER CONES IN LOUDSPEAKERS.

I HOPE TO GOD IT'S A FORM-LETTER SHE SENDS TO ALL THE FANS WHO EMAIL HER. I HOPE TO GOD THAT SHERRI SMALLS IS WRITING PERSONALLY TO ME TO SAY, "YOU BOUGHT AND LIKED MY CD. LET'S HAVE DRINKS."

I'M GLANCING OVER MY SHOULDER IN A MANNER REMINISCENT OF GUILTY FOR A MAN WITHOUT EVEN INTENT TO DO ANYTHING WRONG.

I READ HER NOTE REPEATEDLY. SO FEW LINES, SEEMINGLY IN-NOCENT, BUT I GATHER A MYRIAD NUMBER OF WEIGHTED INFER-ENCES IN BETWEEN THEM.

I'M CALMLY CLOSING WINDOWS, LOGGING OUT, DELETING HIS-TORIES AND ALL BUT ERASING MY HARD DRIVE WHEN CHAN RETURNS LOOKING FOR ME.

HOW'S IT GOING?

HEY! READY TO WATCH A MOVIE?

WE COULD SKIP THE MOVIE AND— *GO TO BED EARLY...*

OH, MY, THE EM-DASH, THE *ITALICS* IN HER VOICE, THE ELIPSE AFTER IT... AND SHE'S NOT WEARING HER OLD-LADY PAJAMAS. I SHOULD HAVE KNOWN. BUT I'M READY TO VOMIT WITH GUILT.

KLAK

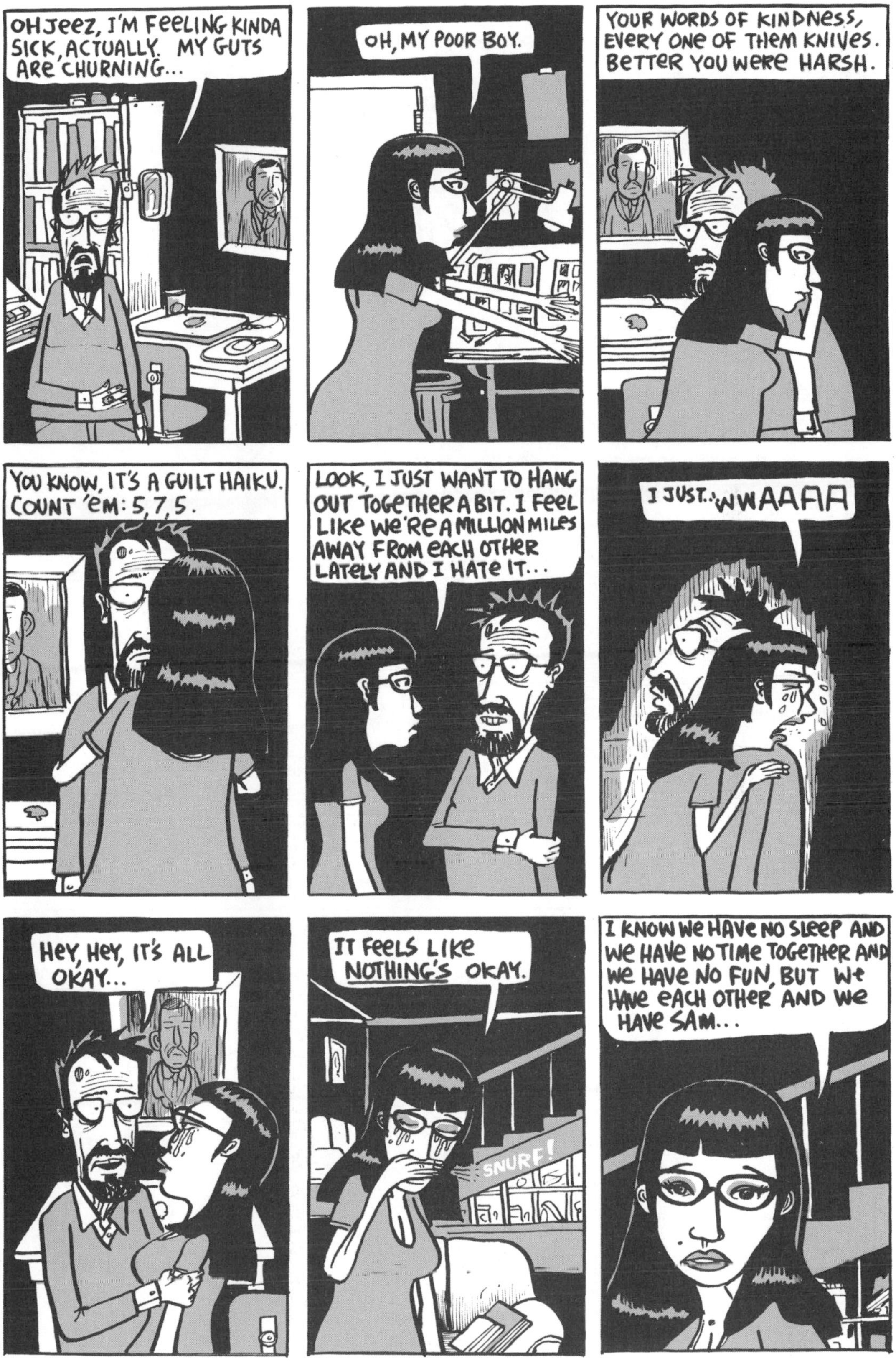
OH JEEZ, I'M FEELING KINDA SICK, ACTUALLY. MY GUTS ARE CHURNING...
OH, MY POOR BOY.
YOUR WORDS OF KINDNESS, EVERY ONE OF THEM KNIVES. BETTER YOU WERE HARSH.
YOU KNOW, IT'S A GUILT HAIKU. COUNT 'EM: 5, 7, 5.
LOOK, I JUST WANT TO HANG OUT TOGETHER A BIT. I FEEL LIKE WE'RE A MILLION MILES AWAY FROM EACH OTHER LATELY AND I HATE IT...
I JUST... WWAAAA
HEY, HEY, IT'S ALL OKAY...
IT FEELS LIKE NOTHING'S OKAY.
SNURF!
I KNOW WE HAVE NO SLEEP AND WE HAVE NO TIME TOGETHER AND WE HAVE NO FUN, BUT WE HAVE EACH OTHER AND WE HAVE SAM...

...OH, I KNOW HE'S A LOT OF WORK, BUT I LOVE HIM SO.

RIGHT, AND I HATE HIM...

PLEASE DON'T JUST GET MAD. CAN WE ACTUALLY TALK HERE? YOU'RE ALWAYS ANGRY ABOUT EVERYTHING LATELY.

I DON'T THINK THAT'S TRUE...

YOU'RE PUTTING SALT ON KRAFT DINNER?! IT'S MADE OF SALT!

AHEM...

WHAT I MEAN IS, WHEN I MET YOU, I HAD GIVEN UP ON THE IDEA OF ROMANTIC LOVE.

BUT WITH YOU AND I, IT WAS A NEW KIND OF LOVE I HAD NEVER EXPERIENCED, YOU KNOW?

I DO KNOW WHAT SHE MEANS. THIS IS THE GIRL THAT CAME ALONG AFTER MY FAILED MARRIAGE, PULLED ME OUT OF THE SINKHOLE OF ILL-ADVISED AFFAIRS AND DRUNKEN DEPRESSION THAT MOST SURELY WOULD HAVE KILLED ME EVENTUALLY.

THIS REMINDER, COUPLED WITH MY "INTENTION OF DOING NOTHING WRONG" HITS ME LIKE A SLEDGE HAMMER IN THE GUTS AND A GROAN ESCAPES ME AND IS ABSORBED INTO HER HAIR.

I KNOW. I'M SORRY, I HAVEN'T BEEN...

LEMME FINISH HERE, NOW THAT WE'RE TALKING... I GUESS YOU TAUGHT ME ABOUT TRUE LOVE AND I THOUGHT IT COULD NEVER GET ANY BIGGER OR BETTER THAN THAT.

BUT THEN SAM CAME ALONG AND I DISCOVERED A KIND OF LOVE THAT IS COMPLETELY UNSELFISH AND PURE AND IT MAKES ME FEEL LIKE I COULD LIFT A CAR IF I HAD TO TO SAVE HIM, YOU KNOW?

AGAIN, I DO. IN OUR DATING DAYS, OUR COOLER, CYNICAL, SMOKING AND EXERCISING DAYS BEFORE SAM, I TRIED TO EXPLAIN THIS SAME KIND OF LOVE I HAD FOR MY DAUGHTER.

AND HOW I WAS PROBABLY NOT DOING ALL I SHOULD FOR THEM AND HOW SICK IT WAS MAKING ME, AND THEN I PROBABLY HAD ANOTHER DRINK. I GUESS YOU CAN ONLY UNDERSTAND THAT LOVE FIRST HAND.

I JUST WANT US TO BE OKAY AGAIN.

I KNOW IT WILL TAKE A LONG TIME FOR THINGS TO GET BACK TO "NORMAL" OR WHATEVER. I KNOW THIS IS HARD FOR YOU BECAUSE YOU'VE BEEN THROUGH IT ALL BEFORE AND YOU'RE...

... UH, GOING THROUGH SOME KIND OF "THING." I JUST REALLY WANT US TO LIKE EACH OTHER AGAIN.

WELL, OF COURSE WE WILL...

HALF OF ME DOESN'T WANT TO HAVE THIS CONVERSATION BE-CAUSE IT'S AS MUCH AS ADMIT-TING THERE'S A PROBLEM IN A RELATIONSHIP WITH THE LOVE OF MY LIFE.

SKRITCH

THE GIRL I MARRIED DESPITE THE FACT THAT I SAID I WOULD NEVER GET MARRIED AGAIN.

...VIRTUALLY MAKING GAY-MARRIAGE LEGAL IN ONTARIO...

PFFFT! GOOD LUCK GAY DUDES.

AND PART OF ME WANTS TO AVOID THIS CONVERSATION BECAUSE I WANT TO GO AWAY TO NEW YORK IN A CLOUD OF UNCERTAINTY AND AN AWKWARD PLACE IN THE RELATIONSHIP SO I CAN JUST-IFY A LITTLE HARMLESS FLIRTING.

UH, MY WIFE DOESN'T UNDERSTAND ME.

WOW

AND THAT PART MAKES ME FEEL A BIT OF A SHIT.

COME ON...

LET'S GET TO SLEEP BEFORE HE WAKES UP.

I SLEEP THE SLEEP OF THE SHITTY, WHICH, AS IT TURNS OUT, IS NOT ALL THAT RESTFUL.

CHAPTER EIGHTEEN:

NEW YORK CITY, WHERE DREAMS COME TRUE, BUILDINGS COLLAPSE, AND MARRIAGES END.

"DISCO" BEAR JULI $10

WHERE THE HELL CAN IT BE, SAM?

WHERE BE.

CHAN, HAVE YOU SEEN MY BLUE SHIRT?

BLUE?

YOU HAVE A BLUE SHIRT?

I'M UNCONSCIOUSLY LOOKING FOR "COOL" CLOTHES. EVERY-THING I OWN IS BLACK PANTS AND BLACK T-SHIRTS, LIKE A BARGAIN-BASEMENT JOHNNY CASH.

BUT I <u>KNOW</u> I HAVE A BLUE SHIRT AND I <u>NEED</u> THAT SHIRT.

IN CASE. FOR THE INTERVIEW. FOR THE MAGAZINE. TO SAVE MY JOB. BECAUSE I'M A GOOD PROVIDER. A FAMILY MAN. A FAMILY MAN, LOOKIN' GOOD IN A "COOL" BLUE SHIRT.

WELL, ALL <u>RIGHT</u>.

WE'LL MISS YOU. CALL US, OKAY?

OF COURSE. SEE YOU THURSDAY. LOVE YOU.

IT GOES LIKE THIS: TAKE A CAB, TAKE A PLANE, WORK ON THE MAGAZINE LAYOUTS ON THE LAPTOP.

TAKE ANOTHER CAB TO THE HOTEL. I HAVE THREE HOURS BEFORE I NEED TO BE BACK AT THE AIRPORT FOR THE PHOTO SHOOT.

THREE HOURS.

CHAN AND I ARE ONLY CON--FUSED LATELY IF WE HAVE FREE TIME. ADDED TO THAT CONFUSION IS THE GUILT I FEEL THAT WHILE SHE IS MINDING SAM ALONE, I'M IN NEW YORK, EYE--BALLING TINY, TEN-DOLLAR BOTTLES OF PLONKY WINE.

OH, RIGHT, AND CONTEMPLAT--ING SOME BRAND OF INFID--ELITY WITH A CHILDREN'S PERFORMER.

THE FACT THAT I DO NOT RAID THE OVER-PRICED COURT--ESY BAR DOES LITTLE TO ASSUAGE MY FEELINGS OF GUILT SOMEHOW.

PROXIMITY, ACTUALLY BEING IN THE SAME CITY, HAS MADE EVERY--THING LESS EXHILERATING AND A GREAT DEAL MORE NAUSEATING.

IN THE HOTEL WI-FI COFFEE SHOP, I WRITE AND DELETE AN EMAIL TO SHERRI SMALLS OVER AND OVER AGAIN. I FINALLY COMPOSE SOMETHING SHORT AND VAGUE AND HIT SEND, TELLING MYSELF I OWE HER THAT COURTESY AT LEAST.

...AND IGNORE THE SMALL VOICE THAT HINTS AT OTHER OBLIGATIONS OF COURTESY I MAY OWE TO OTHER PARTIES, INCLUDING PARTIES THAT I MAY HAVE PROM--ISED ETERNAL FIDELITY TO IN LEGALLY-BINDING SERVICES.

I CALL MY PHOTOGRAPHER AND SHE IS AN ANOMALY: ONE OF THOSE NEW YORKERS WHO OWN A CAR.

SHE OFFERS TO PICK ME UP AND I WAIT OUTSIDE THE HOTEL, CHAIN-SMOKING CAMEL FILTERS. OH YEAH, I'M SMOKING FULL-TIME THIS TRIP. OH WELL, I HAVE WORSE VICES.

MOLLY?

JOHN?

I LOVE THE FACT THAT I'M ACTING OUT SUCH A MOVIE CLICHÉ OF HOLDING A CELEBRITY NAME-SIGN AT AN AIRPORT.

MS. R. FOWLER

SOMETHING I'VE NEVER DONE BEFORE. EXAMPLES LIKE THIS OF MY SHELTERED LIFE KEEP PRESENTING THEMSELVES LATELY.

MS R. FOWLER

OH, I DO KNOW THAT BEING MARRIED AND HAVING CHILDREN AT AGE SEVENTEEN DOESN'T ACTUALLY PRECLUDE ONE FROM HOLDING A HAND-LETTERED SIGN AT AN AIRPORT, IT JUST HAPPENED TO WORK OUT THAT WAY.

COREY HART

BUT THERE WERE OTHER THINGS. IT PROBABLY DID AFFECT. MY TEEN-MARRIED-WITH-KIDS STATUS MAY HAVE CUT INTO MY EXPERIENCES WITH THE LADIES.

OH, WHAT A CUTE... HURRGG!N

HIGH SCHOOL AND UNIVERSITY HI-JINKS AND JOLLY JAPES RE-DUCED TO ALMOST NIL AND PRETTY MUCH EVERYTHING ELSE BUT DRUDGERY, FACTORY WORK, AND A LACK OF SLEEP.

BOOBIE INSPECTOR

BUT, THE OTHER SIDE OF THIS IS THAT THIS WAS A CHOICE THAT I MADE.

R FOWLER

AND, AND THIS IS THE GREAT CATCH 22, ANY COMPLAINT I MAKE ABOUT THE WHACKY COURSE OF MY STUNTED START IN LIFE AND ITS SUBSEQUENT FAILURE WOULD SEEM LIKE A SLIGHT AGAINST THE TWO DAUGHTERS WHO WERE THE POSITIVE PRODUCT OF THAT START.

DAD, SOME KID AT SCHOOL SAID SANTA'S NOT REAL.

YEAH, DAD.

OH GOD.

AND I'VE GAINED SO MUCH FROM HAVING RAISED THEM AND, AN-OTHER MOVIE CLICHÉ, I WOULDN'T CHANGE A THING. EXCEPT THE EIGHTEEN YEARS IN A FAILED MARRIAGE PROBABLY.

IMAGINE IF EVERYTHING WAS TINY FOR THE BARBIES.

MM...

HELL, IF I'M ALONE IN MY THOUGHTS, AND PUTTING ASIDE THE WELL-EARNED BITTERNESS, I CAN EVEN ADMIT TO HAVING HAD A FEW GOOD TIMES WITH THEIR MOTHER BACK IN THE DAY.

DAD, MOM FELL ASLEEP DRIVING AGAIN.

BUT THE GIRLS ARE A PRETTY GOOD REASON TO HALT ONE'S SELF FROM BEMOANING TEEN-AGED LIFESTYLE CHOICES. IT INEVITABLY COMES OFF WRONG.

...NO, WAIT, "REGRET" IS TOTALLY THE WRONG WORD.

WHAT A CUTE KID.

MS. R. FOWLER

I'M CRAZY ABOUT KIDS LATELY. I TURN THIRTY NEXT YEAR. BIOLOGICAL CLOCK IS A-TICKIN'.

MS. R. FOWLER

WOW, THIRTY. THAT IS ANCIENT...

MS. R. FOWLER.

OH MY GOD, SORRY, YOU MUST BE LIKE, WAY OLDER THAN THAT...

MS. R. FOWLER

I'M JOKING.

MS. R. FOWLER

WELL, I DO HAVE DAUGHTERS ALMOST AS OLD AS YOU....

ARRIV

WAIT FOR IT. WAIT FOR THE REACTION...

TWO DAUGHTERS?

OH! HERE COME THE ARRIVALS.

ARRIVALS.IN

...OH BOTHER! IT ALL WORKED OUT TICKETY-BOO IN THE END, SO LET'S US FORGET ALL ABOUT IT, NO?

WELL, ALRIGHT, MS. FOWLER, BUT I CAN'T APOLOGIZE ENOUGH. YOU'RE BEING TOO KIND, REALLY.

OH, DO CALL ME ROWENA, WON'T YOU?

BESIDES, YOUR PHOTO SHOOT PROVIDES A DISTRACTION. IT BEATS GETTING GUTTERED IN THE AIRPORT BAR BY MYSELF! WELL, LET'S HOPE IT DOES. HA HA HA.

ROWENA, I'M HOPING WE'LL HAVE TIME FOR A GREAT PHOTO SHOOT AND GETTING GUTTERED IN THE AIRPORT BAR AS WELL.

MR. OLSEN, YOU'RE A MAN AFTER MY OWN HEART.

OH, DO CALL ME JOHN, WON'T YOU?

IN MY ELEMENT. OLD LADIES LOVE ME. I TAKE WHAT I CAN GET.

WE THOUGHT WE'D LIKE TO SHOOT YOU COMING DOWN THE ELEVATOR FOR A START.

ROWENA, HOW WOULD YOU FEEL ABOUT STANDING IN A FOUNTAIN?

OH, JOLLY!

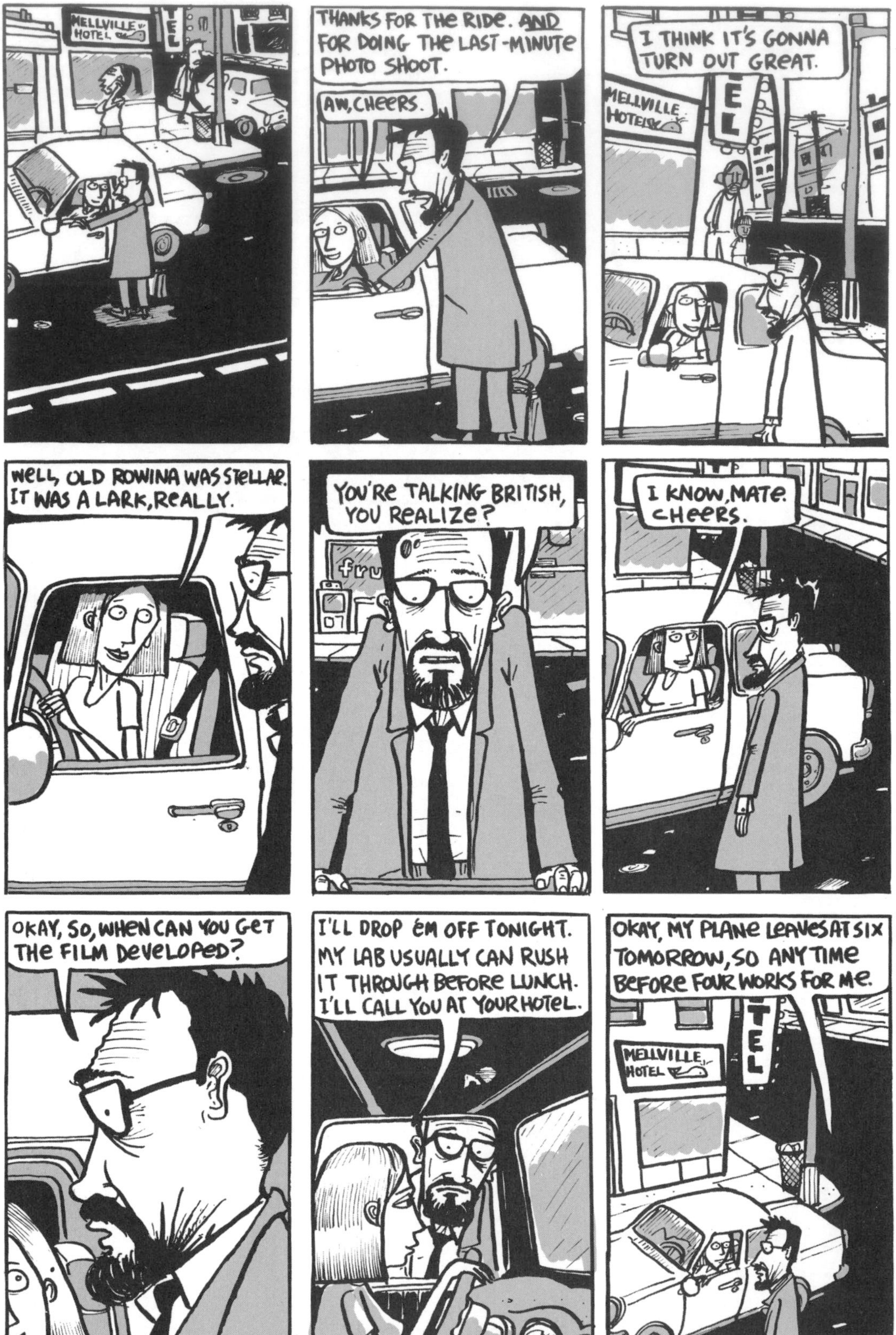
MELLVILLE HOTEL
THANKS FOR THE RIDE. AND FOR DOING THE LAST-MINUTE PHOTO SHOOT.
AW, CHEERS.
I THINK IT'S GONNA TURN OUT GREAT.
MELLVILLE HOTEL
WELL, OLD ROWINA WAS STELLAR. IT WAS A LARK, REALLY.
YOU'RE TALKING BRITISH, YOU REALIZE?
I KNOW, MATE. CHEERS.
OKAY, SO, WHEN CAN YOU GET THE FILM DEVELOPED?
I'LL DROP 'EM OFF TONIGHT. MY LAB USUALLY CAN RUSH IT THROUGH BEFORE LUNCH. I'LL CALL YOU AT YOUR HOTEL.
OKAY, MY PLANE LEAVES AT SIX TOMORROW, SO ANY TIME BEFORE FOUR WORKS FOR ME.
TEL
MELLVILLE HOTEL

I FEEL LIKE A PROFESSIONAL AGAIN INSTEAD OF SOME TEEN-AGER WITH HIS HANDS DOWN HIS PANTS. I'VE BEEN ASSISTING AND SETTING UP SHOTS AND THINKING OF NOTHING ELSE.

I FORGOT HOW MUCH I USED TO ENJOY THIS WORK. OR AT LEAST GIVE HALF OF A SHIT ABOUT IT.

OF COURSE, BY NOW, I'M LIKE A HIGH SCHOOL GIRL RUSHING TO CHECK MY EMAIL.

IT'S ACTUALLY A RELIEF, REALLY, THAT THERE'S NOTHING. DO I NEED MORE TROUBLE IN MY LIFE? NO, I DO NOT.

I'LL GO OUT AND GET SOME NOODLES AND BEER AND I'LL WATCH CABLE TV 'TILL I FALL ASLEEP AND NO SAM TO WAKE ME UP AT 4:30 A.M.

I DECIDE TO CHECK IN WITH CHAN AND SAM AND CALL THE GIRLS BEFORE I GO OUT.

IT SEEMS THAT SINCE THE CANCELATION OF MY POTEN-TIALLY-ILLICIT RENDEZ-VOUS, I'VE BECOME QUITE THE SUPER-DAD-SLASH-FAMILY-MAN.

FIRST CHAN. SHE'S HARRIED AND IS VERY SHORT WITH ME.

I KNOW SHE MUST BE OVER-WHELMED WITH SAM, BUT INSIDE, I'M ALL LIKE: "I JUST DIDN'T HAVE AN AFFAIR ON YOU. HELLOOO?"

MM-HM.

RIGHT, RIGHT...

MARTHA IS MERELY PISSED THAT I'M IN NEW YORK AND SHE'S NOT.

OH, YEAH...

SHE HANGS UP IN WHAT I THINK WAS MEANT TO BE IRONIC, HYPERBOLIC ANGER.

I KNOW...

THE BAR FRIDGE CHASTITY BELT LOCK HAS LONG AGO BEEN SUNDERED.

YEP.

I FARE EQUALLY BADLY WITH LISA.

OH, FOR SURE...

SHE'S MAINLY MIFFED THAT I LEFT TOWN WITHOUT TELLING HER

I'M FEELING LIKE MAYBE NOBODY IS GETTING AN OFFICIAL SOUVENIR OF NEW YORK CITY FROM ME.

IT'S MILLER TIME.

TIME FOR PISSY, WATERED-DOWN, INEXPENSIVE-BECAUSE THE POPULOUS IS UNDER-TAXED AND UNDERSERVICED-AMER-ICAN BEER.

AND NOODLES.

AW JEEZ...

BLINK
BLINK

MESSAGE

UH, THIS IS A MESSAGE FOR JOHN OLSEN...

HEY, JOHN, THIS IS SHERRI SMALLS CALLING...

SO, YOU SAID TO CALL WHEN YOU CAME TO TOWN ABOUT AN INTERVIEW... SO, UH, I'M FREE TONIGHT IF YOU'RE INTERESTED.

...YEAH... NO BIG, EITHER WAY... ANYWAY, HERE'S MY NUMBER. IF YOU WANT 5-2-9-6-9-8-9.

OKAY THEN, CIAO!

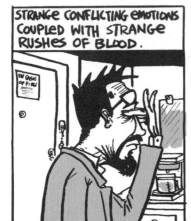

STRANGE CONFLICTING EMOTIONS COUPLED WITH STRANGE RUSHES OF BLOOD.

NOODLES, I CONFESS, ARE NEARLY FORGOTTEN.

FAMILY AND EVEN BEER TOO ARE LEFT BEHIND.

KLIK

UH, THIS IS A MESSAGE FOR JOHN OLSEN...

...OKAY THEN, CIAO! = BEEP =

UH, THIS IS A MESSAGE FOR JOHN OLSEN...

I SHOWER IN NEAR-BOILING WATER FOR OVER TEN MINUTES, PAYING SPECIAL ATTENTION TO MY NETHER REGIONS AND HATING MYSELF FOR THAT.

I TAKE ANOTHER TEN MINUTES TO SUFFICIENTLY GET MY SHIT TOGETHER ENOUGH TO MAKE THE CALL.

SHERRI?

HEY SHERRI!

SHERRI? JOHN HERE.

SLAP SLAP

SHERRI? IT'S JOHN OLSEN... FROM THE MAGAZINE...

HEY! I'M GOOD. YOU?

SUCK!

OKAY, COOL. WELL, I AM FREE.

WHAT HAVE YOU GOT IN MIND?

CHAPTER NINETEEN:
IN OR OUT?

I'M SWEATING.

NO AMOUNT OF ANTIPERSPIR-ANT COULD COMBAT THE KIND OF SWEAT I AM PROD-UCING PRESENTLY.

A PART OF ME WANTS TO DO THE RIGHT THING AND JUST NOT GO TO THIS "MEETING."

THE BARGAINING PART OF MY MIND TELLS ME THERE IS NOTHING WRONG, THIS IS ALL INNOCENT.

BUT IT'S ALSO SAYING, "DUDE, SHOULDN'T YOU BE BUYING SOME CONDOMS, JUST IN CASE?" SO...

THE REASONABLE PART OF MY MIND INSISTS THAT THIS IS ALL INNOCENT.

FOR GOD'S SAKE, I'M ACTUALLY DOING STORY RESEARCH FOR WORK WHILE I'M IN THE MIDDLE OF NEW YORK CITY!

THEN IT SUGGESTS BUYING SOME GUM OR MINTS.

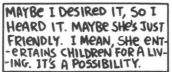
PERHAPS I ONLY IMAGINED HER FLIRTINESS ON THE PHONE.

MAYBE I DESIRED IT, SO I HEARD IT. MAYBE SHE'S JUST FRIENDLY. I MEAN, SHE ENT--ERTAINS CHILDREN FOR A LIV--ING. IT'S A POSSIBILITY.

I HAVE SO LITTLE EXPERIENCE WITH FLIRTING.

OH, I'VE FLIRTED, DON'T GET ME WRONG.

BONJOUR, HI, HELLO.

SALUT, JE VOUS AIDER?

OUI, JE CHERCHE... UH, I WANNA BUY SOME UNDER--WEAR FOR MY GIRLFRIEND.

OF COURSE, WHAT KIND OF PAN-TEES YOU WANT TO 'AVE?

I LIKE THE WAY YOU SAY THAT: "PAN-TEES..."

I SHOULD HIRE YOU TO COME LIVE AT MY HOUSE AND JUST SAY "PAN-TEES" FOR ME ALL THE TIME.

LOOK, EVEN IF SHE'S ALL OVER ME...

I'M NOT SOME MILK-DRINKING TEENAGE-BOY FOLLOWING HIS COCK AROUND LIKE A COMPASS. I'M A FORTY-YEAR-OLD MAN, AND...

OH YEAH, THAT'S WAY WORSE.

I'M NEARLY AT THE COFFEE SHOP WHEN I BACKTRACK TO BUY CINNAMON GUM.

I HATE GUM, BUT OLD MAN HALITOSIS IN A CLINCH IS A REAL COLD SHOWER I WOULD IMAGINE.

CINNAMIN barely masking decay- and poo-breath.

HUH HUH

I'M JUST GONNA DO THIS AND SEE WHERE IT GOES.

beans, beans... coffee, duh... DOG LIBRA

RETAINING MY ORIGINAL RESOLVE TO "NOT EVEN INTEND TO DO ANYTHING WRONG."

fruits.

MY HIPPOCRATIC OATH. MY HYPOCRITICAL OATH.

I SPOT HER IMMEDIATELY.

HER HAIR OVERPOWERS EVERY--THING IN THE ROOM. RED AND LUXURIOUS, AS ONLY EXPENSIVE SHAMPOOS AND SALON VISITS COULD MAKE IT. BUT I SUSPECT IT IS NATURALLY THAT WAY.

I'M AT THE ADVANTAGE HERE.

I'VE MEMORIZED HER FACE FROM ALBUM COVERS, VIDEOS AND WEB IMAGES. SHE HAS NO IDEA WHAT I LOOK LIKE. I CAN STILL JUST WALK OUT OF HERE.

CHAPTER TWENTY: 20 QUESTIONS AND ALMOST AS MANY LIES.

...THAT'S A NEAT, CRUDDY OLD HOTEL. DO YOU TRAVEL TO NEW YORK A LOT?

I NOW REALIZE THAT WHILE I WAS OUT THERE BUYING GUM AND CHANGING OUTFITS LIKE A PROM QUEEN...

SLURP!

... I SHOULD HAVE BEEN SORTING OUT MY "STORY."

WELL, NOT AS OFTEN AS I'D LIKE TO...

(LAST IN N.Y. AT AGE 18, VISITING HIS HIGHSCHOOL CHAPLAIN.)

AM I A FORTY-YEAR-OLD SINGLE GUY, WHICH COULD SEEM ODD AND CREEPY?

AM I DIVORCED WITH TWO ADULT CHILDREN, SAD, ALONE AND ATTRACTIVELY VULNERABLE?

OR AM I PLAYING THIS SCENE STRAIGHT: DIVORCED, RE-MARRIED, TWO ADULT KIDS AND A BABY, I'M JUST A NICE, UN-INTERESTED GUY WHO ONLY WANTS TO INTERVIEW YOU?

I AM AWARE THAT ANY VERSION OTHER THAN THE TRUTH WILL ONLY BE TOLD TO KEEP DANGEROUS OPTIONS OPEN.

SLUP!

THIS IS THE FIRST TIME I'VE BEEN HERE IN YEARS. IT'S A GREAT CITY...

YEAH, I'M SO BLASÉ ABOUT IT NOW.

YOU READ BOOKS AND SEE MOVIES AND THEY TREAT THIS PLACE LIKE IT'S MECCA OR SOMETHING.

I JUST LIVE HERE, YOU KNOW? DO MY LAUNDRY, BUY GROCERIES.

YEAH, YEAH, IT'S LIKE THAT SAYING BY THAT AUTHOR...

- 126 -

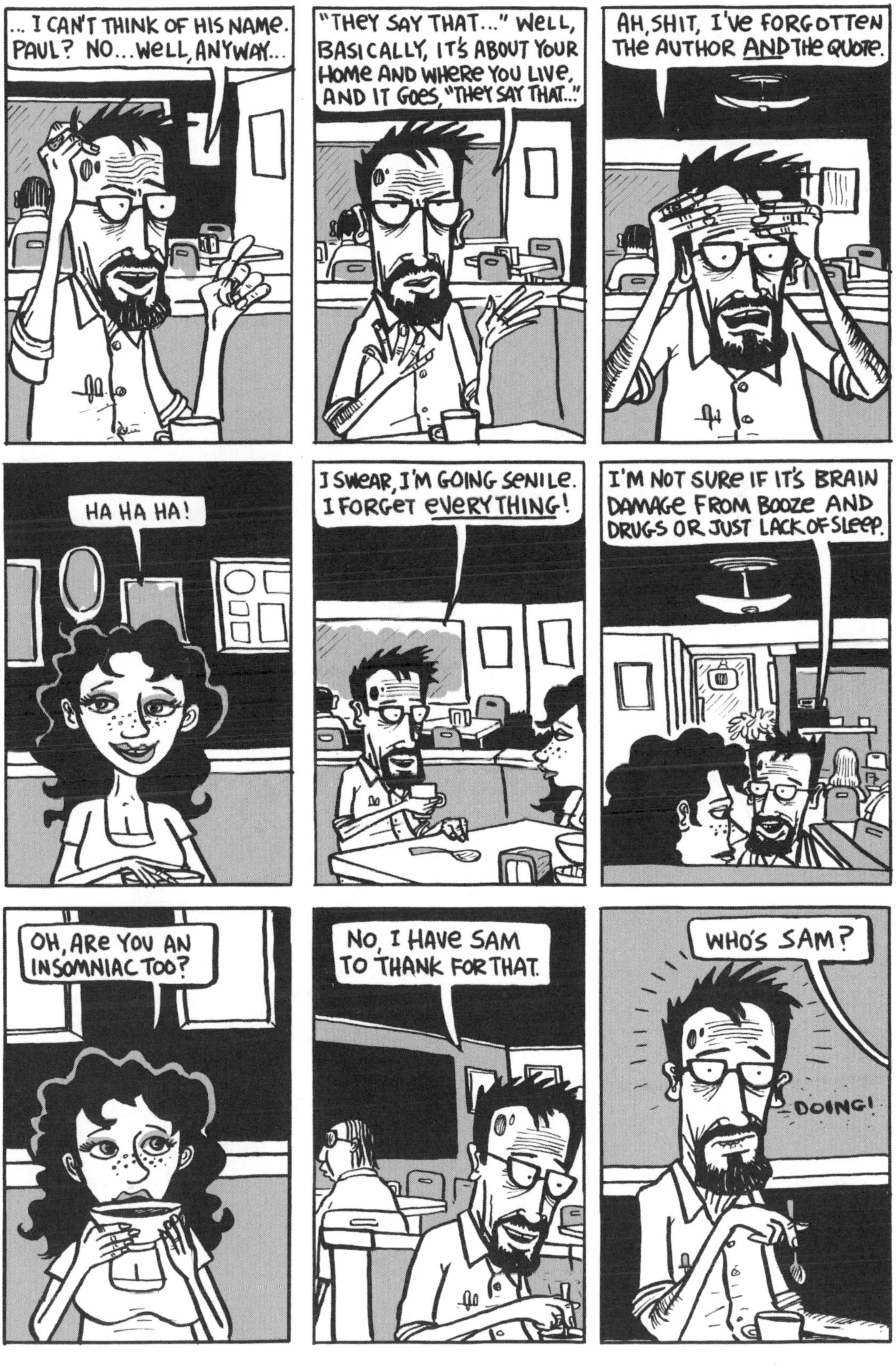

... I CAN'T THINK OF HIS NAME. PAUL? NO... WELL, ANYWAY...
"THEY SAY THAT..." WELL, BASICALLY, IT'S ABOUT YOUR HOME AND WHERE YOU LIVE, AND IT GOES, "THEY SAY THAT..."
AH, SHIT, I'VE FORGOTTEN THE AUTHOR AND THE QUOTE.
HA HA HA!
I SWEAR, I'M GOING SENILE. I FORGET EVERYTHING!
I'M NOT SURE IF IT'S BRAIN DAMAGE FROM BOOZE AND DRUGS OR JUST LACK OF SLEEP.
OH, ARE YOU AN INSOMNIAC TOO?
NO, I HAVE SAM TO THANK FOR THAT.
WHO'S SAM?
DOING!

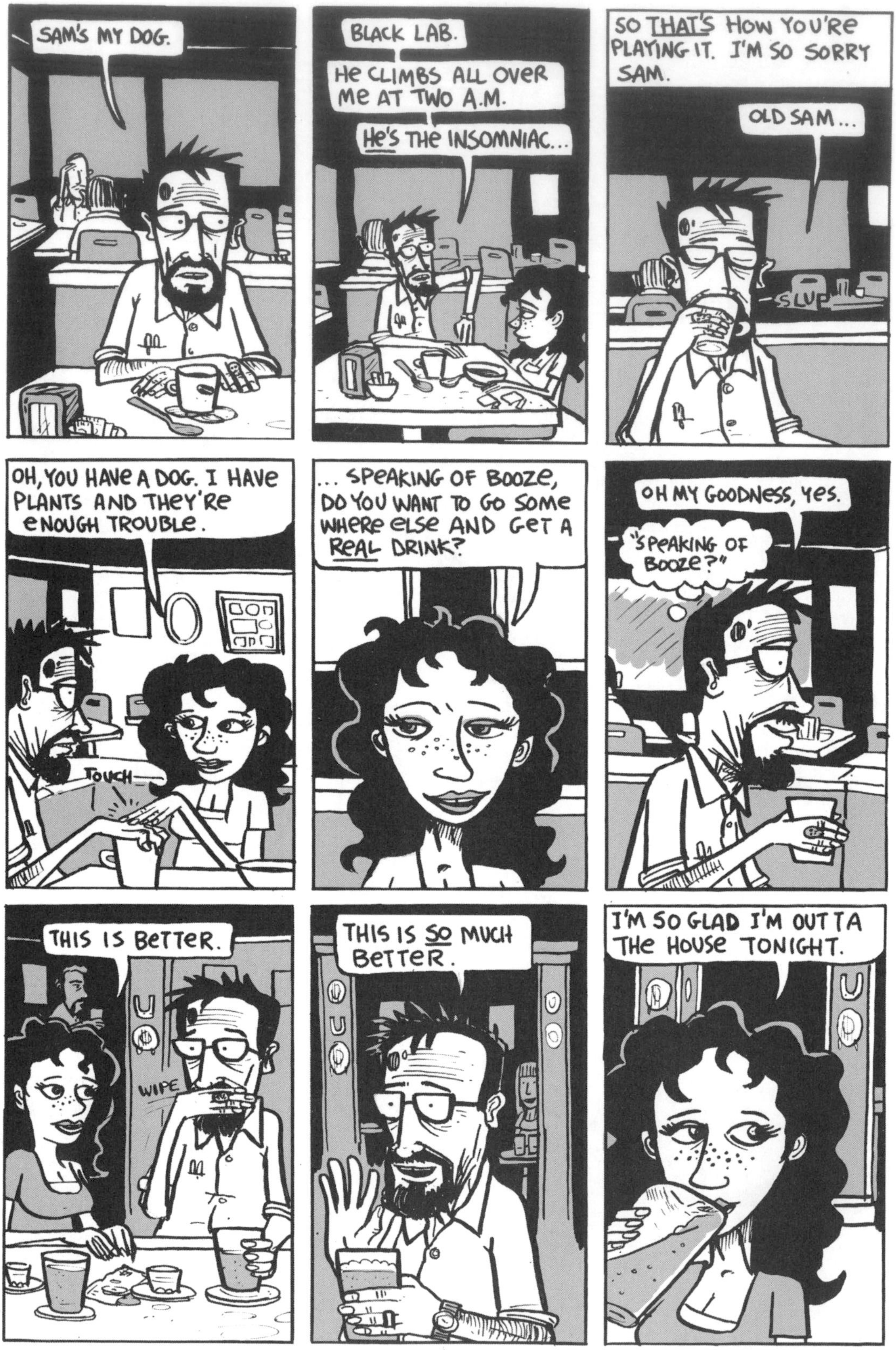
SAM'S MY DOG.
BLACK LAB.
HE CLIMBS ALL OVER ME AT TWO A.M.
HE'S THE INSOMNIAC...
SO THAT'S HOW YOU'RE PLAYING IT. I'M SO SORRY SAM.
OLD SAM...
SLUP
OH, YOU HAVE A DOG. I HAVE PLANTS AND THEY'RE ENOUGH TROUBLE.
TOUCH
... SPEAKING OF BOOZE, DO YOU WANT TO GO SOME WHERE ELSE AND GET A REAL DRINK?
OH MY GOODNESS, YES.
"SPEAKING OF BOOZE?"
THIS IS BETTER.
WIPE
THIS IS SO MUCH BETTER.
I'M SO GLAD I'M OUTTA THE HOUSE TONIGHT.

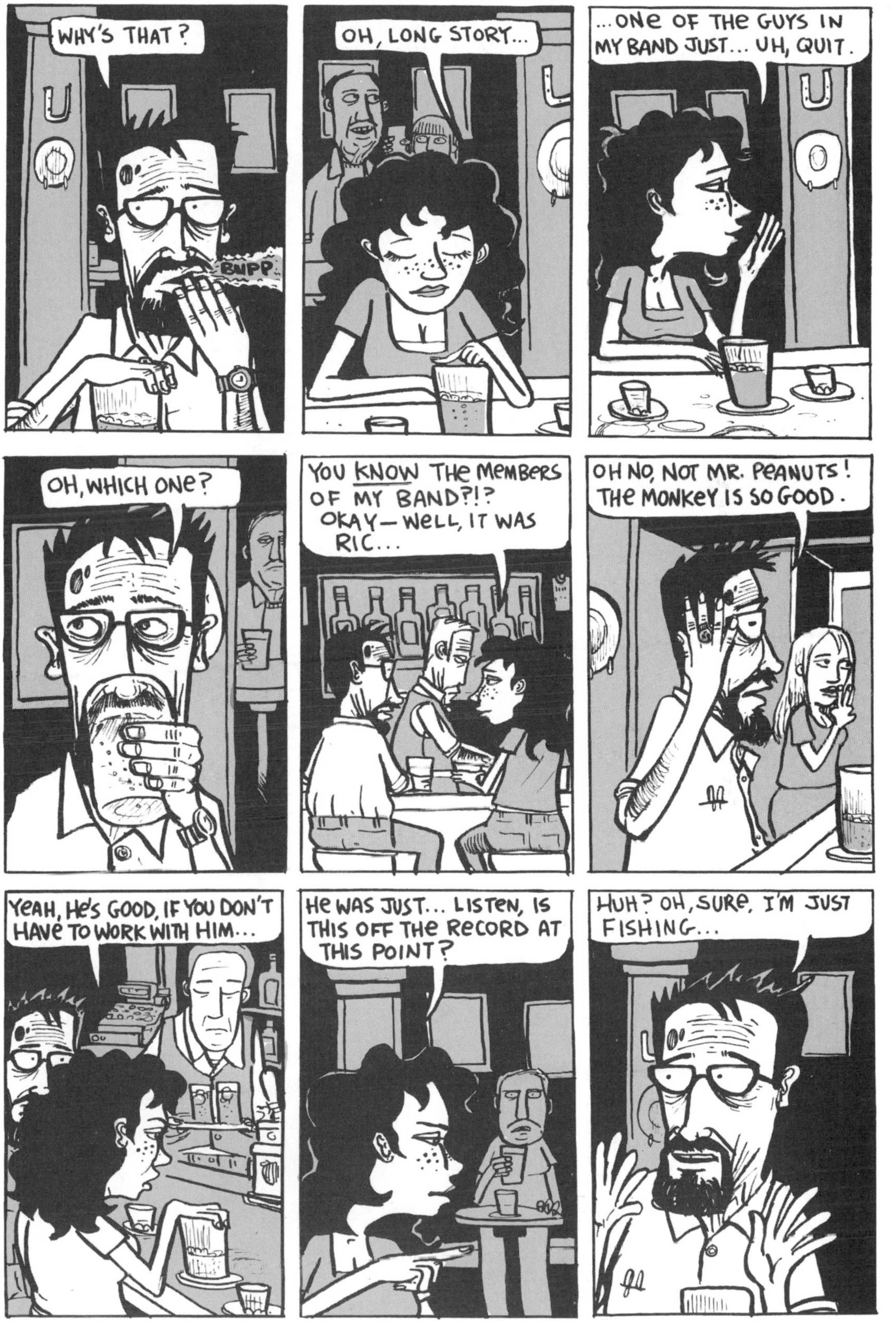
WHY'S THAT?
BNPP
OH, LONG STORY...
...ONE OF THE GUYS IN MY BAND JUST... UH, QUIT.
OH, WHICH ONE?
YOU KNOW THE MEMBERS OF MY BAND?!? OKAY—WELL, IT WAS RIC...
OH NO, NOT MR. PEANUTS! THE MONKEY IS SO GOOD.
YEAH, HE'S GOOD, IF YOU DON'T HAVE TO WORK WITH HIM...
HE WAS JUST... LISTEN, IS THIS OFF THE RECORD AT THIS POINT?
HUH? OH, SURE. I'M JUST FISHING...

IT DOESN'T MATTER ANYWAY, THE PICTURE WAS ALL OVER THE NEWSPAPERS.

SO, RIC WAS BUSTED FOR DRUNK DRIVING.

SECOND OFFENCE, AND WHILE WEARING THE MONKEY SUIT. AND CARRYING COKE AND WEED IN MR. PEANUTS' VEST POCKETS.

WOW.

WOW INDEED. YOUR MAGAZINE SHOULD DO A STORY ABOUT RIC, IT'D BE WAY MORE INTERESTING THAN ME.

SO WHERE DOES THAT LEAVE YOU TWO?

WELL, LIKE I SAID, HE QUIT.

RIGHT, BUT I THOUGT YOU TWO WERE GOING OUT.

YOU'VE DONE SOME RESEARCH.

YEARS AGO WE WENT OUT. <u>YEARS</u> AGO. SO, ON A RELATIONSHIP LEVEL, IT'S FINE.

ON A BUSINESS LEVEL, I NEED A NEW DANCING MONKEY. OOH-OOH-OOH!

YOU HAVE ANY EXPERIENCE IN A MONKEY SUIT, JOHN?

ALAS, I LACK A PREHENSILE TAIL.

AN OLD-WORLD MONKEY.

SADLY, IT'S TRUE. YOU WANT ANOTHER?

YEAH, SURE.

UH, EXCUSE ME...

WHAT ABOUT YOU. ARE YOU MARRIED?

OKAY, SO I'VE ALREADY TURNED MY DEAR LITTLE TODDLER INTO A BLACK LABRADOR DOG AND I THINK I'M ABOUT TO MAKE THE WOMAN WHOM I'VE DESCRIBED AS HAVING SAVED MY LIFE, NEVER TO HAVE EXISTED.

frozen

WHICH WOULD MAKE ME A DEAD MAN TECHNICALLY.

THE GIRLS, I'VE DECIDED, BEING FROM A PREVIOUS MARRIAGE, WHICH LEFT ME BROKEN AND ALONE, STILL EXIST. — I'M GONNA SKIP OVER THE PART WHERE I SAY ALL OF THIS OUT LOUD.

THERE YOU GO, FOLKS...

...SO, AFTER ALL OF THAT, I'VE BEEN SOMETHING OF A LONE WOLF, AS OVERLY DRAMATIC AS THAT SOUNDS.

THIS STORY, THE TRAGIC, FUCKED-UP, CRASH AND BURN, BOOZE-HAZE, HEART-BREAKER STORY OF MY CUCKOLDING AND SUBSEQUENT DIVORCE IS TRUE AND WAS TRUE FIVE YEARS AGO WHEN I FIRST TOLD IT TO CHAN IN A BAR QUITE LIKE THIS ONE.

I'M SICKENED BY MY HYPOC-RISY BUT AM UNABLE TO STOP THIS RUNAWAY TRAIN I'VE SET IN MOTION. ALL I CAN DO IS CHANGE THE SUBJECT.

THAT'S A PRETTY SAD STORY, JOHN...

YEAH.

ARRGHH. THAT SHIT IS DEPRESSING. TELL ME ABOUT THIS TV SHOW YOU MENTIONED.

 WELL, I DON'T KNOW HOW MUCH OF THIS I CAN TELL YOU ABOUT. IT'S ALL UP IN THE AIR.

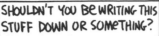 SHOULDN'T YOU BE WRITING THIS STUFF DOWN OR SOMETHING?

 OH, IT'S NOT AN INTERVIEW YET...

 ...TECHNICALLY, I'M JUST FEELING YOU UP AT THIS POINT.

 "FEELING ME UP?"

 PRELIMINARY QUESTIONS FOR A POTENTIAL INTERVIEWEE. IT'S A MAGAZINE TERM.

MM-HM...

 IT ISN'T.

 WELL, I THINK IT'S GREAT YOU'LL BE DOING A SATURDAY MORNING KID'S SHOW. THERE'S NOTHING BUT CRAP OUT THERE.

 OH, WHAT, AND I CAN ADD TO THE CRAP PILE?

OH, HARDLY. YOUR STUFF IS GREAT.

"A, B, C, D, YOU AND ME SITTING IN A TREE. E, F, G, AND H, LET'S FREE THE MONKEYS FROM THEIR CAGE."

THAT STUFF IS GREAT.

WELL, ANY LYRIC WITH MONKEYS OR ELEPHANTS IS AN INSTANT CLASSIC.

I CAN'T BELIEVE YOU CAN SING THAT. I'VE NEVER SEEN SOMEONE WITHOUT KIDS MEMORIZE MY SONG.

HEH, THEY'RE CATCHY.

YEAH — WHAT THE HELL'S UP WITH GROWN-UPS READING HARRY POTTER BOOKS ANYWAY?

YOU WANT ANOTHER BEER?

SURE.

WHERE DID THAT COME FROM?

I WAS JUST THINKING ABOUT IT. I SWEAR, I'D RATHER READ PORNOGRAPHY OPENLY ON THE SUBWAY THAN A HARRY POTTER BOOK.

CAN WE GET ANOTHER TWO OF THESE, PLEASE?

HALF OF ME IS JUDGING MY BEHAVIOUR HARSHLY.

AND THE OTHER HALF IS SELF-CONGRATULATORY ON BEING KIND TO A POTENTIAL INTERVIEWEE FOR THE MAGAZINE THAT I'M "FEELING UP" FOR MY EMPLOYER.

..THAT GREEK SPINACH STUFF WITH PHYLLO PASTRY, SPA-SPAN-

SPANIKOPITA!

RIGHT! THAT STUFF IS AWESOME.

GOOD OL' PHYLLO PASTRY.

YOU CAN WRAP DOG SHIT IN PHYLLO AND PEOPLE WILL LINE UP TO EAT IT.

I'M HAVING FUN HERE, BUT I KNOW I HAVE TO GO.

YEAH, SPANI-POOP-ITA!

I'M A MALE CINDERELLA WITH GLASS SLIPPERS AND A GOWN MADE OF LIES THAT WILL FALL APART AT MIDNIGHT IF NOT BEFORE.

I'M DOING THIS NICE LADY—WHO I FIND INTERESTING AND ATTRACTIVE AND GENUINE AND I CAN TALK EASILY TO—A DISSERVICE BY MISREPRESENTING MY STATUS.

AND, I'M DOING CHAN—WHO I FIND INTERESTING AND ATTRACTIVE AND GENUINE AND I CAN TALK EASILY TO AND WHO I LOVE—A DISSERVICE BY CONTEMPLATING WHATEVER IT IS THAT IS FLOATING ABOUT IN THE AIR AMIDST THE TOO MUCH BEER AND THE ARM-TOUCHES AND THE SOULFUL LOOKS THROWN SURREPTICIOUSLY.

THE EXCITEMENT, INTERSPERSED WITH THE GUILT IS INDUCING CRAZY HOT FLASHES THAT ACTUALLY MAKE ME BREAK OUT IN A SWEAT.

SHE MUST BE WONDERING WHY I SUDDENLY LOOK LIKE AN OLIVE-OIL-SPRAYED MUSCLE-MAN, SANS MUSCLES.

SHERRI...

YOU WANNA KNOW WHAT BUGS ME?

UH... ADULT PEOPLE READING HARRY POTTER?

YEAH, BUT ANOTHER THING...

SHERRI, I GOTTA GO.

REALLY? IT'S SO EARLY...

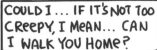

CHAPTER TWENTY-
-ONE:

NO, SERIOUSLY,
IN OR OUT?

IS HE IN A HURRY TO GET ME HORIZONTAL, OR IS HE JUST BEING A BOY SCOUT, WALKING A LADY HOME?

I REALLY _LIKE_ THIS GUY. THIS IS THE FIRST GUY I'VE "CLICKED" WITH IN A LONG TIME. WHATEVER THAT MEANS.

DID YOU EVER NOTICE THAT OUR GENERATION UNCON--SCIOUSLY PUTS QUOTATION MARKS AROUND ANYTHING SINCERE TO PRETEND IT'S IRONIC?

"OH." "DO WE?"

GEORGE ORWELL SAID THAT ENGLISHMEN PROUNOUNCE every FOREIGN WORD WRONG AS A POINT OF PRIDE. MAYBE IT'S A SIMILAR INSECURITY?

IT'S LIKE I'M FLINT AND every GUY I'VE MET HAS BEEN LIKE STRIKING WOOD, PLASTIC, SOAP...

...ANYTHING BUT THE METAL REQUIRED TO MAKE A SPARK, AND THIS GUY IS THE RIGHT KIND OF METAL, I CAN FEEL IT. AND NOW HE'S WALKING AWAY WITHOUT EVEN APPROACHING MY FLINT.

LOTTA DOG SHIT HERE IN NEW YORK...

...WHERE'S ALL THAT PHYLLO PASTRY WHEN YOU NEED IT?

I'D EAT SOME OF THAT RIGHT NOW, I'M _STARVING._

I REALLY THOUGHT WE WERE GETTING ALONG BACK THERE.

I REALLY THINK WE'RE GETTING ALONG RIGHT NOW. SHOULD I INVITE HIM IN? IF HE REJECT-ED ME I'D DIE OF SHAME.

I'M NOT INVITING HIM IN. I'VE PUT TOO MUCH STOCK IN ALL OF THIS EVER SINCE I GOT HIS EMAIL TALKING ABOUT MY OLD MUSIC AT THE SAME TIME I WAS THINKING OF IT.

LIKE THERE'S SOMETHING "MYS--TICAL" OR NEW-AGEY, HOKEY CRAP GOING ON. I DON'T KNOW, IT'S DIFFERENT THAN MY USUAL, WON--DERING IF THE GUY WHO HORKS A GREENER ON THE SIDEWALK IN FRONT OF ME MIGHT BE "THE ONE."

FOO!

IT'S SLIGHTLY LESS PATHETIC ANYWAY.

YOU STILL THERE?

YEAH.

MAN, YOU REALLY SHOULD A BEEN RECORDING ME TONIGHT. I WAS TALKING SOME PRETTY DAZZLING SHIT FOR AN INTERVIEW...

IT'S ALL UP HERE.

BUT YOU TOLD ME YOU'RE GOING SENILE.

I TOLD WHO WHAT?

UH, DO I KNOW YOU?

I HAD SUCH A GOOD FEELING ABOUT ALL OF THIS.

OH, I KNOW THERE WERE COMPLICATIONS; HE LIVES NINE HOURS AWAY, AND IN ANOTHER COUNTRY, I KNOW NOTHING ABOUT HIM AND I'M NOWHERE NEAR READY TO BE IN A RELATIONSHIP.

AND HE COULD BE AN AXE-MURDERER. MONUMENTAL STUFF, REALLY, BUT STILL, THIS "GOOD FEELING." SHEESH.

MISSED!

SHOULD WE GET A CAB OR WHAT?

YOU SAID YOU WANTED TO WALK ME HOME. IT'S JUST THE NEXT BLOCK, LAZY PANTS.

SHERRI...

YOU KNOW WHAT?

WHAT?

WHAT YOU SAID ABOUT HARRY POTTER HURT ME DEEPLY. I LOVE THOSE BOOKS...

YOU'RE A DINK. THAT'S WHERE I LIVE.

I COULD SPEND A LONG TIME HANGING OUT, JOKING AROUND WITH YOU LIKE THIS, JOHN.

PLEASE GIVE ME A SIGN...

WELL, SHERRI, IT'S BEEN REALLY NICE TALKING TO YOU. I'LL BE IN TOUCH.

SUCH A CRAPPY SIGN.

THE INTERVIEW, RIGHT...

YEAH, WELL, WE'LL SEE IF THEY BITE AT THE MAGAZINE.

BE A SHAME TO WASTE ALL THAT "FEELIN' UP."

I CANNOT RESIST THAT FINAL, PATHETIC ATTEMPT AT FLIRTATION.

HEH...YEAH.

HEH.

IT SEEMS TO HAVE THE EFFECT OF A PLACEBO THAT NO ONE EVEN TOLD HIM HE WAS TAKING.

I'LL LET YOU KNOW WHAT THEY SAY. YOU LET ME KNOW WHAT HAPPENS WITH YOUR TV SHOW.

IT SEEMS LIKE YOU'RE AT A CROSSROADS WITH THE CHILDRENS PERFORMER/ADULT PERFORMER THING. I THINK YOU DO BOTH VERY WELL.

THANKS, DR. PHIL. DICKHEAD.

THANKS, JOHN.

I HAD A LOT OF FUN TONIGHT.

GOOD.

ME TOO... WELL, GOODNIGHT.

GOODNIGHT.

OKAY.

SO, I'LL BE IN TOUCH.

YOU REALLY ARE SENILE. YOU ALREADY SAID THAT...

SAID WHAT?

BYE.

BYE.

DON'T GO.

- 142 -

CHAPTER TWENTY-TWO:
THANKFUL FOR CATHOLIC GUILT AND EVEN FOR THE UNCONSCIOUS IN-FLUENCE OF THE COMPETING DOC-TRINE OF CALVINISM.

You can be reasonably sure if you make a decision and you feel miserable and you are having no fun, then you've made the right decision.

And I do feel properly shitty, but it's small con-solation at this time.

So, I did the right thing. Hooray for me.

I don't know where I'd be right now if she HAD in-vited me in...

But yeah, hooray for me, I did the right thing.

I never had the noodles and I'm already drunk, but I want more.

CASHIER CANNOT OPEN SAFE

WHEN A PERSON IS DISTRESSED, THEY WANT POISON AND PRIVATION.

IF IN DOUBT, CALL 911!

NO ONE SAYS, "I'M SO PISSED, I'M GONNA SLEEP EIGHT HOURS AND EAT _FOUR_ SQUARE MEALS TOMORROW.

I'M GONNA CALL MY WIFE, COUNT MY LUCKY STARS, AND THEN DRINK A PINT OF WHISKEY. IN THAT ORDER.

TECHNICALLY, YEAH, THIS STEP IS OUT OF ORDER...

THIS IS GOOD. I'M LUCKY. IT'S EARLY, I'LL DRINK WHISKEY, WATCH TV AND _NOT_ RUIN MY MARRIAGE.

I'M ALREADY FORGETTING THE SILLY SIREN CALL OF THIS CHILD--REN'S PERFORMER, IF IT EVER EXISTED OUTSIDE OF MY OWN MIND. WHAT A LUCKY TV-WATCH--ING WHISKEY-DRINKER I SHALL BE TONIGHT.

...

MESSAGE, MESSAGE...

SHE'S INVITING ME IN.

HEY BABY, IT'S US. I JUST WANTED TO CALL BACK AND SAY HELLO—SAM, SAY HI TO DADDY... NO!

OKAY, WELL, HOPE THE PHOTO SHOOT GOES WELL. SORRY IF WE WERE GRUMPY BEFORE. CALL ME IF YOU GET A CHANCE. I'LL PROBABLY BE ASLEEP THOUGH. OKAY, SEE YOU SOON. LOVE YOU.

I'M ONLY MILDLY DISSAPOINTED—AND ONLY MOMENTARILY—THAT THIS IS THE MESSAGE. I'M A WHISKEY-DRINKIN' TV-WATCHIN' FAMILY MAN, REMEMBER?

THEN THE SECOND MESS-AGE PLAYS... BEEP!

JOHN, IT'S SHERRI HERE. JESUS, I DON'T KNOW— MAYBE MY SIGNALS ARE CROSSED...

MAYBE I'M A KOOK WITH A TOO-HIGH BLOOD ALCOHOL LEVEL, BUT I THOUGHT WE WERE INTERESTED IN EACH OTHER BACK THERE AND THEN YOU LEFT...

I DON'T KNOW, MAYBE I SHOULD HAVE BEEN MORE SUCCINT AND INVITED YOU IN...

I'M DOING THAT NOW... IT'S EARLY. I'M AWAKE. YOU'RE IN NEW YORK. CALL ME.

IF I'M NUTS AND WAY OFF COURSE, JUST FORGET IT... I'M OUT ON A LIMB HERE, JOHN. OKAY, BYE.

GLUG
GLUG
GLUG

GLUG
GLUG
GLUG

IT'S PROBABLY TOO LATE TO CALL CHAN. SHE DID SAY THAT.

OH, PART OF ME IS EXHILER-ATED, I ADMIT IT.

BUT PART OF ME WISHES THAT THESE TESTS OF MY STRENGTH OF WILL WERE OVER FOR TONIGHT. I'M PROBABLY ABOUT TO AT LEAST HALF WAY FAIL THIS ONE.

H-HELLO?!

BEEP! THIS IS SHERRI, CAN'T TAKE YOUR CALL, SO LEAVE A MESSAGE AFTER THE BEEP.

<OH, THANK GOD.>

BIP·BIP·BEEEEEP!

SHERRI, HEY, IT'S JOHN. I THINK YOU'RE PROBABLY NOT A KOOK, BUT...

... I DON'T KNOW WHAT TO DO REALLY... ANYWAY, YOU'RE NOT HOME, SO...

ANYWAY, IT WAS NICE MEETING YOU. UH, OKAY... BYE.

(K-POW.)

THAT WAS SUAVE, JOHN. YOU ARE AN AWESOME CHICK-MAGNET, SIR.

AND YOU KNOW, YOU KINDA LEFT THAT PURPOSELY OPEN DIDN'T YOU? ALL YOU HAD TO SAY WAS, NO THANKS, OR NOT EVEN RETURN HER CALL.

ISN'T THERE A FOLKSY OLD SAYING ABOUT A GUY WHO KEEPS GOING BACK FOR ANOTHER SNAKE BITE?

IF THAT SAYING DOESN'T EXIST, IT MAY BE NECESSARY FOR ME TO INVENT IT.

RING RING

CHAPTER
TWENTY-THREE:

RUN
LIKE
HELL

AH JEEZ, CAN THIS JUST BE OVER?

CLICK!

JOHN. SHERRI HERE. PHONE-TAG... LOOK, I'M COMING OVER THERE.

I GOTTA GET A SHOWER TO SOBER UP, BUT I'M COMING OVER TO TALK TO YOU. I'LL BE THERE IN AN HOUR OR SO.

OKAY. IS THAT OKAY?

IF I WERE BEING GRADED— ONE BEING VERY HAPPY THIS IS STILL ON, TEN BEING VERY DISPLEASED—I GUESS I'D COME IN AT FIVE EXACTLY.

AAAAAAAAAAAA

I DON'T KNOW HOW TO FEEL OR WHAT TO DO. I COULD CALL HER BACK. BUT WHAT TO SAY?

I'LL JUST MEET HER IN THE LOBBY...

MEETING IN THE LOBBY IS COMPLETELY INNOCENT.

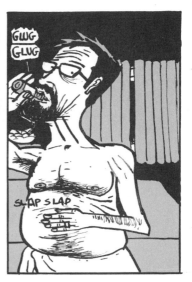

GLUG GLUG

SLAP SLAP

...SPEND A JAW-DROPPING DAY SHOPPING WITH HILTON AND HER GAL-PALS *CLICK*...THEIR MOTOCROSS FANTASY IS ABOUT TO GO... NIGHTMARE!! *CLICK. MINDFREAK, AFTER THIS!

YOU'RE MEETING HER IN THE LOBBY, SO WHAT'S WITH THE PILLOW ARRANGING, HUGH HEFNER?

I GOTTA GET OUTTA HERE. I'LL GO CRAZY WAITING A WHOLE HOUR.

LOURDE

LOURDE

LOURDE

I BROUGHT THE BATHING SUIT IN CASE THE HOTEL HAD A POOL. LIKE ALL MY CLOTHES, THEY'RE A LITTLE TOO TIGHT, BUT THEY'LL WORK FOR RUNNING SHORTS.

I HAVEN'T RUN SINCE SAM WAS BORN, BUT HERE I GO.

A RUN WILL CLEAR MY HEAD.

I'LL BE BACK LONG BEFORE SHERRI ARRIVES... BE A MIRACLE IF I GO FOR EVEN TEN MINUTES.

YEAH, THEY ARE A BIT TIGHT... AND THE SHOES ARE...

STILL, IT DOESN'T LOOK SO BAD...

I'LL ONLY MAKE A COUPLE OF BLOCKS BEFORE THE HEART ATTACK ANYWAY.

ACTUALLY, I REALLY HOPE I DON'T DIE OF A HEART ATTACK IN THESE SHOES AND SHORTS.

IT'S NOT SO BAD.

I MEAN, I KNOW THE FIRST BLOCK FOR THE NEOPHYTE RUNNER IS ALL THE THEME FROM ROCKY AND ELATION.

BUT I'M ACTUALLY NOT IN AS BAD OF SHAPE AS I THOUGHT. —OH, WAIT...

WHEW!

THE ELATION WAS PREMATURE.

PREMATURE ELATION. AHEM. I'VE BEEN TELLING MYSELF THAT THIS IS A RUN TO "CLEAR MY HEAD." NOT SOME PATHETIC, LAST-DITCH EFFORT TO TONE UP MY PATH-ETICALLY OUT OF SHAPE BODY IN CASE SOME ONE SHOULD SEE IT.

BOB'S CH

I TELL MYSELF THAT BECAUSE THAT WOULD BE PATHETIC. GOD, I HATE MYSELF FOR A MILLION REASONS RIGHT NOW.

NA TRAHN VARIETY BEER CIGARETTS

FOOD STAMPS

HMMM?

NU DUDZ

NU DUDZ↑

SORRY, WHAT DID YOU SAY?

NU DUDZ↑

POIT!

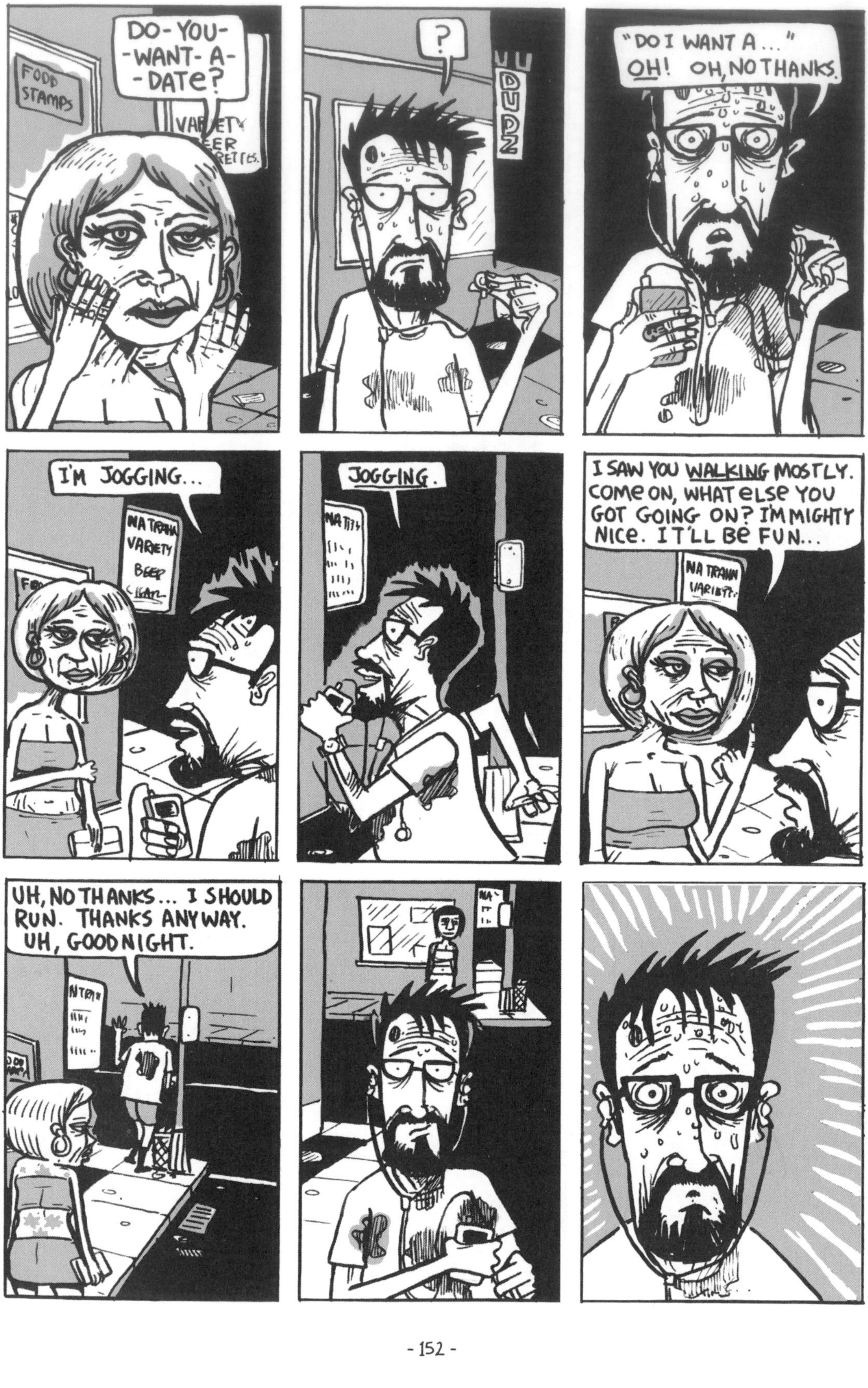
FOOD STAMPS
DO-YOU- -WANT- A- -DATE?
?
DUDZ
"DO I WANT A..." OH! OH, NO THANKS.
I'M JOGGING...
VARIETY
JOGGING.
I SAW YOU WALKING MOSTLY. COME ON, WHAT ELSE YOU GOT GOING ON? I'M MIGHTY NICE. IT'LL BE FUN...
UH, NO THANKS... I SHOULD RUN. THANKS ANYWAY. UH, GOODNIGHT.

WELL, THAT WAS CRAZY.

I'M FUCKING <u>RUNNING</u>, LADY.

IT'S LIKE, I'M OUT FOR A RUN, BUT SURE, I MIGHT BE UP FOR SEX WITH A COMPLETE STRANGER...

...BECAUSE THAT WOULD BE CRAZY... HOOKING UP WITH A COMPLETE STRANGER WHEN YOU'RE HAPPILY MARRIED WITH A FAMILY YOU'D HATE TO LOSE.

-YOU'RE JUST OUT FOR A RUN — THAT WOULD BE...

...RIDICULOUS.

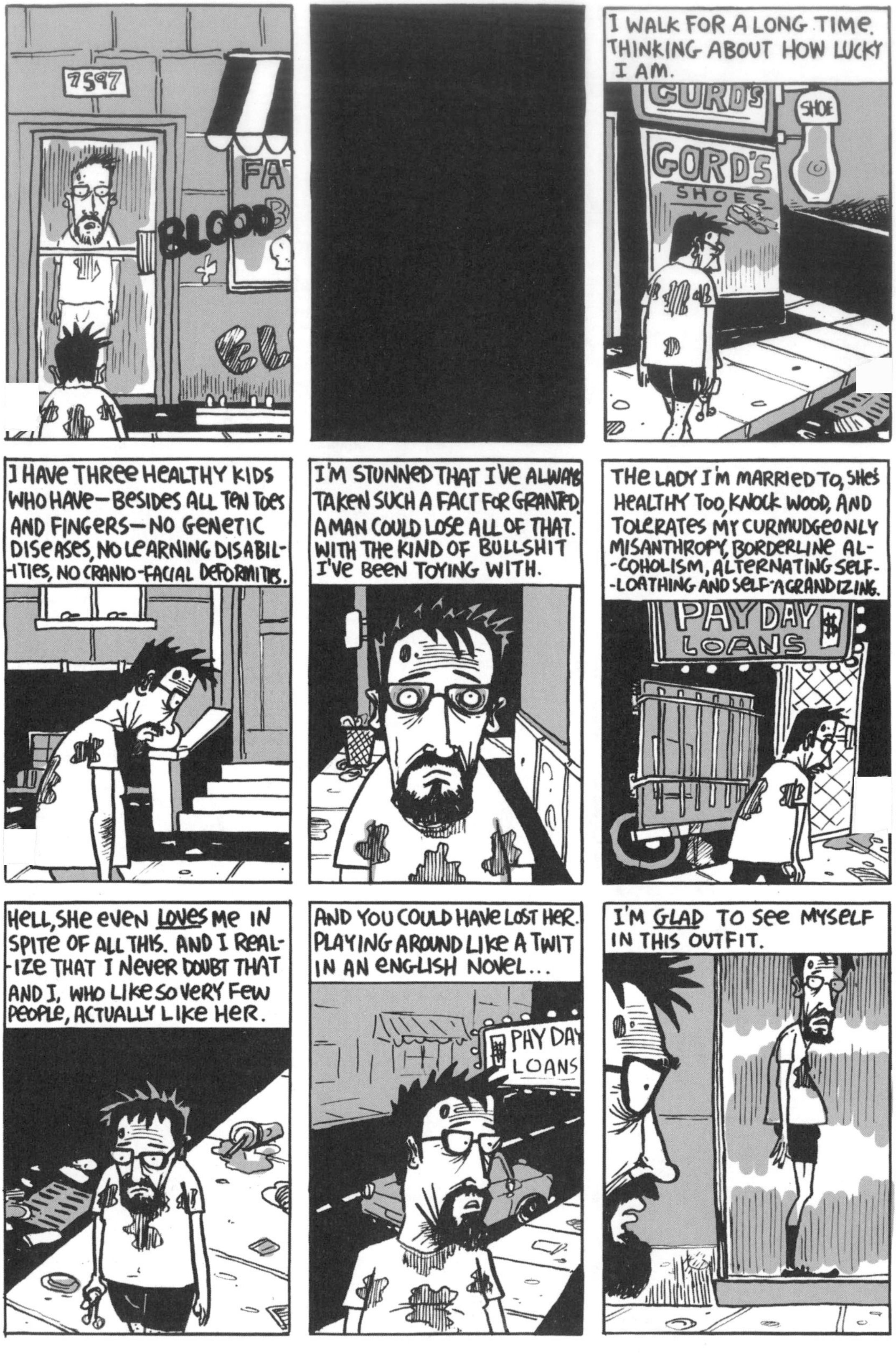
7597
FA
BLOOD
I WALK FOR A LONG TIME. THINKING ABOUT HOW LUCKY I AM.
GORD'S
GORD'S
SHOES
SHOE
I HAVE THREE HEALTHY KIDS WHO HAVE—BESIDES ALL TEN TOES AND FINGERS—NO GENETIC DISEASES, NO LEARNING DISABIL-ITIES, NO CRANIO-FACIAL DEFORMITIES.
I'M STUNNED THAT I'VE ALWAYS TAKEN SUCH A FACT FOR GRANTED. A MAN COULD LOSE ALL OF THAT. WITH THE KIND OF BULLSHIT I'VE BEEN TOYING WITH.
THE LADY I'M MARRIED TO, SHE'S HEALTHY TOO, KNOCK WOOD, AND TOLERATES MY CURMUDGEONLY MISANTHROPY, BORDERLINE AL--COHOLISM, ALTERNATING SELF--LOATHING AND SELF-AGRANDIZING.
PAY DAY LOANS
HELL, SHE EVEN LOVES ME IN SPITE OF ALL THIS. AND I REAL-IZE THAT I NEVER DOUBT THAT AND I, WHO LIKE SO VERY FEW PEOPLE, ACTUALLY LIKE HER.
AND YOU COULD HAVE LOST HER. PLAYING AROUND LIKE A TWIT IN AN ENGLISH NOVEL...
PAY DAY LOANS
I'M GLAD TO SEE MYSELF IN THIS OUTFIT.

FUCKING RIDICULOUS OLD MAN. I'M JUST GLAD THIS WAS STOPPED IN TIME. I'M JUST GLAD THAT NO ONE'S BEEN HURT AND...

...OH SHIT, SHERRI.

SHE'LL BE AT THE HOTEL SOON. WHAT'LL I TELL HER?

I COULD JUST STAY AWAY 'TIL SHE LEAVES... BUT FOR THESE DAMN HOT PANTS: I'M FREEZING.

MAYBE I CAN STILL BEAT HER BACK TO THE HOTEL, SNEAK IN THE BACK WAY AND TELL THE DESK CLERK TO PASS ON THE MESSAGE THAT I'VE CHECKED OUT SUDDENLY.

BACK DOOR

ME

HOTEL

FRONT

SHERRI

IT'S NO JOKE; THAT'S MY BEST PLAN AND THE ONE I INTEND TO ACT UPON.

I HUNCH AND SHUFFLE-RUN, SLAPPING MY ARMS AND LEGS TO STAY WARM. IN A TOWN FAMOUS FOR ECCENTRICS, I'M SURE I'M THE BIGGEST OF FREAKS RUNNING AMOK TONIGHT.

SLAP SLAP SLAP

BUT I'M LAUGHING LIKE SCROOGE ON CHRISTMAS MORN-ING, LESSON LEARNED, A SCROOGE THAT AVOIDED THE GHOST OF MARRIAGE-DESTROY-ING AFFAIRS.

SLAP

SLAP

IF I CAN JUST SORT THINGS OUT WITH SHERRI—IE. AVOID HER AND SEND AN APOLOGETIC EMAIL LATER—I WILL COME OUT OF THIS EXTENDED NIGHT-MARE UNSCATHED.

THE BLOCK BEFORE THE HOTEL, SCOUTING FROM AN ALLEY, I COME AROUND FROM BEHIND, SEEKING A REAR ENTRANCE.

I QUESTION THIS CLEANING MAN IF THERE'S ANOTHER WAY IN. THERE IS!

MORE SCROOGE LAUGHTER; AN EXCELLENT FELLOW, MOST REMARKABLE.

THANKS, MAN.

I SNEAK IN THE BACK, BUT A SIGN ON THE STAIRCASE DOOR WARNS THAT IT IS FOR EMER-GENCIES ONLY.

I WORRY ABOUT ALARMS AND THE ATTENTION THEY WOULD INEVITABLY BRING, SO I RISK SKULKING INTO THE MAIN LOBBY TO THE ELEVATOR.

OH NO, NO, NO...

HE'S STILL NOT ANSWERING... ANY MESSAGE?

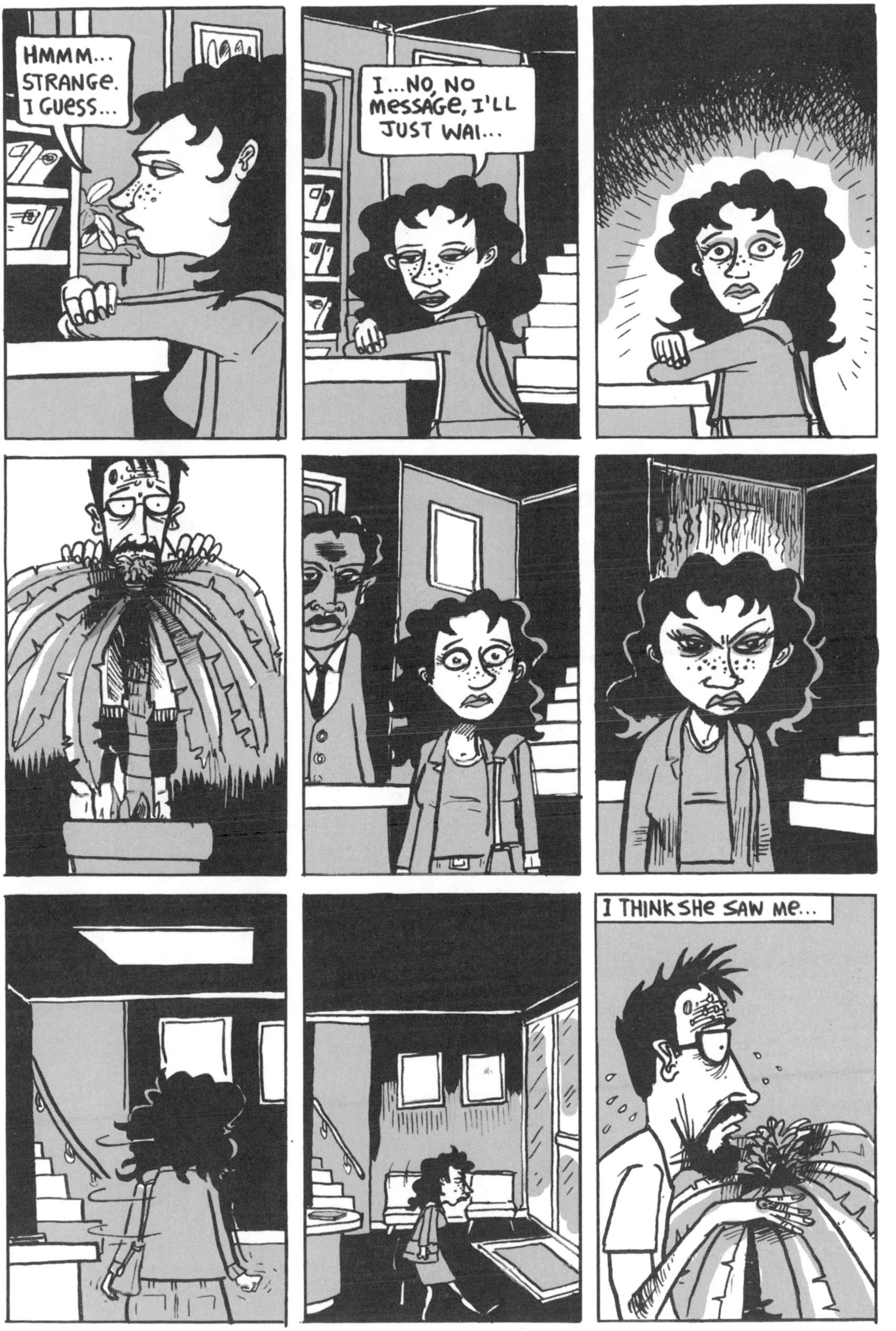
HMMM... STRANGE. I GUESS...
I...NO, NO MESSAGE, I'LL JUST WAI...
I THINK SHE SAW ME...

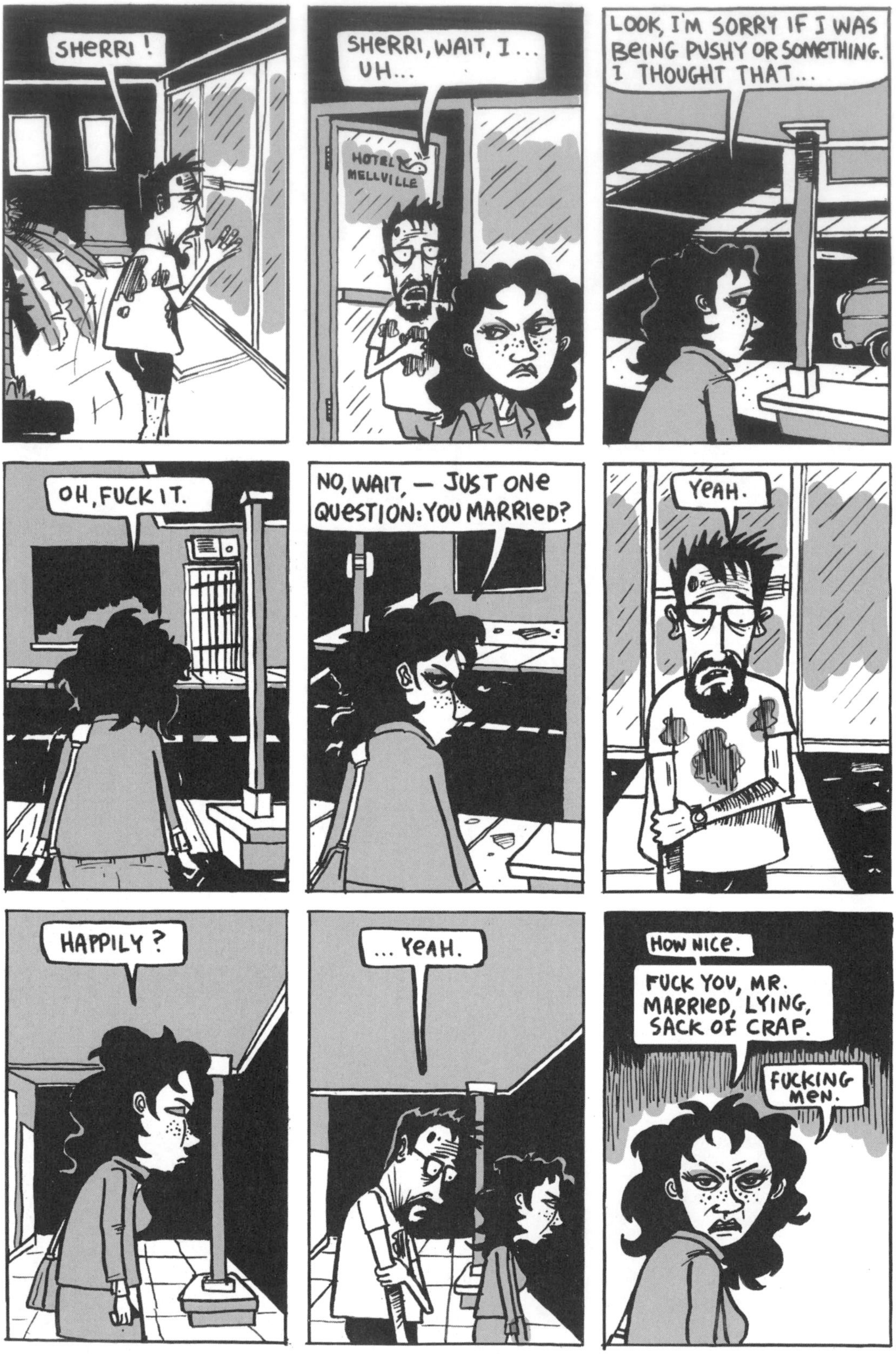
SHERRI !
SHERRI, WAIT, I... UH...
HOTEL MELLVILLE
LOOK, I'M SORRY IF I WAS BEING PUSHY OR SOMETHING. I THOUGHT THAT...
OH, FUCK IT.
NO, WAIT, — JUST ONE QUESTION: YOU MARRIED?
YEAH.
HAPPILY ?
... YEAH.
HOW NICE.
FUCK YOU, MR. MARRIED, LYING, SACK OF CRAP.
FUCKING MEN.

I DON'T EVEN COMMENT ON THE FACT THAT IT SEEMS LIKE I'M SINGLY TAKING THE HEAT FOR ALL THE MEN IN HER PAST.

AND I DON'T FOLLOW HER, I'VE DONE ENOUGH DAMAGE TONIGHT.

FUCKING MIRRORS. COM-PLETE CLARITY, ECCO HOMO. I WISH I WERE DRACULA.

AGAIN, THE MIRROR. OKAY, OKAY, I GET IT.

CHAPTER TWENTY--FOUR:

SHE WON'T GET FOOLED AGAIN.

I THINK THAT HE MAYBE WAS NOT "THE ONE."

YOU MOVE FROM BAD TO WORSE, SHERRI SMALLS.

YOU DON'T DESERVE A CAB. YOU NEED TO WALK HOME.

CAMEL FILTERS, PLEASE. $4.50 YOU HAVE MATCHES?

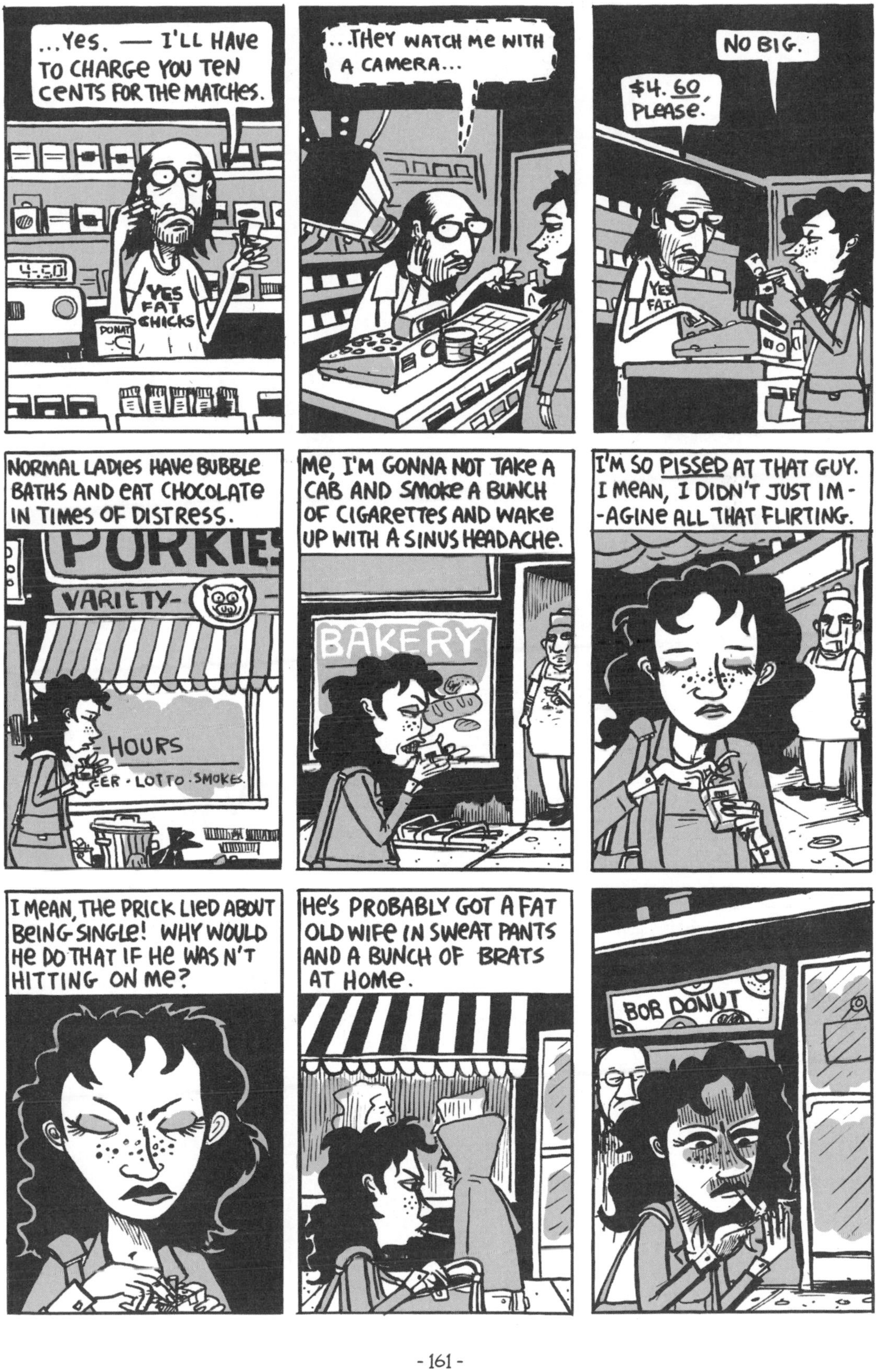
...YES. — I'LL HAVE TO CHARGE YOU TEN CENTS FOR THE MATCHES.
4.50
YES FAT CHICKS
DONAT
...THEY WATCH ME WITH A CAMERA...
$4.60, PLEASE.
NO BIG.
YES FAT
NORMAL LADIES HAVE BUBBLE BATHS AND EAT CHOCOLATE IN TIMES OF DISTRESS.
PORKIES
VARIETY
HOURS
EER · LOTTO · SMOKES.
ME, I'M GONNA NOT TAKE A CAB AND SMOKE A BUNCH OF CIGARETTES AND WAKE UP WITH A SINUS HEADACHE.
BAKERY
I'M SO PISSED AT THAT GUY. I MEAN, I DIDN'T JUST IM--AGINE ALL THAT FLIRTING.
I MEAN, THE PRICK LIED ABOUT BEING SINGLE! WHY WOULD HE DO THAT IF HE WASN'T HITTING ON ME?
HE'S PROBABLY GOT A FAT OLD WIFE IN SWEAT PANTS AND A BUNCH OF BRATS AT HOME.
BOB DONUT

AND WHY AM I SO JEALOUS OF THAT?

NOT A FAT LADY IN SWEAT PANTS SPECIFICALLY, BUT JUST SOMEONE AT HOME WAITING FOR ME.

AND WHY AM I JEALOUS OF THAT, IF IT SUCKS SO BAD HE'S OFF FLIRTING WITH ME ON A BUSINESS TRIP?

HE PROBABLY DOESN'T EVEN WORK FOR ANY MAGAZINE. HE DIDN'T EVEN HAVE A TAPE RECORDER! YOU'RE STUPID AND DESPERATE, SHERRI.

STILL, I HAD FUN TALKING TO HIM AND I DIDN'T JUST IMAGINE SOME KIND OF CONNECTION OR SOMETHING THERE...

...LIKE I FEEL WITH NINETY-PERCENT OF THE MEN— MEN LACKING OVERT DEFORMITIES-WHOM I SPEND LONGER THAN TEN MINUTES WITH.

BAGEL TIME

YOU MUST REEK OF DESPER-ATION, SHERRI.
YOU MUST STINK OF NEEDY.

BAGEL TIME

FLICK!

YOU MUST LOOK LIKE MAGNIF-IED VELCRO HOOKS, LOOKING AT EVERYONE LIKE THEY ARE MAGNIFIED VELCRO HOOPS.

I KNOW THIS SOUNDS NEW--AGEY AND STUPID AND LIKE SOMETHING A WHITE, SUBUR-BAN YOGA INSTRUCTOR WITH A SANSKRIT NAME WOULD SAY...

... BUT I REALLY GOTTA FIND OUT WHAT THE FVCK IS THE VOID IN ME THAT I'M SO DESPERATELY TRYING TO FILL.

Heeeeey PRETTY, PRETTY!!! YeAAGH!!!

WAIT, COME BACK. YOU WANNA BE MY BOYFRIEND? I'VE DONE WORSE IN THE PAST. I'VE DONE WORSE ONLY TEN MINUTES AGO...

I THINK I NEED TO CONCENTRATE ON DEALING WITH THE FACT THAT THE LONG, LIMPING DEATH SCENE WITH RIC IS FINALLY OVER.

AND THERE'S THIS TV SHOW THING THAT I DO WANT TO DO. ALL THAT HAPPY HORSE SHIT I SPOUTED OFF TO RIC IS ALSO TRUE. I CAN MAKE A LOT OF MONEY DOING SOMETHING I'M GOOD AT, AND TAKE THE MONEY AND RUN.

I COULD WRITE ANOTHER BUNCH OF SONGS FOR GROWN-UPS. THE ONE GOOD THING ABOUT THIS DICKWEED, JOHN, IS HE REM--INDED ME THAT PEOPLE STILL LIKE MY OLD MUSIC. UNLESS HE LIED ABOUT THAT AS WELL.

I'VE ACTUALLY BEEN WRIT--ING LYRICS IN MY HEAD THAT DON'T RELY ON MONKEYS, DUCKS, CHICKENS OR BANANAS. LYRICS FOR GROWN-UPS.

SO THAT'S GOOD.

SO, I'M GONNA KNUCKLE DOWN AND HAVE SOME QUALITY ALONE TIME. NOT BE SUCH A DES--PERATE VENUS FLY TRAP.

ALL THE TIME REALIZING THAT THIS NEW WORLD-VIEW STILL INCLUDES THE POS--SIBILITY THAT EVERYONE ALWAYS FINDS THE RIGHT PER--SON FOR THEM EVENTUALLY, RIGHT?

HAPPILY EVER AFTER, RIGHT?

1900

BLINK! BLINK

OH GOD DAMNIT. IF IT'S A MESSAGE FROM THAT MAR--RIED SACK OF CRAP, I'M JUST GONNA DELETE IT...

...AFTER I LISTEN TO IT.

TAK!

TWO... NEW...MESSAGES.

FIRST... MESSAGE... BEEEEEP

SHERRI, DARLING IT'S KARL. IF YOU'RE THERE, PICK UP, WON'T YOU?

OH KARL, YOU'VE GONE STRAIGHT AND WANT TO MAKE BABIES WITH ME. YAY!

SO, I HAD A STRANGE CALL FROM THE HAND--SOME GARY FRIEDKIN.

HE FEELS YOU DON'T LIKE HIM AND HE'S HEARTBROKEN. I FEEL LIKE I'M IN HIGH SCHOOL AGAIN; I THINK HE'S GOT QUITE A CRUSH ON YOU.

HE WANTS TO WORK WITH YOU AND FEELS HE'S DONE SOME--THING TERRIBLE AND WANTS TO CORRECT IT.

OH SHERRI, WHAT DO YOU WANT TO DO ABOUT THIS NETWORK DEAL?

THE WORLD—OR AT LEAST THE WORLD OF CHILDREN'S ENTER--TAINMENT—IS YOUR OYSTER. WILL YOU SUCK OUT THE MAR--ROW AND EXTRACT THAT OYSTER OR NOT?

DO CALL OLD KARL AT YOUR EARLIEST CONVENIENCE, WON'T YOU, SHERRI?

HOPE YOU ARE OKAY OVER THERE... BYE.

BEEEP! NEXT...MESSAGE...

HEY SHERRI, IT'S, UH, GARY FRIEDKIN HERE.

I HAD CALLED YOUR MAN KARL TO ACT AS A PEACE EMMISARY, THEN I REALIZED THAT WAS KIND OF WIENER-Y AND DECIDED TO CALL YOU MYSELF.

SHERRI, I GENUINELY ADMIRE THE WORK YOU DO AND I REALLY WANT TO WORK WITH YOU AND TRANSFER THAT WORK TO TELEVISION.

I THOUGHT WE WERE HAVING A GREAT LUNCH THE OTHER DAY, AND I THOUGHT WE WERE GETTING ALONG LIKE FRIENDS UNTIL I THINK I CAME OFF LIKE A HOLLY-WOOD SLIMEBALL ABOUT HAND--LING RIC...

I'M SORRY ABOUT THAT.—LOOK, I'M IN TOWN AGAIN NEXT WEEK AND I'D LIKE TO MEET WITH YOU AND LET YOU KNOW THAT WE AT THE NETWORK WANT YOU ON YOUR TERMS...

...WHATEVER THEY ARE, INCLUDING RIC, IF HE'S STILL IN THE MIX. (KARL MENTIONED HE WAS LEAVING). BUT WHATEVER YOU WANT—WITHIN REASON...

I'D LOVE TO GO BACK TO THAT RESTAURANT AGAIN, START OVER, AND TRY NOT TO BE AS SLIMY THIS TIME.

GIVE ME A CALL AND LET ME KNOW. I HOPE TO SEE YOU AGAIN. BYE.

OKAY, SO I CONFESS: MY LOINS WERE STIRRED BY THAT. BUT THEY ARE ALSO DECIDEDLY GIRDED.

THE GUY SOUNDS MORE DES-PERATE THAN I DO.

OVERALL, I FEEL PRETTY GOOD TONIGHT AND WITHOUT A WHOLE BOTTLE OF RED WINE TO MAKE IT SO.

I KNOW I HAD, LIKE, TEN BEERS EARLIER, BUT THAT SEEMS AGES AGO AND A TECHNICALITY.

I FEEL ELATED, VAGUELY HOPEFUL AND I CAN'T RE-MEMBER IF I SAID I WAS THROUGH WITH RELATIONSHIPS OR LOOKING FOR A NEW ONE...

SIGH...

CHAPTER TWENTY-FIVE:

OLD, ALONE AND WEARING AN INCONGRUOUS RUNNING COSTUME

I KNOW I SHOULD BE HAPPY AS HELL RIGHT NOW.

GRATE FUL TOO, AND I AM. I DECIDE THAT'S MY NEW PERSONA: GRATEFUL AND POSITIVE.

I'M NOT ONLY GONNA NOT BITCH WHEN I MISS MY BUS, BUT ALSO BE THANKFUL WHEN I DO CATCH IT. THAT'S WHAT MY LIFE HAS BEEN MISSING: APPRECIATING WHAT I HAVE.

(FOR CREDIBILITY'S SAKE, I STILL HATE NEW AGE ANY--THING AND SELF-HELP---WHATEVER.)

OKAY JOHN, I THINK YOU'VE BEEN CHASTISED ENOUGH, YOU CAN TAKE OFF THE RUN--NING OUTFIT NOW.

I REMIND MYSELF I'M NOT SHOWERING BECAUSE I'M SWEATY FROM RUNNING - WHICH WOULD BE MANLY...

I'M SHOWERING BECAUSE I'M COLD FROM WALKING AROUND IN THAT RUNNING OUTFIT - WHICH IS NOT MANLY.

MY POSITIVE TAKE ON ALL OF THIS IS THAT MY BODY IS FALLING APART. PERFECTLY NORMAL FOR A MAN OF MY AGE.

AND AT MY TIME OF LIFE, A DIGNIFIED MAN IS MEASURED LESS BY HIS PHYSICALITY AND MORE ON THE BASIS OF HIS INTELLECT AND ACHIEVMENTS.

OFF!

I PLAN TO WORK ON DEVEL--OPING THESE TWO.

I DON'T ALLOW MYSELF THE LUXURY OF CALLING AND WAKING UP CHAN. I DESERVE TO SWEAT THIS OUT A BIT 'TIL I GET HOME AND HAVE A LOOOOONG TALK.

I ALSO DO NOT LET MYSELF OFF EASY AND WRITE THE INEVITABLE APOLOGY EMAIL TO SHERRI TONIGHT. I LEAVE THAT FOR ANOTHER DAY AND CONTEMPLATE CONSEQUENCES.

WHICH SOUNDS HEALTHILY GROWN-UP, REALLY.

I'M JUST LYING HERE THINKING OF ALL THE GOOD THINGS IN MY LIFE.

AND THIS IS NOT SOME SUDDEN, NEW-AGEY CONVERSION. I'VE ALWAYS BEEN AWARE OF THE GOOD BEFORE, I JUST TENDED TO FOCUS ON THE MUD AND THE STRUGGLE IT TOOK TO GET TO THESE DIAMONDS IN THE ROUGH.

LITTLE SAM IS JUST STARTING TO TALK AND HIS PERSONALITY BEGINS TO REVEAL ITSELF AND MY LOVE FOR HIM CHANGES WITH IT.

FROM THE PRIMITIVE CAVEMAN DESIRE TO KILL THINGS TO PROTECT THIS LITTLE CREATURE-CARRIER OF MY D.N.A.-TO SOMETHING MUCH DEEPER.

DRUNKS AND JUNKIES.

SAVAGE DOGS

I MISS HIM AND I WANT TO BUY A MECHANICAL BEAR IN THE SUBWAY FOR HIM LIKE I DID FOR MATTY WHEN I WAS IN NEW YORK YEARS AGO IN A COMPLETE NEW YORKER CARTOON MOMENT.

"Disco" BEAR ONLY $10

IT'S ALL THE SAME AND ALL DIFFERENT WITH SAM AS IT WAS WITH THE GIRLS. IT'S LIKE DOZING DURING A MOVIE. YOU WAKE UP AND SOMEHOW THE PLOT HAS ADVANCED; AND THEY'RE GROWN-UP.

OFF TO UNIVERSITY.

HUH?

NOW THEY'RE ADULTS WITH THEIR OWN THOUGHT PATTERNS, NO LONGER INFLUENCED BY MY OVERBEARING OPINIONS AND PHILOSOPHIES.

EHH, TEACHERS ARE COWARDS, TEACHING MEMORIZED CRAP TO THEIR INTELLECTUAL INFERIORS...

intellectual inferiors...

LIKE PEOPLE I'D MEET AT A PARTY AND SAY: "WHAT CHARMING YOUNG GIRLS...

... I DISAGREE WITH SOME OF THEIR OPINIONS ON POPULAR CULTURE."

I RESPECTFULLY DISAGREE. I DO NOT THINK MADONNA IS "GOD."

I'VE DECIDED TO TALK TO THEM ABOUT THE DIVORCE.

A SUBJECT THEY'VE ALWAYS ATTEMPTED TO AVOID.

LA-LA-LA-LA-LA-LA!!

I WANT THEM TO UNDERSTAND HOW IT WENT DOWN AND HOW IT BROKE ME. HOW I HAD- WHAT SEEMS IN RETROSPECT- TO HAVE BEEN A FIVE-YEAR NERVOUS BREAKDOWN.

OL' DRUNKY LIQUOR

I WANT TO SAY THE WORDS OUT LOUD: THAT I KNOW I WASN'T THERE FOR YOU AFTER THE DIV- ORCE AND I KNOW I FAILED YOU.

SAYING THOSE WORDS WILL BE A SHITTY KIND OF GOOD I THINK.

AND I'M GONNA TALK TO MY WIFE AND THANK HER FOR TOLERATING ALL OF MY "EN- -DEARING FOIBLES."

I'M GONNA TELL HER WHAT WENT DOWN HERE AND WHAT DIDN'T AND SEE WHERE THAT LEAVES ME.

BOOT!

PERHAPS IN A CARDBOARD BOX ON THE STREET.

TAKE YOUR TIME, BUT I DO HAVE A COUPLE SEEING IT THIS AFTERNOON.

↑ THIS END UP
♿ FRAGILE

MAYBE IN A NEW START WITH MY NEW POSITIVE SELF.

HOLEY MOLEY! THE PAIN SURE LETS YOU KNOW YOU'RE ALIVE!

I'LL TELL HER NOT TO WORRY; I'LL STILL BE MOSTLY BITCHY.

SOMEHOW, I FEEL PRETTY GOOD. CALMER THAN I HAVE IN MONTHS.

RING!

WELL, THIS COMPROMISES MY SENSE OF WELL-BEING... IS IT SHERRI?

HELLO?

JOHN? THIS IS MOLLY.

OH, YES, I – UH... WHO IS THIS?

MOLLY, FROM THE PHOTO SHOOT TODAY...

OH, RIGHT! HOW'S IT GOING, MOLLY?

NOT SO GOOD ACTUALLY... I,.. I.. MY CAR GOT BROKEN INTO. THEY STOLE MY CAMERA BAG AND... I LOST YOUR FILM... I'M SO SORRY! I HAD A TWO-THOUSAND-DOLLAR CAMERA IN THERE, TOO.

I GUESS I'M JUST NEW TO THIS BUT I'M STRUGGLING TO FIND THE POSITIVE SPIN ON THIS...

THE END

ACKNOWLEDGEMENTS

THANKS TO CHRIS OLIVEROS WHO I HOPE ONE DAY I WILL BE BRAVE ENOUGH TO CALL "THE CHIEF." PEGGY BURNS, A VERY FINE LADY TO HAVE IN YOUR CORNER IN MARKETING A BOOK. TOM DEVLIN, WHO BROKE MY BALLS AND MADE ME REDRAW A LOT OF BAD DRAWINGS. YOU, THE READER, SHOULD THANK HIM TOO. MY AGENT, SAMANTHA HAYWOOD; PETER BAGGE, A HERO OF MINE, A BRILLIANT CARTOONIST AND A GENEROUS MAN FOR PROVIDING A QUOTE FOR THE BACK OF THIS BOOK; SETH, A TRUE GENTLEMAN, WHO SETS THE STANDARD AND SHOWS THE WAY; ANDY BROWN, THE BIGGEST AND HAIRIEST HEART IN THE WORLD; TODD STEWART AND BILLY MAVREAS, MY MAN-DRAWING SALON COMRADES; DAVE COLLIER; MIKE O'CONNOR; MY PARENTS, THOUGH THEY DO NOT APPEAR IN THIS BOOK THEY ARE ALWAYS IN MY THOUGHTS AND KEEP ME SOMEWHAT ON THE RIGHT PATH; LUKE AND OWEN (NOT THE WILSONS, BUT THE OLLMANN-SMITHS, MY GRANDSONS); WAYNE GLASS, MY DEAR OLD PAL UNDERGROUND; BROTHER JAMES THORNTON, CSC, I MISS YOU OLD FRIEND.

NOTES

WHEN I WAS WRITING THIS STORY, I HAPPENED TO READ IAN BROWN'S *GLOBE AND MAIL* ARTICLE ABOUT LIFE WITH HIS SEVERELY DISABLED SON, WALKER. BROWN'S UNFLINCHING HONESTY AND COMPLETE LACK OF SELF-PITY IN THE FACE OF GENUINELY OVERWHELMING DIFFICULTIES AFFECTED ME MORE THAN ANYTHING I HAD READ IN YEARS. THAT ARTICLE MADE ME RE-EXAMINE MY LIFE, AND CEASE SOMEWHAT, MY BOURGEOISIE WHINING AND INCIDENTALLY, AFFECTED THE DIRECTION OF THIS BOOK.

I DECIDED WHEN I STARTED THIS BOOK THAT I WOULDN'T MUCH DISCUSS WHAT PARTS ARE TRUE OR FICTION. BUT THERE IS ONE FICTION IN THIS NARRATIVE THAT I WANT TO MAKE CLEAR—EVEN MORE IMPORTANT THAN CLARIFYING IF THE CHARACTER'S AFFAIR IS REAL OR FICTIONAL—IS THAT WHILE I WAS ART DIRECTOR AT A MAGAZINE FOR SIX YEARS, I WAS NOT FIRED FOR ANY KIND OF FICTIONAL INCOMPETENCE AS OCCURS IN *MID-LIFE*, BUT AS PART OF WHAT CAME TO BE CALLED THE "PENIS-PURGE OF 2007" OR THE FIRING OF ALL THE MEN AT THE MAGAZINE I WAS EMPLOYED BY. IT WAS A YOGA MAGAZINE. LONG STORY. ANOTHER BOOK. STAND BY...

RAFFI. IF YOU ARE NOT CANADIAN OR, YOU ARE CANADIAN BUT WERE NOT ALIVE BETWEEN 1980 AND 1995 AND ARE READING THIS, YOU SHOULD KNOW THAT RAFFI WAS THE REAL DEAL IN CHILDREN'S RECORDS DURING THIS TIME. WITH A NOD TO SHARON, LOIS AND BRAM, AND OF COURSE, SIR FRED PENNER (I'M HOPING I'M PREACHING TO THE CHOIR HERE) RAFFI WAS **THE** MAN IN SONGS ABOUT BANANAS, MONKEYS AND ELEPHANTS. I'VE SEEN HIM IN CONCERT AND CAN ATTEST TO THE MAN'S SINCERITY, PLUS, HE'S A DEDICATED CRUSADER FOR PEACE AND THE ENVIRONMENT, HE'S PALS WITH THE DALI LAMA AND, OH YEAH, HE WROTE A LITTLE SONG CALLED "BABY BELUGA." DON'T NOBODY MESS WITH THE RAFFI. (P.S. HE'S **NOT** THE REAL-LIFE CHILDREN'S PERFORMER THAT I HAD A CRUSH ON.)

(Also thanks to La Nobella wine, which greatly aided the production of this volume...)

(AND, AS OF THIS WRITING, IN 2010, I'M STILL FIRING "LIVE AMMUNITION," LADIES AND GENTLEMEN... BUT, PLEASE, SPAY AND NEUTER YOUR PETS!')

CLINIQUE MÉDICALE
MÉDECINE FAMILIALE ET SPÉCIALISÉE

Tél.: ▮ • Fax: ▮
• Tél.: ▮

Pour: Joseph Ollman
Adresse:
Date: Aug 26/06

Rx

Dr Andrew Steinberg
Urology

- Father of 3 request
vasectomy

186412

PAS DE SUBSTITUTION

RÉPÉTITION	1	2	3	4	5		NR

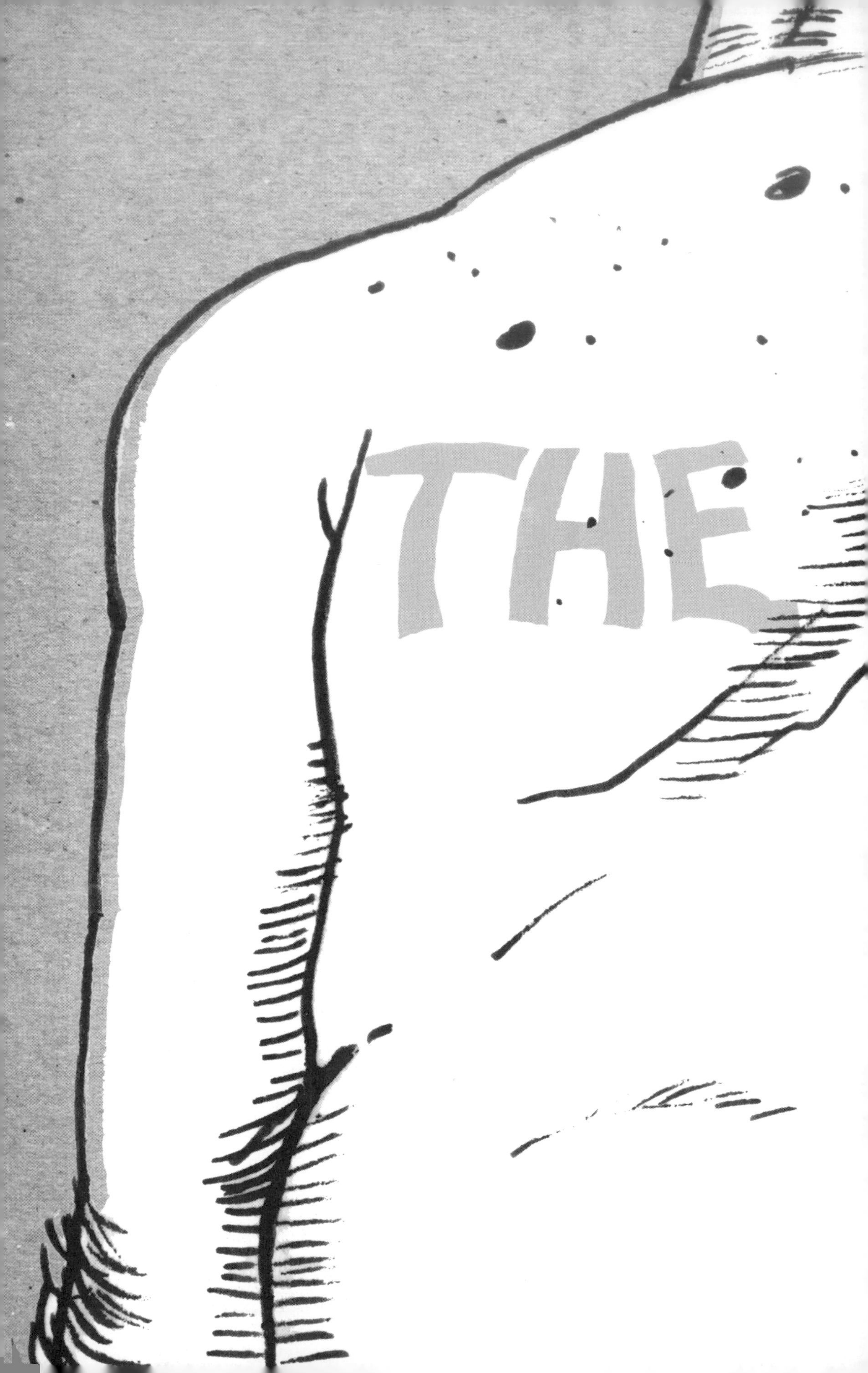
THE

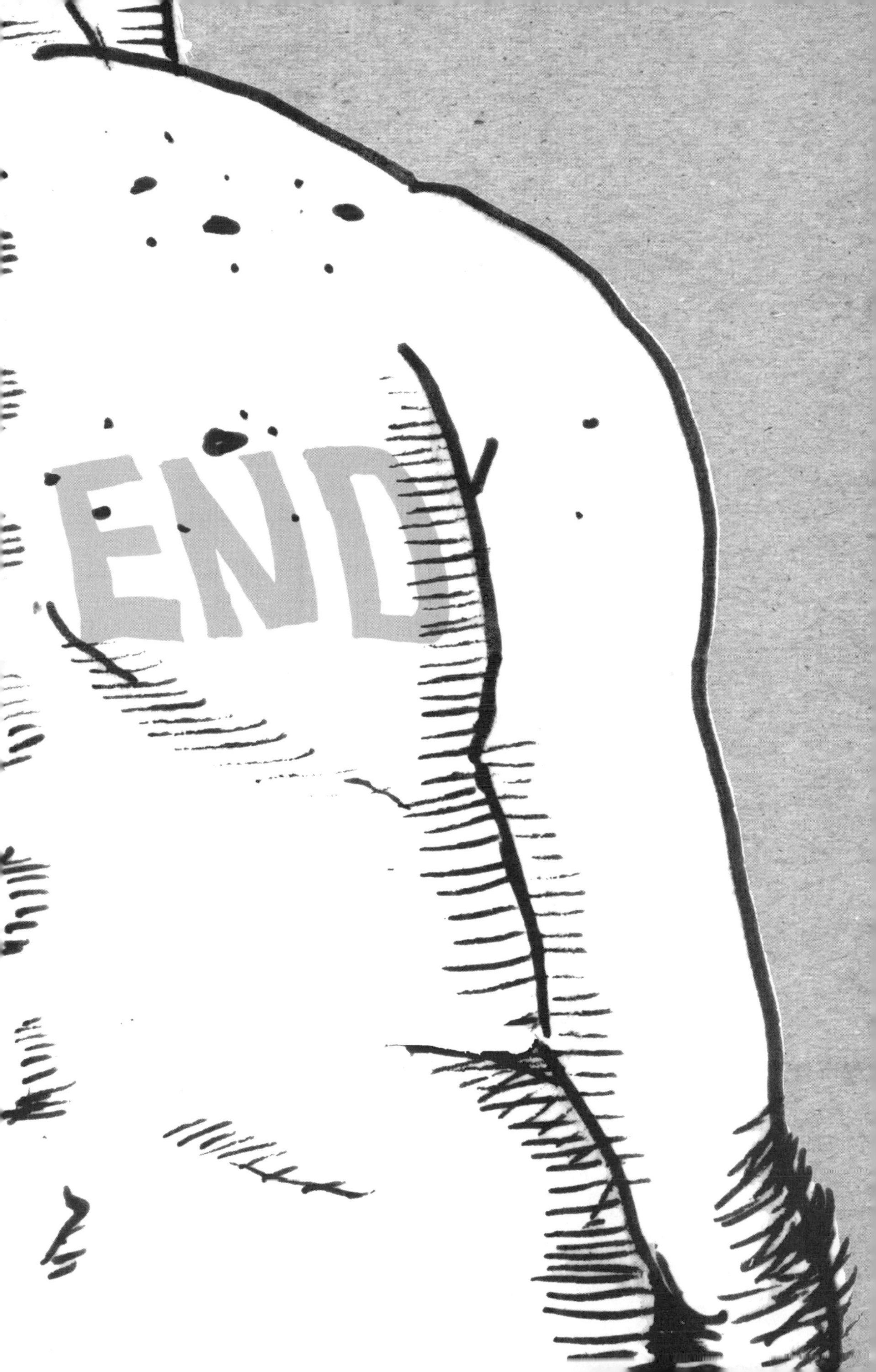
END

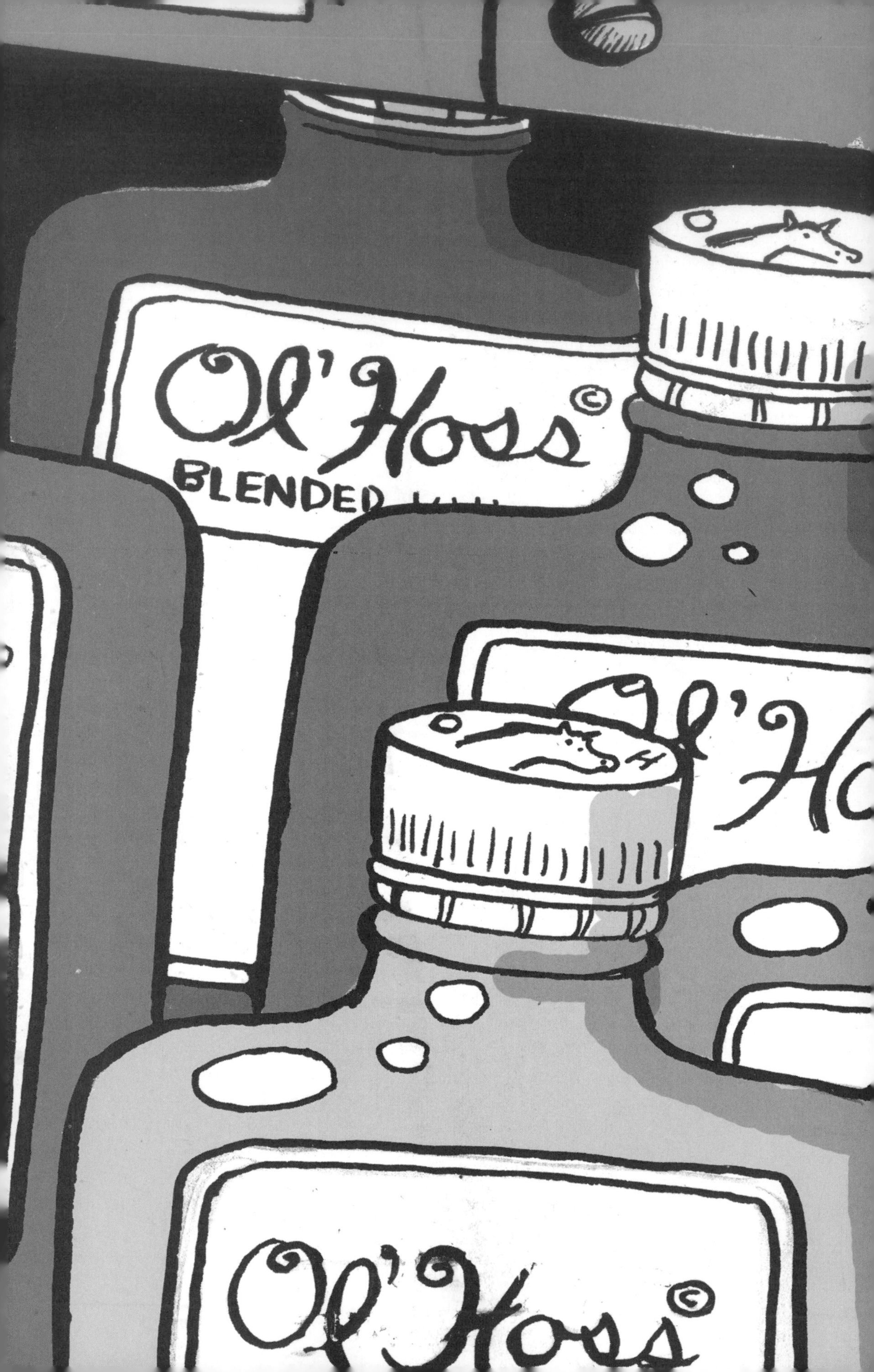
Ol' Hoss©
BLENDED
Ol' Hoss©